THE JAMESON RAID

DR. JAMESON
(From a cartoon by LESLIE WARD in *Vanity Fair*)

(*frontispiece*)

THE JAMESON RAID

BY
HUGH MARSHALL HOLE
C.M.G.
Formerly Civil Commissioner of Bulawayo
Author of 'The Making of Rhodesia,' 'Lobengula,' etc.

1930
PHILIP ALLAN

TO THE MEMORY OF
J. A. C. G.

INTRODUCTION

Hugh Marshall Hole's book, *The Jameson raid* possesses a dual significance, which clearly justifies its republication after almost 70 years since its first appearance. First, one has the authoritative insights of a writer whose career introduced him to the very heart of the political scenario of Central and Southern Africa, as his biographical profile makes clearly apparent. Second, the themes and motifs which inform the narrative exercised an enduring impression upon the Afrikaans political consciousness; shaping the Afrikaner's perceptions and values for the greater part of the succeeding century. The year 1999 represents the anniversary of the outbreak of the 2nd Anglo-Boer War, the climax of a century of tension between the Boers and British in South Africa; lending the republication of this work a further special appositeness.

This introductory essay is moulded by these twin considerations. The first part examines the author's credentials as an authoritative observer of the events that he narrates. The second part relates the Jameson raid - within the context of 19th Century South African history - to the ensuing century of the country's turbulent political development; against the background of the peculiar character of the Afrikaner state which emerged after 1948, with its driving undercurrents of ideology and religion, and the pressures of the new imperialism, which shaped the motives of Rhodes and his confederates. It should be borne in mind that, at the time that Hole's book was published, the mythologies that attained fruition during the apartheid regime (1948-1994) were still in the process of germination. The vantage point of their imperial antagonists is also examined in depth; against the background of the late 19th Century 'new imperialism' and the political, economic and 'moral' imperatives that were its inexorable driving forces. It is apparent that the former theme - the social and political psychology of the Afrikaner - dominates the introductory essay. If the reader accepts that the object of an introduction is not to compete with the writer - thereby undermining the integrity of the author - but, rather, to supplement and enhance his/her themes by exploring facets which present the work in new perspectives, then the fact that the present introduction is weighted in this manner is justified. For the dissection of the 'soul of the Afrikaner' (ie the political and social psychology of the Boers) is central to an understanding of the conflict with the British; yet this dimension is not treated by Hole.

The Writer

Lt Col Hugh Marshall Hole, CMG (1865-1941) was born on 16 May 1865. Educated at Blundell's School and Baliol College, Oxford (whence he graduated with a BA degree in 1887), he entered the service of the British South Africa Company in 1890 (ie during its infancy) and joined the civil service of Rhodesia (as it then was) in 1891, as secretary to its administrator, Dr Leander Starr Jameson. Between that date and 1914 he filled many public offices in that territory; including that of Civil Commissioner of Bulawayo, acting Administrator of North West Rhodesia (1903-1904 and 1907), Chief Native Commissioner for Matabeleland and Chief Secretary of Southern Rhodesia. A close friend of Rhodes, he took charge of the arrangements for the latter's funeral and interment in the Matopos hills in 1902. In 1901 Rhodes had sent Hole on a special mission to Arabia; in order to devise means for the introduction of Arabs for employment in Southern Rhodesia. In 1909 he was employed on similar missions in Nyasaland and Portuguese East Africa (now Malawi and Mozambique respectively). Hole retired from government service in Rhodesia in 1913,

INTRODUCTION

but returned as secretary to the Native Reserve Commission (May-November 1914).

He saw extensive military service; viz in the Matabele rebellion of 1896, the Anglo-Boer War of 1899-1902, and World War I; serving with the 4th Battalion of the Norfolk Regiment between 1915 and 1919 and being mentioned in despatches on several occasions. He was created a Commander of the Most Distinguished Order of St Michael and St George (CMG). Following the termination of his military service he rejoined the British South Africa Company in London. He represented Rhodesia on the Headquarters Council of the British Empire Service League. His publications were extensive; consisting - in addition to the present re-published volume: *The making of Rhodesia* (1926); *Old Rhodesian days* (1928); *Lobengula* (1929); and *The passing of the black kings* (1932). He was the joint author of *Reports on native disturbances in Rhodesia* 1896-7; in addition to numerous articles and pamphlets relating to Rhodesia. He died on 18 May 1941.

It is apparent from the foregoing outline of his career that Hole's professional life was almost entirely and inextricably interwoven with the earliest phase of white controlled Rhodesia and the events within South Africa which inexorably moved that country to war in 1899. As both administrator and soldier he had been a deeply involved personal witness to the turbulence and ethnic tensions which followed in the wake of the British imperial credo. As such, Hole was closely acquainted with the characters and events which precipitated the Jameson raid. Nevertheless, the work is presented with an extremely high degree of objectivity. However, a significant feature of the work is the restricted frame of reference, or narrow parameters within which the narrative is presented. In other words, Hole focuses almost entirely upon the immediate political, social, economic - and psychological - context within which the events unfold. He does not relate the narrative to the broader cultural-historical background underpinning the conflict between Boer tribalism and the new imperialism. There are several notable illustrations of this approach. He does not, for example, discuss the preceding six decades of Anglo-Boer relations, characterised by bitterness and conflict; or the peculiar tribal cultural values of the Boers. Nor does Hole analyse the pressures of the new imperialism, which did so much to shape the ideology of Rhodes and his followers. Similarly, whilst Kruger's response to the uitlander grievances is scrupulously documented, the extent to which he embodied the collective consciousness of the Boers is not discussed. It is this feature - the narrowly circumscribed canvas - that has largely shaped the introductory essay, which seeks to supplement the work by the provision of this overall context of underlying historical forces. In this sense, the Jameson raid is presented, not as a specific event fixed in time, but related to a continuing stratum of South African history.

Central themes in the work

To reiterate, *The Jameson raid* was originally published in 1930. At that point in time, it is extremely doubtful as to whether he was aware that the events which he so lucidly and skilfully narrates - and the leading characters of which are so forcefully and clearly delineated - were not entombed in a sealed past but were to form vital skeins in a mythical tapestry which was to shape South Africa's history for the ensuing six decades. It would certainly have demanded remarkable foresight to conceive of a regressive political/social ideology - rooted in the credo of a 17th Century Dutch/Flemish peasantry - shaping the most powerful state in Africa; commanding vast economic resources and presiding over a huge military-industrial complex. (One must, of course, bear in mind that hindsight is an extremely exact science).

That phase of Afrikaner history is now permanently sealed by a development which was totally inconceivable (indeed anathema) to both parties in the protracted Boer-British conflict; viz black majority rule. It is highly improbable that Hole himself could have imagined a black president elected by universal suffrage; a process which attained expression in 1994, when Nelson Mandela was thus elected. In actual fact, assuming that one accepts the domino theory, that momentous event was foredained after the accession to power of a black majority government, headed by Robert Mugabe, within Rhodesia (now Zimbabwe); and the victory of the South West Africa People's Organisation (SWAPO) within modern Namibia. These developments within the Zambezi salient and South West Africa - driving the South African whites to their inexorable fate - were undoubtedly equally inconceivable to Hole. The ultimate masters of the sub-continent were thus the victims of the 'kaffir' mentality shared by both antagonists in the Boer-British conflict; both of whom bequeathed to their black and coloured victims virtually a century of exploitation and codified victimisation; and whose rivalries and aspirations were fundamentally irrelevant to the vast majority of the country's inhabitants.

A little people: the pressure cooker of Afrikanerdom

It is, for obvious reasons, notoriously difficult to define the central features of a particular ethnic group. It comprises so many differing individual personalities that the approach towards such a definition inevitably involves the danger of stereotyping. The possibility is exacerbated by subjective, purely personal impressions ('value judgements'); ie certain traits of character or speech which colour the interpreter's critique. Nevertheless, such an analysis - possessing a high degree of objectivity - is possible in the case of the Afrikaner. This is mainly due to the fact that the sustaining power of the myths forged during the 19th Century - and enjoying renewed vigour following the Nationalist Party's ascension to power in 1948 - has most powerfully shaped Afrikaner perceptions and attitudes (especially with regard to the crucial issue of race relations) with a remarkable degree of homogeneity and clarity for the greater part of the 20th Century. It is, indeed, this element of homogeneity - of the unity of shared cultural values - which justifies the appellation of 'tribe' when discussing the Afrikaners and their Boer ancestors. The other central characteristic and driving force of tribal society - insularity - is, of course, implicit in such a homogeneous value system. In contrast, the indigenous (as opposed to immigrant) English speaking element - whose forebears were the 1820 Settlers - possessed no such tribal complexion; due to the fact that its value system was grounded in their British homeland and, most importantly, that their values altered and adapted in response to those of English society. Thus, English speaking South Africans avoided the insularity of the tribal Afrikaner, and developed no sustaining mythology to harbour and reinforce such insular modes of thought.

The central role of myth in Afrikaner history

The welcome opportunity to write the introduction to this republished work has awakened many personal recollections (by no means universally pleasant). The writer was engaged at the South African National Museum of Military History, Johannesburg, for 15 years. As such, he was consistently exposed to the historical sensitivities and myths fostered by the Afrikaner. As is characteristic of insecure and beleaguered peoples, the Afrikaner became veritably obsessed with the history of their besieged homelands. This, in turn, generated a virtual mania with cultural hegemony; centred upon history and the Afrikaans language. At the centre of this web of prejudices was the cultivation of a national identity anchored in the struggle between the Boer republics of the Transvaal and Orange

INTRODUCTION

Free State on the one hand; and the British government on the other. This skein of myth has its starting point in the 'Great Trek' of the 1830s, the migration of Boer families (the *voortrekkers*) from the British controlled Cape into the interior; this Boer diaspora leading to conflict with the native tribes and eventually to the creation of the republics of the Transvaal and Orange Free State (in 1852 and 1854 respectively).

It bears reiteration that the conflict between Boer tribalism and British imperialism shaped the perceptions of Afrikaner political thought throughout the 20th Century. An incisive view of the role of myth in Afrikaans culture - the manner in which the nation's history has been mythologised or distorted, in order to enhance a political ideology - is contained in Graham Leach's work, *The Afrikaners: their last great trek* (London: Macmillan, 1989). The author discusses the Boer victory over the Zulus at Blood River (1838). The victory is commemorated by the 'Day of the Vow' (16 December) (later retitled 'Dingane's day'). A speaker's address in 1938 inferred that:

> 'The victory at Blood River shows us ... that God wants a white civilisation in South Africa. It is historically incorrect to state that South Africa belongs to the bantu [black] race ... God gave South Africa to the Afrikaners - it is our country. Here a white civilisation must rule forever.'

Leach quotes the views of Professor F A Van Jaarsveld, whose research has demythologised the traditional Afrikaner interpretation of Blood River:

> 'He maintains that the vow at Blood River, far from being a solemn and binding covenant, was romanticised to serve as a powerful tool of Afrikaner survival, not during the trek itself, but only years later, when the Afrikaner was at his lowest point, defeated

and dejected and in urgent need of a history, a tradition and a heritage to cling to. It was only after the first Boer War against the British in 1880, when Afrikaner nationalism came to the fore, that Blood River - the deed itself and the Boer commandos who fought - became the stuff of Afrikaner legend. After the second Boer War of 1899-1902, when thousands of Afrikaners fled poverty in the countryside to compete alongside British and blacks in the cities, the glorified image of the *voortrekker* leaders evoked a nostalgia for what they conjured as a heroic past, a time when the Afrikaner was forging his own destiny on land which he had made his own. The Boer War had resulted in a disruption and discontinuity to the Afrikaner's way of life. He was desperately seeking to maintain his identity. Rewriting history to strengthen Afrikaner nationalism was one way of doing it ...

During the late 1930s, prime ministers Jan Smuts and J.B.M. Hertzog tried to unite Afrikaners and English-speakers within a common South African nationality, and therefore had hoped that "Dingane's Day" would be celebrated by all whites as an "ordinary" public holiday. After 1948, however, the Nationalist Government was not interested in 16 December as an occasion for the binding together or reconciliation of all South Africans: they saw it rather as a tribal Afrikaner "holy" day. It deteriorated into an annual emotional jamboree for the narrow pursuit and promotion of Afrikaner nationalism...

According to Professor van Jaarsveld, Afrikaner nationalism was historically orientated and had a strong religious sense. It arose from the alleged similarity between the Great Trek and the exodus of the Israelites from Egyptian bondage and their settlement in Canaan. The history of the *voortrekker* was not only theological but regarded with nostalgia. After the Boer War the defeated Afrikaners came to venerate and romanticise their agricultural pioneers. The myth and the legend afforded legitimacy to the twentieth century Afrikaner nationalists.'

The physical embodiment of Afrikaner mythology is embodied in the hideous *Voortrekker* monument, opened on 16 December ('The Day of the Vow') 1949 and situated near Pretoria. It is a shrine to the embittered racial memories of the Afrikaner.

This mythological web's principal focal points, in addition to the Great Trek and its consequences, are: the 'theft' of Natal by the British in 1842; the annexation of the Transvaal by Disraeli's government in 1877 and the resultant 1st Anglo-Boer War of 1880-1881 (popularly termed the 'First South African War of Independence'); climaxed by the Boer victory at Majuba in February 1881 and the regaining of Transvaal independence. The 2nd Anglo-Boer War of 1899-1902 represents the apotheosis of this mythological tapestry; in which the Jameson raid of 1895 occupies a pivotal position. As is well known, the raid involved the ill-conceived and pathetically organised invasion of the Transvaal by a British mercenary force based in Rhodesia; and spearheaded by the quixotic Dr Jameson, with the connivance of his confederate and mentor, Cecil John Rhodes. The issues which had precipitated the raid - the question of political rights for the immigrants into the Transvaal ('uitlanders') - was the immediate pretext for the outbreak of war in 1899.

The enduring legacy of the 2nd Anglo-Boer War

It bears reiteration that the conflict between Boer tribalism and British imperialism shaped the perceptions of the Afrikaner political consciousness throughout the ensuing century.

The famous American novelist, F Scott Fitzgerald, stated

that for his countrymen there were no second acts. There was, indeed, a second act to the Anglo-Boer War of 1899-1902; viz the creation of the Republic of South Africa in 1961. This theme is explored in Brian Bunting's book, *The rise of the South African Reich* (International Aid Defence Fund for Southern Africa, 1986; originally published by Penguin, 1964. The author writes:

> 'For the Boers the war was the climax to a "century of wrong", a century of British expansion, oppression and meddling, which had finally goaded them beyond the limits of endurance. There rose up before them as they fought the memory of the past, of the colony which had been annexed [ie Natal], of the slaves which had been freed, ... of the battle of Majuba, of the thousand and one defeats and humiliations to which they had been subjected ever since the British presence established itself in South Africa. For a while they had been able to escape from British rule into the security of their own two republics, but now these too were threatened with destruction. Everything for which they had lived and struggled was endangered - their freedom, their language, their possessions, their racial supremacy, their very existence as an independent people with their God-given right to manage their affairs and their chattels as they pleased. The people of the two republics felt that the cup of bitterness was too full to be borne. They threw themselves into the struggle feeling themselves ready to die rather than submit...
>
> The bitter-enders among the Afrikaners never accepted the finality of defeat and looked forward to the time when, through internal schism or external intervention, they would be able to re-establish the Boer republics... This provides a clue to Afrikaner nationalist thinking and action.'

INTRODUCTION

For dedicated Afrikaner nationalists, South African history had ended in 1902, with the British victory in the 2nd South African War and the occupation of the two republics; to be reincarnated in 1948 and attain its fruition in 1961; the intervening period (1902-1948) exemplifying a political desert. In this respect, the Republic of South Africa (RSA) was fundamentally regressive. It reincarnated the inward-looking, essentially tribalistic complexion of the Boer mentality. The obsession with cultural hegemony, referred to above, was an integral platform in that outlook. At the heart of that drive for cultural dominance one has the ideology of apartheid; a ruthless doctrine of racial segregation and discrimination, first clearly formulated into a systematic legalised dogma by Dr Verwoerd, the (then) South African prime minister, in the early 1960s. It was, of course, the relentless pursuit of this policy which transformed the Republic of South Africa into a political pariah and excited global revulsion. The South African Republic's masters embodied the reassertion and reincarnation of Boer republicanism; powerfully interlaced with an element of revenge against its former English speaking conquerors. It bears reiteration that language was a most powerful instrument in such a policy. Language was the force which ensured, for example, the domination of Afrikaner political-cultural perception in the public services (notably education) and the armed forces (which, together with the police force, was often defined as the Nationalist Party in uniform). [This obsession with language was underpinned by a central myth in Afrikaans culture. A tongue which was essentially a hybrid patois fusing a coloured/Malay dialect, Dutch and Flemish, was elevated by self-righteous and politically motivated academics as the 'most recent prince of the Indo-Germanic languages']. Thus, the tribal base of the Afrikaner - so vividly exemplified in Kruger's republic - remained firmly in place.

The Republic of South Africa embodied one of the most curious political aberrations of the 20th Century; viz an anachronistic 17th Century ideology superimposed upon a technologically and economically sophisticated power. That ideology was buttressed by the dogma of the Dutch Reformed Church, anchored in the 16th Century creed of Calvinism, which, characteristically, became totally divorced from (and, indeed, totally ostracised by) its liberal and progressive counterpart within its Netherlands homeland. There have been several examples of fundamentalist religious sects establishing communities, over which they exercised political hegemony; in effect theocracies. The Puritan states of 17th Century New England immediately spring to mind. A further illustration is John Calvin's establishment of a theocratic state in 16th Century Geneva. The Afrikaner furnishes the sole example of a powerful modern state being controlled by an ideology rooted in an archaic religious fundamentalism. The Afrikaner government, sensitive to the escalating pressures of isolation, became increasingly aware of the growing and insupportable cost of this debilitating anachronism. Hence, one has the increasingly 'cosmetic' treatment applied to the doctrine and practice of apartheid. This process is partly exemplified in the field of terminology: apartheid became redefined as 'separate development'; the bantustans were redesignated 'homelands''; and 'bantus' retitled 'blacks'. Most notably, the pathetic endeavour to render apartheid palatable to the outside world was expressed in new political structures; viz the creation of a tripartite system of parliamentary chambers for whites/coloureds/Asians and Indians during the late 1970s; co-existing with independent governments of the homelands (Transkei, Ciskei, kwaZulu, Lesotho, etc). 'Grand apartheid' in this manner superseded 'petty apartheid', characterised by the minutiae of social segregation, which was considerably relaxed during the final decade of white rule in South Africa. As is well known, there are three types of power; viz coercive, compensatory and conditioned. Coercive power consists of the rule of fear (such as is found in prisons and totalitarian states);

compensatory power is that possessed by the capitalist, in his determination of the living conditions of his/her employees; conditioned power implies legitimacy (the consent of the governed). The power of the Boers over their non-white servants was largely conditioned, rooted in a patriarchal culture in which such divisions were implicitly absorbed by the collective consciousness of non-whites. The 20th Century destroyed this conditioned power, against the background of the rise of black nationalism (the African National Congress being founded in 1912). In response, the Nationalist governments of the first three decades of its rule adopted coercive powers, expressed in punitive laws. Realising that the vast weight of numbers of the indigenous population, combined with the escalating pressures of a hostile world opinion, rendered the exercise of such power ultimately untenable, the Afrikaners sought to cultivate conditioned power, in order to gain legitimacy. The cosmetic treatment applied to apartheid thus embodies the shift from coercive to conditioned power. However, as we shall see, the innate character of Afrikaner ideology rendered such a transition impossible.

This ostensible retreat from traditional apartheid created an ideological vacuum. The desire for an anchor within such a void - in which traditional points of reference had been shed - fractured the political unity of Afrikanerdom; expressed in factions and parties which denounced a 'reformist' Nationalist Party as 'treachery'. Such factions/ parties were exemplified by the Conservative Party (founded by the late Dr Treurnicht), the rival Herstigte Nationale Party (HNP) and the para-military, extra-legal AWB.

Afrikaner tribalism has often been defined as white nationalism, but this is essentially a misleading conception. The heavily introspective character of Afrikaner nationalism was equally contemptuous of, and indifferent to both the non-European inhabitants of South Africa and its non-Afrikans white neighbours positioned on the country's borders; ie the Rhodesians and Portuguese, and both confronted with insurgency movements. The South African government's indifference to the Portuguese defence of their colonies in south east and south west Africa (Mozambique and Angola respectively) and the white Rhodesian struggle in the Zambezi salient can be largely explained in terms of this inward looking tribalism. (Indeed, a substantial body of Afrikaner opinion was actually hostile to the white Rhodesian posture; feeling that the struggle had no connection with South Africa and that, in any event, the white Rhodesians had opted for dominion status in 1922, as opposed to incorporation within South Africa). Ultimately, it was this 'tunnel vision' which sanctioned the policy of sacrificing South Africa's essential buffer zones - both Rhodesia and South West Africa - in a curious re-enactment of Chamberlain's appeasement policy in central Europe during the 1930s. This 'strategic glaucoma' was a critical element in the eventual collapse of the South African Reich.

Destructive ironies and paradoxes within Afrikanerdom

At the heart of this reincarnation of the Boer republics in 1961, there is a profound irony. The Nationalist Party which seized power in 1948 determined to extend its control into the traditional preserves of the uitlanders of the 19th Century. In this process it was overwhelmingly successful; and, as a result, its Afrikaner acolytes surrendered to the culture and values of their former conquerors. In economic terms this process was reflected in the emergence of South Africa as a 'one crop' economy (the 'crop' in question being, of course, gold); and the considerable decline in the gold price since the late 1970s was a key factor in the weakening resistance of South Africa's political masters to the outside world). Johannesburg - the economic capital of post-Nationalist South Africa - in the 1990s would have been readily recognised by the uitlanders of the 1880s and 1890s. The city bore all the hallmarks of a freebooter capitalist ethic; ruthlessly indifferent to the social and cultural needs of a dense urban population. The expression of the Afrikaner surrender to alien cultural values was the emergence of a vicious obsession with unrestricted capitalism; compared with which Thatcherism appeared almost socialist. The development of this trait eventually involved the total abandonment of the Nationalist Party's traditional power base; viz the poor whites. Policies such as job reservation, which had underpinned the Party's allegiance with this social sector during its formative years and earlier decades of rule, were abandoned during the dying phases of the regime. The privatisation of the huge Afrikaner dominated industries and bureaucracies, which for four decades had provided an employment haven for Afrikaners, was a central plank in this programme of unrestricted capitalism. During the 1980s the government's privatisation programme, which extended to ESCOM (the electricity supply industry) and even to hospitals) raised the spectre once more of the 'poor whites', who had swelled the urban proletariat during the 1920s. In this respect, a further cleavage was introduced into South African society; overlaying the traditional polarisation between whites and non-whites. This was the class division within white society itself; an increasingly oppressive white elite (in which the values and aspirations of privileged English speaking South Africans and Afrikaners were indistinguishable, modelled upon American culture) was indifferent to the increasing swell of their impoverished and disadvantaged compatriots. The early years of the 1980s witnessed the worst economic recession for whites since the 1920s. Whilst the figures for registered white unemployed in 1981 was a little in excess of 6 000, in 1986 it had increased to 32 000; whilst insolvencies quadrupled in the four years leading to 1985. It should be borne in mind that 19th Century Boer society was characterised by a traditional and deeply entrenched social cleavage between the property owners (burghers) and landless agricultural labourers (bywoners). The destruction of the burgher class by the Anglo-Boer War of 1899-1902 is at the root of the impoverishment of the Afrikaner, reducing him to a landless agricultural - and soon urban - proletariat. Whilst this class provided the original power base of the Nationalist Party, during the 1920s and 1930s, its revival during the last two decades of the present century - with far greater and infinitely more frightening dimensions - was a direct consequence of the Party's policies and attitudes during this period.

Indeed, one may justifiably argue that the eventual surrender of the Afrikaner to black majority rule is anchored in the erosion of his/her cultural base - that of a rural peasantry - and the absorption of values that were fundamentally alien to that heritage. In this respect, the fate of Afrikanerdom vindicates the thesis of Oswald Spengler's *Decline of the West*; viz that an ethnic group faces ultimate extinction when it uproots itself from its socio-cultural values.

Yet, embedded in this irony, there resides a more profound paradox. The regressive character of the Nationalist Party's regime could not possibly survive in a modern world. (The concrete expression of this profound inadequacy was the total inability of the Afrikaans language to compete with English in the international business world. Its survival was totally dependent upon the artificial stimulus afforded by the obsession with cultural hegemony). It may with justice be argued that, confronted with this insoluble paradox, the Afrikaner chose ultimately to abdicate power to the black majority. Within the context of this argument, it is essential to bear in mind that the fundamentally regressive, atavistic character of Afrikaner ideology could permit of no adaptation or response to new challenges. It is for precisely this reason that the retreat from apartheid's original dogma - characterised by the minutiae of social segregation and the total political exclusion of non-whites - could only end, ultimately, in the total abdication of power. As will be discussed below, in several important respects.

Afrikaner nationalism bears a close resemblance to fascist ideology; in so far as it is anchored in the creed of the cultural nationalist (viz that citizenship must be restricted to those who share a common ethnic background). Fascism has, in the 20th Century, revealed remarkable powers of flexibility and renewal; evidenced in such ideologies as the neo conservatism of the New Right, which has enjoyed such a widespread vogue (especially in the United States and Thatcherite Britain) during the last two decades of the present century. Afrikanerdom, however, was not capable of such flexibility; due to its narrow racial base, which is the centre of its ideology.

This point is underscored by Graham Leach, in his book, *The Afrikaners: their last great trek*, cited above. Writing of the period in which the whites still retained power, he states:

> 'The *laager* [the traditional encampment of wagons assembled in a defensive circle] is an expression of the Afrikaners' failure to adjust completely to the land in which they live.
>
> The Afrikaners' argument that they are an African tribe wishing to live as Africans among their black compatriots is not convincing. The Afrikaners have never really been able to meet Africa on its own terms. Their language, rich in African idioms, is for blacks the language of the squad car and of the oppressor, not a language of reconciliation between peoples. It is one of the many African tragedies that Afrikaans, spoken by thousands of blacks and mixed-race people, has come

to be associated with racial exclusiveness... Yet Afrikaans could so easily have become a medium of healing between the races because of which it has drawn from the rich soil of Africa. Not for one moment have Afrikaners thought how they might set their language free and remove it from the straitjacket of apartheid ideology so that blacks and others would be proud to use it. Afrikaans is a young language born on the African continent, but a language which might one day be lost because of its identification with Afrikaner power and privilege.

The Afrikaners over three centuries have failed to learn the great...quality of humility...; they have proved extraordinarily insensitive to the hopes, fears and feelings of black Africans. The deeper meaning of the continent - its tides, its flows, its way of doing things - have left little impression upon Afrikaners because, at the end of the day, they return to their European roots.'

The final phrase, 'they return to their European roots' underscores the enduring legacy of a 17th Century Dutch-Flemish culture; insulated against succeeding generations of European enlightenment. This view was echoed by Nina Overton, Professor of Communications at Rand Afrikaans University (Johannesburg); a 'detribalised' Afrikaner who stated:

'We come from European fanatics...We are still fanatics...a group of Europeans placed in a harsh, unforgiving continent.'

Ultimately, it was this problem - the isolation of Afrikaner culture and values from the mainstream of European progressive thought - which had shaped its history and development. Thus, the Great Trek was fundamentally motivated by the reaction to the British Government's

INTRODUCTION

legislation to abolish slavery within its imperial possessions in 1833 (probably one of the most humane and enlightened acts of the 19th Century). (One of the Boer families which undertook the trek was incensed by the fact that they were answerable in law for the mutilation of their coloured servant). As Bernard Bunting writes:

> 'The desire to be free of British rule was not merely the manifestation of a spirit of national independence. It was also prompted by the wish to continue to own slaves, to be able to discriminate between White and Non-White, to re- establish the parochial relationship between master and servant which had existed from the time of van Riebeeck [ie Jan van Riebeeck, the representative of the Dutch East India Company, who founded the first white settlement in South Africa, at the Cape, in 1652] and which now looked like being destroyed for ever. The new republics which were set up in the Orange Free State and Transvaal enabled the Dutch to refashion for themselves their old way of life.'

The determination to exclude the uitlander from the civic and political life of the Transvaal during the last two decades of the 19th Century was motivated by the desire to insulate the Boer republic from the 'contamination' of an alien culture rooted in contemporary European and American cultural values. Similarly, apartheid was shaped by the drive to insulate the Afrikaner from the effects of a modern multi-ethnic society. Isolation and insularity are thus the fundamental and consistent driving forces of Afrikaans history and culture. Within this context, Bernard Bunting writes:

> 'Afraid of domination at first by the British, later by the African, the Afrikaner nationalist has tended always to seek safety in isolation'.

Ultimately, Afrikanerdom was faced with the same dilemma as that which confronted traditional Communism within the Soviet Union; viz reform was incompatible with survival, the original ideology not permitting any manoeuvrability. [The analogy between the Afrikaner state and Communism is most apposite. It was ironic that a state so vociferously committed to combating Communism reveals several important points of convergence with the Communist regime. First, one has the one party state (the Nationalist Party enjoying uninterrupted rule between its first electoral victory in 1948 and the final demise of white rule in 1994). Second, one notes the recurrent resort to intimidation and extra legal activity by the government; exemplified in such practices as detention without trial (sanctioned by 'states of emergency'), the use of torture by security personnel and, indeed, assassination of the state's dissidents. The totalitarian state, characterised by contempt for the rule of law, proved to be the hallmark of both Communism and Afrikanerdom (and, of course, fascism). A further feature of totalitarianism is apparent in the Afrikaner state; viz cultural sterility. The artistic establishment - the most vocal and articulate sector of the anti-apartheid lobby - could never transcend an ethno-centric and parochial plane of expression (largely confined, in terms of subject matter, to the moral dilemmas confronted white South Africans). It proved incapable of expressing central universalist themes in the manner of the European cultural tradition].

The pathetic attempt to redefine Afrikanerdom in terms purely of language (thus encompassing non-whites) during the dying years of the Nationalist Party regime, was regarded as nothing less than a hollow mockery and apology by the regime's opponents. To quote the words of the Roman poet Horace, 'little people deserve their little fate'.

The fundamental - and insoluble - problem which confronted the Nationalist Party during its benighted rule (spanning virtually half a century) was thus the

INTRODUCTION

reconciliation between its traditional culture and ideology, and its place in the modern world. It was the impossibility of procuring this reconciliation which sealed the fate of the white tribe. Within this context, a highly perceptive comment was made by Andre Zaaiman, a conscientious objector, when he stated:

> 'The Afrikaner is going through an existential crisis. He is beginning to reject apartheid but has no reference point.'

In this respect, the liberal Afrikaner (eg of the stamp of Frederick van Zyl Slabbert, the former leader of the Progressive Federal Party (PFP), or the well known writer, Laurens van der Post) occupied a cultural and intellectual wasteland. The liberal philosophy - with its underlying premise of pluralism and cultural diversity as being integral aspects of a unified state - was fundamentally antithetical to Afrikaner ideology.

[It is hardly surprising that a substantial body of Afrikaners expressed a marked sympathy with Nazism during World War II; expressed in the widespread support for the covert fascist organisation, the *Ossewa Brandweg* ('flaming brand'). Nazi sympathisers had heavily infiltrated the Railways Police, and also several Afrikaner regiments, necessitating their drastic restructuring. Afrikaner nationalism - characterised by the tribalist atavistic obsession with cultural/ethnic hegemony and mastery - has its assured place in the lineage of fascism. In this respect, Kruger's republic is, indeed, a prototype and ancestor of the fascist state. This theme is pursued in depth in Brian Bunting's work, *The rise of the South African Reich*. The writer draws several important analogies between South Africa during the 1960s and the Third Reich. Important points of convergence included: the programme of indoctrination undertaken in the schools with the object of permanently impressing the exclusive claims of Afrikaner ideology; and the legal framework of apartheid. The latter was expressed in: the Mixed Marriages Act (1949); Immorality Acts (1927/1950/1957/1967); Group Areas Act (1950/1957/1965). The statutory foundations of apartheid are interpreted as the South African counterpart of the Nazi Nuremberg laws, enacted during the 1930s, founded upon racial discrimination against the Jews. It is the peculiar characteristic of the South African state that, in 1948 (a point in time which, for obvious reasons, witnessed the global revulsion against Nazi ideology), the principal tenets of the Third Reich's political credo were embodied in the cardinal tenets of Nationalist Party policy. The *Ossewa Brandweg* in fact experienced a reincarnation in the form of the *Afrikaner Weerstandbewiging* (AWB), whose tactics and objectives were similar to the notorious Ku Klux Klan in the United States, and whose leader was the notorious Eugene Terre Blanche].

The profound incompatibility between Afrikaner political-cultural values and the pressures of the modern world assumed diverse forms. The most obvious manifestation - and the source of the country's exclusion from the international community - was, obviously, the political exclusion of non-whites and the systematic programme of racial discrimination. There were, however, other expressions of this dangerous insularity on the part of the ruling elite. A highly significant expression of this incompatibility was the total inability to cope with the multiple problems associated with urbanisation. The provision of adequate social services, for example, was totally beyond the comprehension of successive Nationalist governments. The social fabric of South African cities - characterised by the chaotic, slum ridden townships (of which Soweto was a prime example), influx of squatters, lawlessness and appalling levels of unemployment - was disintegrating at least a decade prior to the final abdication of white power. The priorities of such governments were symbolically and most graphically expressed in vast

INTRODUCTION   xxiii

luxurious military complexes (such as that which housed the South African Defence Force, near Pretoria). In this respect, the Republic of South Africa mirrored - on a far more extensive scale - the main features of its 19th Century predecessor; the hallmarks of which were gross corruption and massive inefficiency. Such negligence affected both blacks and increasing numbers of disadvantaged whites. (The memory of extremely aged white ladies - rendered homeless by soaring rents and sectional title - scavenging in the gutters of the mean, narrow Johannesburg streets produced an ineffaceable impression upon the writer; as also did the queues of the homeless and unemployed - many of them white - awaiting the meals dispensed in the streets by charitable religious organisations). In the face of such problems the white government adopted, initially a policy of denial (the falling gold price becoming the preferred culprit) and, ultimately, abdication of power.

One is now in a position to appreciate the extent to which Afrikanerdom contained the seeds of its own destruction, in two fundamental respects. First, its extremely narrow ideological base permitted of no flexibility, and hence its attempts at reconciliation with the pressures of the modern world contained the dynamics of self-destruction. Second, from a military-strategic viewpoint, the tunnel vision of Afrikaner tribalism generated the domino process within central and southern Africa which foredained the inevitable abdication of white power within the Republic.

The imperialists

What of the Boers' antagonists during the late 19th Century, the architects of the Jameson raid? Arguably, they exemplify the point that the moral issues in history reflect, not black and white, but subtle spectrums of grey. The Boer-British conflict of the last decades of the 19th Century embodies a dispute between a regressive tribalism and the forces of what might be termed a gangster capitalism. The driving pressure of the uitlander leaders was the new imperialism; viz the linkage between the extension of imperialism and desire to ruthlessly harness new fields of investment. European technology was the key to this expansion; undertaken invariably at the expense of non-European peoples. (To a large extent, the long catalogue of military disasters, which characterised the British Army's involvement in the 1st and 2nd Anglo-Boer Wars - is rooted in the failure to distinguish between the Boers and the primitive tribes over which cheap victories were secured).

The character of the new imperialists is succinctly defined by David Thomson in his work, *Europe since Napoleon* (London, New York, etc: Penguin, 1960):

> 'The quest for markets in which to sell manufactured goods was important. But...the political factor was no less important than the purely economic. Until 1870 British manufacturers of textiles, machinery and hardware had found good markets in other European lands. After 1870, Germany, France, Belgium and other nations were able to satisfy their own home markets, which they began to protect against imports from Britain by tariff barriers. They even began to produce a surplus for which they sought markets abroad. With increasing saturation of European markets, all tended to look for more open markets overseas, and in the competitive, protectionist mood of European politics they found governments responsive enough to national needs to undertake the political conquest of undeveloped territories. For this purpose, Africa and Asia served admirably. It was in these economic and political circumstances that the urge to exploit backward territories by the investment of surplus capital could make so much headway. It began especially after 1870 and gained rapidly in momentum until 1914. (Of the annual investment of British capital

between 1909 and 1914, thirty-six per cent went into British overseas territories). By then the main industrial countries had equipped themselves with an abundance of manufacturing plant, and the openings for capital investment at home were more meagre. The vast underdeveloped areas of Africa and Asia offered the most inviting opportunities, provided that they could be made safe enough for investment, and there seemed no better guarantee of security than the appropriation of these lands.'

The Witwatersrand embodied one of the most important receptacles for such investment. The output was almost 500 000 ounces in 1890 and 1 210 865 ounces in 1892. It superseded the goldfields of California and Alaska (both of which had become exhausted by the end of the century); and, indeed, the gold seams of the Witwatersrand - which were to dominate the world's economy for the greater part of the 20th Century - remain unexhausted to the present day. By 1890 there were 450 mining companies on the Rand, capitalised at £11 million. A major channel of this investment was Rhodes's company, De Beers Consolidated Goldfields, which soon controlled a large share of the business. In 1888 the amalgamation of De Beers and Barnato diamond interests gave the De Beers Corporation, under Rhodes, a virtual monopoly of the industry. By 1914 the major European powers had become heavy investors in the overseas territories (much of it undeveloped). British capital flowed mainly overseas, to the Americas and Africa (almost $86 bn being directed to Asia, Africa and Australia, and over $6 bn to the United States); French mainly to eastern Europe and Russia; German mainly to south eastern Europe, Turkey and the Far East, although also to the Americas. Together, they held $30 000 m in loans and investments abroad. In addition the Dutch invested heavily in the Netherlands East Indies and smaller countries such as Belgium, Scandinavia and Switzerland also participated in this process. The flow of capital led to extensive development of hitherto undeveloped territories. Economists generally agree that the new imperialism is explicable in terms of a 'glut of capital' seeking safe investment, much of it lost or spent in World War I.

The new imperialism was overlaid by intense competition between the major European powers, focusing upon Anglo-German rivalry. As David Thomson further writes:

> 'Again governments were responsive, for reasons that were not exclusively economic. The ports of Africa and the Far East were valuable as naval bases and ports of call, no less than as in-roads for trade and investment. Given the tangle of international fears and distrusts in Europe during these years, and the ever-present menace of war, no possible strategic or prestige-giving advantage could be forfeited. Once the scramble for partitioning Africa had begun, the powers were confronted with the choice of grabbing such advantages for themselves or seeing them snatched by potential enemies. The 'international anarchy' contributed an impetus of its own to the general race for colonies.'

Thus, in 1885 the British Government had annexed southern Bechuanaland in order to prevent the possible link-up between the Transvaal and German South West Africa. In 1887 the British annexed Zululand, in order to block the effort of the Transvaal government to establish territorial connections with the sea. The isolation of the Transvaal was completed in September 1894, when the British annexed Pondoland, thereby connecting the Cape Colony with Natal. Hence also the British Government's covert support for the Jameson raid, both developments being grounded in Kruger's strong predilection for Germany. The relationship between the Transvaal and Anglo-German rivalry was highlighted on 3 January 1896, when the Kaiser despatched to Kruger a telegram congratulating the latter on his success in suppressing the insurrection. This step created an acute crisis in the relations between Britain and Germany.

Lenin's thesis - contained in his pamphlet, *Imperialism: the highest stage of capitalism* (1916) - is substantially correct. Lenin argued that the new imperialism was mainly impelled by the desire to find and exploit new outlets for investment, rather than markets. His argument is flawed, however, in so far as he advocated that the competitive imperialisms was the source of the Great War of 1914-1918. Rather, the reverse was the case; viz the menace of war had led to imperialism.

The dynamics of the new imperialism were encouraged - rather than planned or directed - by governments. The central and immediate driving force was provided by individuals. In this respect, the movement is highly individualist in character. (Did these individuals exemplify the 'traditional values' so espoused by the neo conservatives of the late 20th Century?) Such individuals were represented by the great colonial proconsuls; eg Lord Cromer in Egypt, Lord Lugard in Nigeria, Lord Milner at the Cape, Marshal Lyautey in Morocco, Karl Peters in German East Africa. An invaluable instrument in the development of the new imperialism was the chartered company, which were either the sponsors or creations of such individuals. Obvious examples included the International African Association, founded in 1876 by King Leopold II of Belgium. This organisation had despatched Henry Morton Stanley on explorations into the Congo between 1879 and 1884, where Stanley made treaties with the native chiefs and established Leopold's influence over vast areas of the interior. In 1885 the African Association converted itself into the Congo Free State, with Leopold as its absolute sovereign. The success prompted other powers to establish chartered companies to develop other African regions. Such enterprises, granted by their governments monopoly rights in the exploitation of various territories, became the general media of colonial commerce and appropriation in the subsequent decade. Thus, the German and British East African Companies had been created by 1888; the Italian Benadir Company developed Italian Somaliland in 1892; and the Royal Niger Company developed Nigeria. Central to the story of the Jameson raid is, of course, the British South Africa Company, created by Rhodes in 1888, with the object of developing the valley of the Zambezi salient. The company in effect appropriated the territories subsequently designated southern Rhodesia; governing the territory until 1922.

The moral sanction for the new imperialism

The new imperialism was shaped by a climate of European thought and culture which appeared to lend moral sanction to the vast expansion of western influence over the globe. Two key elements in this process were scientific advances on a massive scale, and Darwinism.

With regard to the former, achievements in the sphere of mechanical engineering attracted immediate admiration during this period. These were manifested in such phenomena as: the quadrupling of the world's railway mileage between 1870 and 1900, including such triumphs as the Forth Bridge in Scotland, the Trans Siberian and Canadian Pacific Railways; the erection of the first skyscrapers in New York and Chicago, and the Eiffel Tower in Paris; the construction of the Suez, Kiel and Panama Canals; the great new oceanic liners; and the exciting consequences of the invention of the internal combustion engine, which made possible both automobiles and aeroplanes. There were also signs of an impending conquest of the dimensions of space when, in 1895, the Irish-Italian inventor, Guglielmo Marconi, first used radio waves to transmit messages by wireless telegraphy. It is

INTRODUCTION

important to bear in mind that these revolutionary advances in mechanical engineering were manifested in the sphere of military technology. During the last quarter of the 19th Century the face of war experienced a momentous transition. Until the mid-19th Century weapons technology had remained essentially static for some two centuries. Single shot muzzle loading muskets propelled their balls at extremely limited range; muzzle loading bronze cannons were similarly inaccurate and short range weapons, firing their shot in flat trajectories. However, from the 1860s onwards the pace of military technology had experienced a phenomenal acceleration. By the late 1880s, bolt action rifles had appeared (exemplified by the Lee Metford and Mauser), capable of rapidly delivering their rounds at ranges of up to 1 000 yards. Above all, the water cooled machine gun - the product of the inventive genius of Hiram Maxim - had come to dominate the battlefield scenario; together with rapid firing, rifled breech loading artillery. The British South Africa Company's conquest of Matabeleland and Mashonaland (the future Southern Rhodesia) was due in no small measure to the maxim gun and magazine rifle. Next in esteem ranked the exploration of the world's surface, facilitated by the modern resources of transport and medicine. The infamous African interior was penetrated, whilst the earth's poles were explored.

With reference to Darwinism, Charles Darwin's epochal theory of evolution was, during the generation prior to 1914, the most far reaching and controversial of all scientific theories. Darwin's *On the origin of species* had been published in 1859, and *Descent of man* in 1871. Darwin, in endeavouring to explain the development and diversity of species, propounded a theory in which the emergence of man in the world was not due to a cataclysmic act of divine creation, but simply to a process of selection through a relentless struggle for survival. The clear implication of Darwin's theories was that man was simply the product of the law of the jungle. Darwinism presupposes an endless sequence of minute mutations, one vast continuum in time and space, effected - not by the inheritance of characteristics acquired by deliberate efforts (as previous biologists had conceived - but by the impersonal process of natural selection. This selective process derives from the struggle for survival - the very will to live - and it selects by favouring those individuals who happen to possess variations of immediate advantage to them in their environment. These individuals tend to survive and breed. The same process, repeated countless times for each succeeding generation, results in accumulated minute variations that account for the differentiation of the species. The contribution of geologists to this theory was their proof that the earth had existed for billions of years, during which this biological process could have occurred. One can readily appreciate the manner in which Darwinist thought afforded the moral sanction - indeed imperative - for the exploitation of undeveloped 'primitive' peoples by 'superior' European civilisation; the new imperialism appearing to re-enact the dynamics of the 'survival of the fittest'.

Conclusion

One is now in a position to analyse the dimensions - political/strategic, economic, philosophical - within which the Boer-British conflict was enacted. On the political/strategic plane one has the new imperialism's relationship with nationalist rivalries; in this particular instance, Anglo-German rivalry for strategic assets in Africa. The tensions between Britain and an aggressive expansionist Wilhelmine Germany were overlaid by the presence of a pro-German white republic in the midst of British territory after it had been hemmed in on the west, east and north; by the acquisition of Bechuanaland, Zululand, Pondoland and Rhodesia. The economic dimension - the imperative of the new imperialism to seek new outlets for capital investment - had been lent an

INTRODUCTION

irresistible momentum by the discovery of inexhaustible gold deposits within the Transvaal Republic. On a broader, philosophical plane, one can readily understand how the antagonists of the Boers regarded Kruger's republic as the obscurantist and atavistic obstacle to an irresistible tide of European expansion; sanctioned by both technology and the Darwinist credo.

One is also placed to appreciate the peculiar resonances and echoes which the Boer-British conflict possesses, in the light of subsequent history. The Transvaal Republic is the prototype of the fascist state which disfigures the succeeding century. The seminal features of the Boer ethos - a fanatically defended ethnic homogeneity, racial exclusiveness underpinned by an outmoded Calvinist dogma and the total political exclusion of those who were not members of the 'volk' - conform closely to the fascist ideology. The legacy which attained its climax in the 2nd Boer War (and extends back to the Great Trek of the 1830s), were to buttress the ideology and myths of the Afrikaner credo; heightened and enhanced during the Nationalist Party's regime of 1948-1994. The imperialist antagonists of the Boers also have their 20th Century descendants. In seeking to destabilise and ultimately destroy their hosts through their machinations and manipulative policies, Rhodes and his colleagues possess distinct connotations of the multi-national corporations of today. Further, the base of the Jameson raid - Rhodesia - was to serve as a destabilising factor in African history during the 1960s and 1970s, generating a protracted insurgency war in the Zambezi salient.

S Monick
February 1999

CONTENTS

CHAP.		PAGE
I.	THE SEED GROUND	1
II.	A STAR IN THE ASCENDANT	11
III.	THE SOWERS	25
IV.	GERMINATION	34
V.	GETTING READY IN RHODESIA	42
VI.	THE 'JUMPING-OFF GROUND'	51
VII.	UNDERGROUND WORK	62
VIII.	JOHANNESBURG COMES IN	71
IX.	THE PLAN OF CAMPAIGN	79
X.	PITSANI AND MAFEKING	93
XI.	CROSS-PURPOSES	109
XII.	UNION JACK OR VIERKLEUR	124
XIII.	THE DAMP SQUIB	134
XIV.	READY TO BOLT	143
XV.	THEY'RE OFF!	153
XVI.	THE RAID	163
XVII.	THE SURRENDER	180
XVIII.	WARNINGS	192
XIX.	THE REFORM COMMITTEE	203
XX.	TROUBLES OF THE REFORM COMMITTEE	213
XXI.	REVERBERATIONS	225
XXII.	HUMILIATION	241
XXIII.	KRUGER'S MAGNANIMITY	259
XXIV.	REGINA VERSUS JAMESON	269
XXV.	THE AFTER-COST	277

Appendices

I.	THE LETTER OF INVITATION	287
II.	COMPOSITION OF DR. JAMESON'S FORCE AND DETAILS OF CASUALTIES	289
III.	THE 'SUZERAINTY'	296
	INDEX	299

ILLUSTRATIONS

DR. JAMESON	*frontispiece*
(*from a cartoon by Leslie Ward*)	
DR. F. RUTHERFOORD HARRIS . . .	*facing page* 8
COLONEL FRANK RHODES	,, 48
SIR GEORGE FARRAR	,, 100
LEANDER STARR JAMESON IN 1895 . .	,, 148
SCENE OF JAMESON'S SURRENDER . .	,, 188
PAUL KRUGER	,, 244
CECIL RHODES	,, 284
MAP OF THE TRANSVAAL AND ADJOINING TERRITORIES IN 1895	,, 163
MAP OF THE KRUGERSDORP DISTRICT . .	,, 182

CHAPTER I

The Seed Ground

No episode of modern history has been so fertile in riddles as the Jameson Raid. A generation has passed, but the speculations which exercised men's minds when they first began to consider it in cool blood have not yet ceased to vex them. We are still unable to comprehend the motives which prompted people of sound judgment in ordinary affairs to mix themselves up in a plot ill-conceived from the outset, and ill-managed as it progressed. The searchlight of official enquiries, the examination of contemporary documents, and the 'revelations' of those professing to have been behind the scenes leave us still in the dark as to the complicity of this and that highly placed personage, either in the general scheme of revolution within the Transvaal or in the special plan for intervention from outside. Opinions still differ as to the ethical justification for the plot itself and as to the defensibility, according to accepted standards of honour, of some of the actions by which it was engineered. These questions have been thrashed out from nearly every conceivable angle, and the principal actors – Rhodes, Kruger, Jameson and the leaders of the Reform Committee – have found their champions, each striving to defend the conduct of an individual or party at the expense of the others. But all discussions of the subject close with a note of interrogation.

One line of investigation only seems to have been somewhat neglected. Perhaps it would have been a difficult line to pursue while so many of those concerned were alive, and, in some cases, holding public positions.

Nevertheless, no study of the chain of events which culminated in the Raid can be complete without a study of the characters, the temperaments and the psychology of those who guided the rank and file, and, with what appears to be an utter disregard of the ordinary canons of good sense, compassed the ruin of their own cause.

Take, for example, Dr. Jameson himself. When Rhodes was first startled by the news that he had invaded the Transvaal he is said to have exclaimed, " Jameson has taken the bit between his teeth and bolted ". We understand this phenomenon in horses. We know that some are apt to get above themselves – especially in company – while others remain steady, even in the hunting-field or on a race-course. It may be something in their training, or the way they are handled, or their individual character or in a combination of all three which makes them act differently. We recognise the influences and make allowance for them. And so in Jameson's case it is well worth while to apply the test suggested by this metaphor of Rhodes's and to see if we cannot trace the growth in him of certain temperamental peculiarities, which existed perhaps from the beginning, but were intensified by a series of unusual experiences and fostered by the influence of those who immediately surrounded him. The same process may be applied with advantage to some of the others involved.

Mr. Ian Colvin, in his admirable biography,[1] has clearly discerned that the real turning-point in Jameson's career came at Kimberley, in 1889, six years before the Raid, when he forsook his lucrative medical practice on the diamond-fields to throw in his lot with Rhodes's schemes for the northern expansion of British South Africa. So many of those who afterwards took part in these schemes

---

[1] *The Life of Jameson*, by Ian Colvin, Vol. I., p. 90.

were at Kimberley at the same time that no apology is needed for taking a backward glance at the conditions there when Rhodes was maturing his plans for carrying the British flag up to the River Zambesi, and beyond it.

Kimberley was then the northern terminus of the railway-line from the Cape which has since been extended to the Belgian Congo. It was the jumping-off ground for all whose business took them to the gold-fields of Witwatersrand, where the new township of Johannesburg was springing up like a mushroom, and for the traders, hunters and adventurers who were pushing their way up to Bechuanaland and the regions beyond – then generally known as 'the interior'. It was also the focus of most of the financial activity of South Africa. The share-brokers and speculators formed the most vital section of the community. Their business might have been reduced when Rhodes brought about the amalgamation of the diamond interests into one big concern – the De Beers Consolidated Mines – a stroke which, while it placed the industry on a solid basis and in many other ways inaugurated a new era of prosperity for the town itself, limited the opportunities for dealing in diamond shares – but, almost simultaneously, a fresh impetus had been given to speculation by the discovery of gold on the Rand, and the flotation of numerous mining and exploration companies to develop it. The share-dealing fraternity acquired a new lease of life and, for the time being, Kimberley continued to be the headquarters of the financial magnates. The most active brains in the Colony were collected there. Capetown no doubt remained the centre of culture, education and politics, but Capetown was old-fashioned and unprogressive, besides being too far away from the ganglions of the mining industry to keep touch with the new forces which were gathering strength irresistibly in the north. Johannesburg itself was still more or less out in the wilds, and had barely risen above the status of a mining-camp. Three years earlier the Rand had been a bare stretch of inhospitable veld, with hardly a mud shanty to mark the future site of the richest city in the world. The deep levels had not yet been proved and the whole business of gold-mining was still looked upon as something of a gamble. Even to get to Johannesburg was an adventure, involving a risky and intensely uncomfortable journey of sixty hours in a lurching and lumbering American coach, and no one undertook it except with one object – to make money quickly, and get back. Dwelling-houses were almost unobtainable. Sir Lionel (then Mr.) Phillips and his wife, who reached the place in 1889, thought themselves fortunate in succeeding to the 'mansion' of Mr. Hermann Eckstein – a bungalow of corrugated iron, containing four rooms, a veranda and a kitchen.[1] Newcomers had to take what they could get, and it was a common occurrence to have to make one's bed under the billiard table of one of the so-called 'hotels' while a game was going on overhead. Very few had then conceived the idea of settling down in a place whose permanence was so uncertain.

Kimberley was a solid reality, however, and so far from damaging its prospects the Transvaal gold-fever revivified them. In those days it was the rallying-point of the most progressive elements in South Africa.

When Griqualand West was absorbed in Cape Colony, Kimberley had retained its High Court, with a full complement of officials, giving employment to a number of barristers and solicitors. Several of the latter were young men destined to make their mark later on. Charles

[1] *Some South African Recollections*, by Florence Phillips, 1899.

Coghlan, twenty-five years afterwards first Prime Minister of Southern Rhodesia, and H. C. Hull, who became Minister of Finance for the Union of South Africa, were both practising as attorneys, notaries and conveyancers. In the medical profession, besides Jameson, was Frederick Rutherfoord Harris, a man in the prime of life and, like Jameson, possessed by that demon of restlessness which seems always to have haunted Englishmen in South Africa. Most of the diamond-buyers and a good proportion of the share-brokers were Jews, but there was a sprinkling of Frenchmen, Germans and British. Mr. Abe Bailey was just starting in a small way as a financier, but Cecil Rhodes, Alfred Beit and ' Barney ' Barnato had ' arrived ', and all were said to have passed the million mark.

When the writer first saw Kimberley, early in 1889, the great Johannesburg boom had reached its peak. During the preceding twelve months the excitement had been continuous, and every man and woman in Kimberley – for it was there that most of the speculation went on – had been swept along in a tide of wild gambling. Clerks, who a little time before had been content to stand behind a bank counter and cash cheques on salaries of £20 a month, had been lured away to keep the books of brokers at £50, £60 or £70, with a commission on deals. In some cases they soon started business on their own account, and deemed themselves on the high road to fortune. Money was spent like water. The old galvanised iron cottages were giving way to handsome brick houses full of expensive furniture from London. In the diamond market and round the Stock Exchange there were constant scenes of excitement. News would come down of some rich strike on the Rand and at once the street would be crowded with brokers shouting out the prices like bookies on the rails before the start of a big race. In the evening business was transferred to the bars and lounges of the hotels, which were thronged with eager buyers and sellers. Even at the new club, which was the most luxurious and up-to-date in Africa, one could not get away from the atmosphere of money-making. Gold-reefs, shares and flotations were the main topics of conversation, and champagne the ordinary beverage, of the members, who were one and all absorbed in the cheerful game of making a pile.

For all that, there was a small group of men who kept their heads and were looking beyond the immediate things close at hand, beyond the Rand and the Transvaal, to distant regions in the north, on which the avaricious eyes of Germany, Portugal and the Boers were also fixed, and where rumour said there were immense tracts of fertile country fit for European settlement, and gold reefs compared with which the Rand would become insignificant. The dominant figure of this group was Cecil Rhodes, who moved serene and detached from the crowd of speculators, yet forming part of them; knowing them all, but confiding in only a chosen few his dreams for a greater South Africa. Charles Dunell Rudd, his mining partner; Rochfort Maguire, the All Souls don, and Sir Charles Metcalfe, the railway engineer, both friends of Oxford days; Alfred Beit, in whom he discovered a spirit of enterprise and an imagination not uncommon in a race which has produced a Disraeli and a Nathan Rothschild, though rare in that mob of money-grubbers: these were some of the young men – they were all young then – to whom Rhodes revealed his far-reaching plans, and, above all, Leander Starr Jameson, whose quarters he shared in a rather dingy bungalow opposite the club.

Jameson was then at the zenith of his professional career. Apart from his surgical skill, which was of an unusually high order, and his faculty of quick diagnosis, he had achieved an enormous popularity by his attractive and magnetic personality. One of the qualities which helped him was his flow of good-humoured banter. Few can indulge in this habit without overstepping the mark and giving offence, yet Jameson seemed privileged, and though he was outspoken to the extent often of downright rudeness he found that people tolerated and even encouraged his propensity. They recognised that his chaffing, joking manner was only a mask, and that beneath it was a very real and human sympathy. He was brutally candid, and did not hesitate to tell his patients, when necessary, that their ailments were trivial or imaginary. Yet he never lost one, and his practice, especially among women, with whom he was always a favourite, increased by leaps and bounds, until by 1888 it must have been worth £6,000 or £7,000 a year. He ought to have been saving money, for his mode of living was by no means extravagant, and he seemed to have no taste for stocks and shares, but he was careless about accounts, took little trouble to collect his fees and never bothered to check his expenditure. He was, moreover, a daring gambler, of the kind that is always trying to bring off a risky coup and finds no pleasure in playing for safety.

Under his nonchalant and slightly cynical exterior the fever of ambition and restlessness was constantly and secretly burning. When he could climb no higher the incessant rounds of a general practitioner began to bore him. His daily work was hard, and on the whole humdrum. He longed for new excitements, but although he was the repository of Rhodes's cherished plans for capturing the North he did not at once conceive the idea that there was any place for himself in those plans, and it was an accident, more or less, that turned his thoughts definitely in that direction.

Early in 1889 Rhodes had it in his mind to make a trip to Matabeleland. Three months before, his agents, Rudd, Maguire and Thompson, had secured from Lobengula, the King of that country, a valuable mineral concession, which Rhodes had submitted to England for consideration by the Imperial Government. But there were reports that a determined opposition was being organised in London, and his presence was urgently needed there to deal with certain powerful financial groups, and others, whose interests would have to be absorbed or eliminated before he could be free to proceed with his own schemes. He could not be in two places at once and he was obliged to postpone the visit to Bulawayo, where, in spite of the fact that Rudd had come away with the concession, he felt that the position was safe in the hands of Maguire and Thompson, his other two representatives. Matters would doubtless have been allowed to take their course there had it not happened that at the end of January there passed through Kimberley a deputation of two Matabele headmen who, it was rumoured, had been despatched by Lobengula on a secret mission to Queen Victoria. What was more significant was that they were in charge of a gentleman known to be acting for one of the aforesaid groups of London financiers and to have been for some time negotiating for a concession on their behalf, and that the interpreter with the party was connected with another rival group. While it thus became more important than ever that Rhodes should be in England – and he did in fact start four weeks later – it was equally imperative

Dr. F. RUTHERFOORD HARRIS

(*face p.* 8)

that someone in whom he could trust should proceed to Matabeleland to find out if possible something of the King's intentions in sending this mission, and it at once occurred to him to ask Jameson, who was entirely in his confidence, to go up in his stead, to find out how the land lay and to do what he could to smooth over any doubts or difficulties in the King's mind.

It was a novel task to impose upon a man whose life had been passed in sick-rooms and operating-theatres, and who had no previous experience of natives or up-country conditions, but its very novelty appealed to Jameson, who happened to be greatly in need of a change and rest from doctoring, and he jumped at the suggestion. It was undesirable that the real purpose of his journey should become known and so, although the pursuit of game was entirely out of his line, he called it a shooting-trip, and, to lend colour to the idea, decided to take with him a full equipment of guns and rifles, and a sporting companion.

His choice fell upon Dr. Frederick Rutherfoord Harris, who afterwards cut such a prominent figure in connection with affairs in the north and with the actual Raid that some account of his personality may here be given. Unlike Jameson, he had not made a success of his medical practice in Kimberley. He was an ardent sportsman, and spent a good deal of time in coursing buck and shooting, to the detriment of his professional work. Realising that he would never make a fortune as a general practitioner, he turned his attention to gold-mines, and had a finger in several of the new companies floated in the early days of the Rand, but he was not particularly lucky in his ventures, and when the slump came he found that he had lost the bulk of his modest capital. He was, however, a man of boundless enterprise and resource, and when Jameson suggested that he should join him in the trip to Matabeleland he was glad to seize the opportunity of learning something about the new developments there, for he saw that if he played his cards adroitly he might get some sort of foothold in the select circle of Rhodes's entourage, of which at that time he was little more than a hanger-on. Jameson, for his part, wanted a cheerful and energetic fellow-traveller, who would help him with the transport and not jib at a little hard work, and Harris exactly filled the bill. He was compact of courage, initiative and driving-power, but lacked the altruism which inspired Rhodes and the magnetism which enabled Jameson himself to become a leader. In default of these finer qualities his irrepressible self-confidence and pluck made him a useful lieutenant in any business which required a cool head and a contempt for the beaten tracks of convention.

Whether Rhodes intended it to be so or not, this expedition proved to be a sort of trial trip. It had in itself no direct bearing on subsequent events in the Transvaal, but it had a very important effect in shaping the course of Jameson's career. It was the first of a series of personal adventures which, during the next seven years, swept him forward from one triumph to another, but in the end lured him to disaster. It was the beginning of his metamorphosis.

CHAPTER II

A Star in the Ascendant

THE two doctors lost no time in getting away. Less than a week after Lobengula's 'envoys' had passed through Kimberley they started on their 700-mile trek, travelling at first by mule cart so as to catch up some waggons despatched a short time before by Rhodes to carry the first consignment of the 1,000 rifles which were part of the price he had agreed to pay for his mineral concession. It took them two months to reach Bulawayo, and Jameson found that the position there called for all his powers of tactful handling.

Thompson was fidgety and full of vague apprehensions. Maguire was bored to death. His surroundings were hopelessly uncongenial. He had nothing in common with the other white men who infested the kraal, plying the King with presents and flattery in the hope of winning his favour. He could not speak the native language and had therefore no influence with the King's *indunas* and councillors. He assured Jameson that he could do more good by returning to help Rhodes in the task of dealing with the importunate demands with which he was now being pestered. The concession had been the signal for an outbreak of a species of blackmail on the part of all sorts of adventurers, most of them obscure nobodies who had been paying their addresses to Lobengula, and now claimed to have received promises of rights to dig for gold or special privileges for trading or farming, or to stand in such favour at the 'court' that they could not be ignored. The majority of these claims were fictitious, and they were all put forward with the idea of extorting money, but they threatened to become a serious clog on Rhodes's freedom of action. Jameson, agreeing that Maguire's evidence might be useful in disposing of them, and believing that his presence in Bulawayo was no longer essential, assented to the suggestion that he should return with himself and Harris.

As for the King, Jameson found him sick both in body and mind. He was suffering from gout and ophthalmia, aggravated by the nauseous messes of the native witch-doctors, and as Jameson had a supply of drugs he was able to give him great relief. Having by this means gained his confidence, he proceeded to ease his mind, which had been disturbed by the insinuations of interested parties that he had been the victim of trickery. It transpired that the mission to England had been prompted by a report spread by some Boer hunters that the 'Great White Queen' (Victoria) had no real existence, and that the British Resident, Mr. J. S. Moffat, who had for some time been living at Bulawayo, but was now absent, was a sham. About these and other disquieting reports Jameson was able to reassure him. His open jovial manner and his disdain of the obsequiousness used by other white men in order to curry favour with Lobengula immensely strengthened his influence. He employed the same methods with the old savage as he had so often utilised with his patients at Kimberley, and with the same result. The King was completely won over, and when, after ten days at the kraal, Jameson took his leave he received a pressing invitation to come again.

Apart from his intercourse with the King, Jameson sought every opportunity of making friends with the white men at the kraal, and trying to convince them that they had all to gain, and nothing to lose, by throwing in their lot with Rhodes. Here too he was generally successful, though there was a small party which kept him at arm's length and proved impervious to his powers of persuasion. On the whole, however, he was satisfied, and even elated, at the result of his first flight as a diplomatic agent, and he returned to Kimberley in high feather. He resumed his interrupted practice with the air of one who had merely been on a holiday, but in reality his heart was no longer in his work. He had felt his power over men. He had tasted up-country life and adventure, and was greedy for more.

Rhodes in the meantime had succeeded in reconciling conflicting interests in England and, having seen everything in train for the grant of a Royal Charter, also returned to Kimberley, arriving in the middle of August.

All seemed to be going smoothly for the northern programme when suddenly a bombshell burst which threatened to wreck it completely. The group of irreconcilables whom Jameson had left at Bulawayo were the agents of a German financier who had political as well as commercial aims, and was prepared to go to any lengths to prevent Rhodes from acquiring a foothold in Matabeleland. These men had no nice scruples as to the methods they employed, and as soon as Jameson's back was turned they set to work to undo the effect of his success with the King. They poisoned his mind by asserting that he had sold his country to Rhodes, whose next step would be to bring up an army to drive him and his people out of it. Their insinuations gained weight through indiscreet letters from both the British Government and the Aborigines Protection Society, brought out by the headmen who had visited England. The King's suspicious nature took fright, and in his rage he sought a scapegoat. One of his chief councillors who had favoured the concession was ordered for execution and was barbarously murdered with his whole family. Thompson, now the solitary representative of Rhodes's interests, thought he was destined to be the next victim and incontinently fled down country. There was an imminent risk that the King would repudiate the concession altogether, in which case all the ground secured by Rhodes would be lost. Again he turned to Jameson, the only man who might be able to save the situation, and again, but this time with more alacrity because there was a real crisis to be faced, Jameson started for the scene. He expected to be away a few weeks only, but the trouble proved even more acute than he had anticipated, and the weeks lengthened into months. He left Kimberley in the middle of September, 1889, and did not return till the following March.

It is unnecessary to give a detailed account of the prolonged and almost daily conversations by which he gradually restored confidence in the mind of the distracted Chief. He achieved in the end a real triumph, for when, after four months of patient diplomacy, he left Bulawayo he had secured permission, not only for preliminary prospecting in Matabeleland, but for the entry in the dry season of an expedition to start gold-mining operations on a definite basis in Mashonaland.

Preparations for this expedition were already well advanced in Kimberley, where Rutherfoord Harris was installed as secretary of the Chartered Company, and Jameson, though for a few weeks he made a desultory effort to recover the threads of his practice, found it impossible to resist the temptation to join it. This time it was a burning of his boats. The lure of the North had gripped him, as it did many others at that time. Kimberley, his medical career, all considerations of material gain were jettisoned. He sloughed off his old life and threw himself heart and soul into the wider sphere which promised so much more movement and excitement.

He first paid a final visit to Bulawayo, where Lobengula was suffering from another attack of nerves owing to the assembling of troops near his border, for detachments of the Pioneers and of the military police force which was to march with them and afterwards to garrison the country, were already arriving there, and the young braves of the Matabele army were getting restive and clamouring to be allowed to wipe them out with their assegais. The resourceful Doctor applied the usual soothing syrup. He explained in a convincing way that the column would follow a route which would avoid all Matabele kraals and cattle-posts, and repeated his assurances that the object of the expedition was purely a peaceful one. The King, though only half reconciled, and still suspicious of the military character of their outfit, realised that it was now too late to stop their advance. His chief anxiety was to prevent an armed collision, but his people were excited and hard to keep in hand, and the air was charged with dangerous possibilities.

At the end of May, Jameson left for the police camp in Northern Bechuanaland, and there he made his first acquaintance with one who came to be his closest ally and the chosen partner in some of his most daring exploits – including the Raid. This was Sir John Willoughby, the second-in-command of the police. He was an officer in the Royal Horse Guards, who had gained laurels both on active service and in sport. He had been with his regiment in the cavalry charge at Kassassin and at Tel-el-kebir, but was probably best known at the time as the owner of a horse which, in 1884, had run a dead heat for first place in the Derby. It was generally rumoured that he had dropped a good bit of money on the Turf, and was anxious to get away from England for a while and to economise. The expedition to Mashonaland suited both purposes, with the chance of some fighting and a little speculation in gold mines thrown in.

Though the friendship which sprung up between the two men was a very genuine and constant one, it is difficult for anyone who knew them at the time to discover what constituted the mutual attraction. Their early training and social connections had been utterly different – an inherited fortune, Eton, the Blues, the Turf, in the one case; narrow means, a Scottish university, the diamond diggings and a hard professional struggle in the other. In character they were no less dissimilar. Jameson was an opportunist with a strong dash of genius; careless in money matters and ambitious of glory rather than gain. Willoughby was of a more calculating nature; without any outstanding brain capacity, but with one eye always open for a chance of profit. Both, however, were endowed with a sort of piratical craving for adventure and in both the gambling instinct was a powerful motive.

Jameson joined the Pioneer column in an unofficial rôle, but with the confidence that he would have Rhodes's support in any course he saw fit to undertake. He was a free lance in a company which was organised on rigid military lines. He was not even enrolled as a member, and was merely a civilian attached for rations. Nevertheless, he at once made his presence felt, and it came to be tacitly understood that he was the guiding spirit of the whole project and had authority to decide all matters of policy. It was a position fraught with risk, and

A STAR IN THE ASCENDANT

although, strangely enough, the soldier element in the force accepted it without demur, it did eventually lead to friction between him and Mr. Colquhoun, the only other civilian in the expedition, an ex-officer of the Indian Government, selected by Rhodes for the task of forming the nucleus of an administrative service in the new territory. When the column reached its destination, where Fort Salisbury was founded, Colquhoun assumed charge and objected, not perhaps without justice, to the authority which Jameson arrogated to himself — declined, in fact, to recognise him as holding any superior powers. Had Colquhoun been in an assured position he must have been upheld, but he was no match for the other, and in the long run had to resign. For the time being it suited Jameson's purpose to leave Colquhoun in control and to avoid provoking an open breach by taking himself off on a number of hazardous and disconnected missions on behalf of Rhodes, which for nearly a year kept him busily engaged in other fields, and of these a rapid outline must now be given.

He first started off to explore a route from Mashonaland to the east coast of Africa, and after a most arduous journey of 400 miles – partly on foot and partly in a canoe – and many perilous adventures,[1] he arrived with two white companions, one of them Major Frank Johnson, the commander of the Pioneers, at the mouth of the Pungwe River, where the port of Beira was afterwards established. A steamer had been sent to meet him and he made his way by sea to Cape Colony. A fortnight at Kimberley and he was off again over the long pioneer road of 1,000 miles to Fort Salisbury, which he reached on Christmas Day of 1890. It was the height of the worst

---

[1] This and the journey to Gazaland are graphically described by Colvin in his biography.

rainy season in living memory, but within three days Jameson departed on a new errand – this time to Gazaland, where Rhodes had agents trying to secure a concession from the King, Gungunyana, in defiance of the Portuguese, who claimed that he was their tributary. The country over which Jameson – again with two white companions – had to travel for 700 miles was in many parts swampy and malarious. Food was unobtainable and the rains were torrential. It was by far the most trying experience he had so far undergone, and the fatigue and exposure told severely on his health. When he eventually reached his destination he was suffering from a sharp attack of fever, but he braced himself for the encounter with the King, who was wavering between the British and the Portuguese, and by the sheer force of his magnetic personality induced him to put his sign manual to the concession, giving the Chartered Company mineral and other rights over his whole country.[1] This document he immediately despatched by a safe messenger overland, while he himself went down to the Limpopo River to join a small steamer sent by Rutherfoord Harris in anticipation of his arrival there. No sooner had he embarked than the steamer was boarded by the commander and crew of a Portuguese gunboat which had been shadowing it. Jameson and his party were made prisoners and taken to Delagoa Bay, where, as no compromising papers were found on them, they were ultimately set free. After this audacious exploit Jameson spent a few weeks in Cape Colony consulting with Rhodes as to further plans, and in May he started once more for Mashonaland, taking with him this time full powers to act in Rhodes's place as Managing Director of the Chartered Company. Before he had time to

[1] This concession was subsequently disallowed by the Imperial Government.

A STAR IN THE ASCENDANT

settle, however, a new crisis called him down to the Transvaal border, where an armed force of Boers was preparing for an organised attempt to cross the Limpopo River and occupy the southern portion of the Company's territory. On this occasion he was supported by a detachment of police with a machine-gun. He met the Boer leaders and reasoned with them; assured them that if they tried to force an entry they would be fired on, but that if they chose to accept the Company's authority and enter as ordinary settlers they would be admitted. As usual his subtle gift of suasion prevailed. The Boers were induced to abandon their intentions, and their commander actually accepted a post in the Company's service!

The varied excursions above described had all taken place within nine months from the date of the occupation of Mashonaland. Jameson had not come through them scatheless. The incessant travelling, the exposure to bad weather and the constant shortage of food supplies had told heavily on his constitution. He never spared himself, and when he returned to Fort Salisbury in August 1891, he suffered from repeated attacks of malarial fever and was a martyr to piles.

In that month Colquhoun, realising that, with the divided control, he could no longer retain his position with dignity, resigned, and Jameson, at Rhodes's request, stepped into his place as Administrator and Chief Magistrate. He was absolutely without training or experience, judicial, financial or executive; he had a difficult community to handle, mainly composed of happy-go-lucky young Englishmen with very vague ideas of what they were there for and inclined to be impatient of discipline. Some of them were prospecting or farming in an amateur sort of fashion, some trading with the natives, or riding transport, while a good few were idle and liable to get into mischief. There was a certain amount of discontent and disappointment, for the gold was not proving so easy to find as had been expected; mining tools, foodstuffs and the ordinary necessaries of life were scarce, and the conditions extremely rough. The heartbreaking journey of 1,000 miles from the nearest railhead was the chief obstacle to progress. Yet somehow or other Jameson managed to infuse a spirit of optimism and hopefulness into the situation, and by his ready intuition was able to tackle the daily problems inseparable from a colony in the making. For a few months he had the assistance of Rutherfoord Harris, but the latter was rather unjustly saddled by the settlers with the responsibility for the shortage of food supplies, and his unpopularity became so marked that Jameson thought it wise to send him down country. The decision was made easier by an accident. Harris was unlucky enough to be badly mauled by a crocodile while bathing, and narrowly escaped with his life. As soon as he was fit to move he left to resume the secretaryship of the Company at Capetown, and Mashonaland saw him no more.

For nearly two years Jameson carried on the work of administration. He had promised Rhodes to see the young colony through its birth throes, and was loyal to his word. There can be no doubt that he was the right man for the task. He was prone to take short cuts and had an utter disregard for official formality, but his rough and ready methods were well suited to the conditions, and he succeeded where an experienced and orthodox Governor of the regulation type, such as Colquhoun, would have failed. Nevertheless, he found the life too hampered by routine for his taste, and was beginning to sigh for fresh fields to conquer, when an event occurred which altered the whole of his outlook, and was the means of raising him within a few months to the pinnacle of fame.

The Matabele had for some time been chafing at the restrictions on their old freedom to raid the tribes of Mashonaland. Men of experience knew that, sooner or later, a conflict was bound to occur. Several minor acts of aggression on the part of irresponsible bodies of natives had already been smoothed over when, in July 1893, a force of 2,000 or 3,000 of Lobengula's soldiers, sent to punish an unruly local chief near the agreed border, got out of hand and invaded the mining township of Victoria, pursuing the inoffensive Mashona on to the commonage lands, killing fugitives and burning and looting villages within sight of the white men. The very existence of the settlement was threatened, and all work came to a standstill. Jameson hurried to the spot, sent for the leaders of the Matabele and peremptorily ordered them to retire. A patrol sent to enforce the order found a party still raiding and fired upon them, inflicting severe loss.

During the next few weeks attempts were made by the Imperial authorities, and even by Lobengula himself, to patch up some reconciliation, but matters had gone too far. It was clear that no abiding peace could exist between a barbarous nation of warlike instincts and a body of high-spirited young colonists such as the Pioneers of Mashonaland, and had not official sanction been given the latter would have taken matters into their own hands. The Matabele were a menace to civilisation. In Rhodes's words, "We either had to have war or to leave the country."[1]

---

[1] Speech at annual meeting of shareholders of the B.S.A. Company in London, 18th January, 1895.

Although it would be untrue to say that Jameson sought or provoked the Matabele war, it would be equally false to deny that he was thoroughly alive to the advantage to be gained by occupying the country. If he pushed the quarrel to a head he only anticipated by a few years what was inevitable in the long run. He did, in fact, use his utmost efforts to secure permission to attack the Matabele in their own stronghold. He began to train his volunteers, in full confidence that he would get his way, and after some procrastination on the part of the authorities he got it.

The expedition which he led into the field was, from a military point of view, absurdly weak. Experts had warned him that nothing less than a force of 5,000 would be sufficient to deal with the Matabele, who were considered as dangerous as their parent tribe, the Zulus. Jameson flew in the face of the experts and of those in the country who remembered the Zulu war, and went into the fray with a force of less than 700 miners and farmers. It was a gamble – and, by the aid of Providence, it came off. Within two months he led his small army triumphantly into Bulawayo, and Lobengula, with the remnant of his fighting men, fled into the wilderness.

The command of the Mashonaland force had been entrusted to Major Forbes of the 6th Dragoons, the senior regular officer in the country, but he was not allowed a free hand, for the general direction of the plan of campaign was retained by Jameson, who had, moreover, taken with him Sir John Willoughby, in the capacity of 'Military Adviser',[1] and it was Willoughby who furnished the official reports to the Imperial Government. Forbes, unfortunately, suffered a loss of prestige through the disaster which befell the patrol under Major

---

[1] In the Company's report for 1892–4 he is styled 'Senior Military Officer.'

Allan Wilson at Shangani, and, though responsible for the success of the initial operations, got little of the credit. That went to Jameson, who became the hero of the whole affair. He deserved every word that was said in his praise for what, making allowance for a strong element of luck, was a notable feat of arms. The design was his, and the campaign would never have been undertaken, nor could it have been brought to a victorious conclusion, without his inspiration. But it is impossible to disregard the effect of this culminating achievement on the psychology of the man himself.

Towards the end of 1894, having seen Matabeleland settled, new towns founded and mining work started, he came to England and found himself the man of the hour. He was greeted with rapturous enthusiasm in the City of London and was lionised in society. The Queen conferred on him the Order of the Bath – the only special decoration or reward, by the way, that was bestowed on any of those engaged in the Matabele campaign. He delivered an address at the Imperial Institute before a notable gathering presided over by the Prince of Wales. With Rhodes – Prime Minister of Cape Colony and now a Privy Councillor – sitting on his right, he foreshadowed the future which, between them, they had mapped out for South Africa – a commercial federation of which Rhodesia was to be the keystone. Only a handful of Transvaal Boers stood in the way of this consummation. He left it to his audience to infer that that obstacle would soon disappear.

Rhodes also said a few words. Those listening realised that they had before them two Englishmen of the Elizabethan type – men who had made history and were determined to make more. Both had a great reception, and in the case of Jameson, a romantic figure, whose Matabele victory compensated for a long series of British failures in Africa, it amounted to an ovation. It may have helped to intoxicate him with an exaggerated estimate of his own powers. In less than six years he had risen from an obscure professional position to be the darling of the public. As an explorer, an administrator – as a military leader even [1]– he had brought off every venture he had embarked on. He had never failed. It is hardly surprising that he should have conceived the notion that he never *could* fail.

[1] *Cf.* Earl Grey, in a speech to the Chartered shareholders about that date: "I am using no empty phrase when I say that Dr. Jameson's exploits as an administrator have rivalled his exploits as a general."

CHAPTER III

The Sowers

From the casual and airy reference which Jameson, in his address at the Imperial Institute, made to the Transvaal Boers – 15,000, he called them, amid a population of 50,000 Englishmen and Cape Colonists – it would never have been guessed that they were occupying much of his thoughts. They were a fly in the ointment, certainly, but not of such overpowering importance as to warrant doubts as to the speedy attainment of the great scheme of South African federation which had been painted in such glowing colours. Jameson's audience (of whom the present writer happened to be one) would have been surprised to learn that the situation in the Transvaal and the attitude of President Paul Kruger and his Government, both towards the other states of South Africa and the growing alien community – mainly British – within their own borders, had, in the last three months, become the absorbing interest in the minds of Jameson and Rhodes.

Up to the previous September (1894) Jameson had been too much engrossed in the details of the settlement of Matabeleland – recently placed under the direct control of the Chartered Company – to give attention to outside affairs. In that month he was joined by Rhodes, who had managed to tear himself away from his duties as Prime Minister of the Cape for a short visit to Rhodesia, and had brought with him Mr. John Hays Hammond, an eminent American mining engineer, whose opinion of the mineral prospects of the new territory he was anxious to obtain. This was Jameson's first meeting with

Hammond, who was employed by the Goldfields of South Africa, Ltd., one of the leading companies operating on the Rand, of which Rhodes was joint Managing Director. The three men then made a tour of a few weeks through Matabeleland and Mashonaland, inspecting all the principal gold properties on their way.

According to the evidence given by Jameson two and a half years afterwards before the Parliamentary Committee in London, it was on this tour that his interest in the affairs of Rhodesia's southern neighbour was awakened. 'The position of the Transvaal and the grievances of the Uitlanders in Johannesburg', he said, 'were freely discussed by us, Mr. Hammond asserting that it was impossible for the economic condition of the Rand to continue, and that unless a radical change was made there would be a rising by the people in Johannesburg.'[1]

He added that he was 'much impressed' by the talk; the truth probably being that he scented the possibility of a fresh excitement and began to coquet with the idea of having a hand in it.

The conversations also made an impression on Rhodes, who referred to them in his evidence before the same committee:

'Hammond . . . told me about the whole condition and situation there; that it was impossible to go on, that the poorer reefs would not pay on account of the taxation. We used to discuss this the whole time we went through Mashonaland. I then came back by Beira to Delagoa Bay and came up to Johannesburg. Then I saw a number of people, and the situation was that a number of them had that feeling which is peculiar to

[1] Report of the Select Committee on British South Africa – Evidence. Question No. 4513.

our race, that they must have a share in the government of the country where they were paying taxes.'[1]

There was this difference between the two. Rhodes, apart from his dreams of the federation of South Africa, was closely affected, as a Director and large shareholder in one of the most important mining groups on the Rand, by the heavy burdens which President Paul Kruger and his Government were heaping on the gold industry, and had therefore a solid excuse for employing every effort to lighten them. Jameson had no such direct incentive. It is probable that the grievances of the Uitlanders did not weigh very heavily on his mind. It is possible that he did not care two straws about them. What he did see was that 'Krugerism' was an obstacle – the only obstacle – in the way of Rhodes's political aims, to which he had now dedicated his life. It is more than likely that he was fascinated by the thought that he might be able to play a leading part in bringing about the removal of this obstacle, and that – either then or later – it dawned upon him that in the Chartered Company he had, ready to hand and to a great extent under his thumb, an instrument which he could use for this purpose. One wishes it were possible to acquit Jameson of an ambition for a further personal triumph. It is difficult, in the light of after-events, to banish the suggestion.

What were these 'grievances' which were engendering so much discontent that they might provoke a 'rising of the people in Johannesburg'?

The *Uitlanders* (foreigners), as President Kruger called and consistently treated them – the population concentrated on the Rand and a few other mining centres – were mostly of British origin, but all had come from

[1] Select Committee, No. 709.

countries with free institutions. What was galling them – goading them, in fact, to desperation – was that they – an intelligent majority, owning the mines, the bulk of the town property and much of the land; providing the whole of the commerce and five-sixths of the public revenue – were in the clutch, and at the mercy, of a minority composed almost entirely of uneducated burghers, scattered about on isolated farms, with a mental outlook and a standard of living which had hardly changed at all since the country was seized by their grandfathers, the *Voortrekkers*, fifty years before.

It is difficult to estimate the size of the burgher population, but it is certain that by 1895 it was greatly exceeded by the Uitlanders, whose numbers along the Rand alone were more than 100,000. The Boers themselves had no interest in gold mining as an industry. The more ignorant among them would have been glad to see it collapse and the Uitlanders take themselves elsewhere. There were others, like Kruger, shrewd enough to realise that the development of the mines had not only pulled their country out of bankruptcy and raised it to affluence, but was constantly providing them with opportunities of personal enrichment. Kruger, apart from his hatred and dread of the British who had gradually encircled the Transvaal from outside and shut up his people, as it were, in a cattle kraal, had only two thoughts about those who had settled inside his boundaries: to appropriate the profits of their industry for the benefit of himself and his burghers, and to exclude them from any voice in the government or politics of the Republic. As their numbers grew he tightened his grip. By 1894 the conditions had become wellnigh insupportable.

The grievance that was made the most of was the

denial of the rights of citizenship to any but the Boers of the Transvaal. Petitions, signed by many thousands of Uitlanders, for the right to become naturalised and to have the vote were more than once rejected in the *Volksraad* with sneers and derision. Their only result was the introduction of new legislation making the restrictions more rigid. It is doubtful, however, whether this disability was so acutely felt by the alien community at large as was made out. Mr. Lionel Phillips,[1] one of the leaders of the mining industry, in a letter to Mr. Alfred Beit in June 1894, wrote that he 'didn't think many people cared a fig for the franchise'.[2] There were certainly other grievances affecting them more directly and less easy to bear. Every effort, for instance, was made by the authorities to repress the use of the English language, both in the schools and in official business. The absence of any provision for the decent education of their children hit the less monied classes severely. Acts were passed curtailing the liberty of the Press and the right of public meeting. The Government made a regular practice of granting concessions for utility services, such as water supply and electric lighting, to individuals who were ready to bribe the members of the Volksraad in order to secure favours. The most scandalous of these was the dynamite concession, which put into the hands of a group of foreign speculators a monopoly worth upwards of half a million a year, and provided one member of the State Executive with an annual income of nearly £10,000 – all of which came out of the pockets of the mining companies.[3] The railways were controlled by another body of concessionaires, domiciled in Holland, who, in co-operation with Kruger, imposed the most outrageous

[1] Now Sir Lionel Phillips, Bart.
[2] Select Committee Report, Appendix No. 12.
[3] Fitzpatrick, *The Transvaal From Within*, p. 59.

rates on all machinery, foodstuffs and other goods imported for the use of the mining community. The Courts of Justice were exploited for the benefit of the Boers and to the detriment of all others. More than once Kruger attempted to tamper with the independence of the judges, who were grossly underpaid and held office at his pleasure. Only burghers of the Republic were eligible for jury service, so that an Englishman was heavily handicapped in any case where he was in conflict with a Boer. The control of public funds, wrung from the Uitlanders by inequitable taxation, was disgracefully mishandled, and large amounts were appropriated for 'secret service' and unaccounted for. The Civil Service was incompetent and venal. From the Executive Council down to the petty district officials the Government was rotten and corrupt.

Perhaps the most sinister aspect of the situation – at any rate, that which caused the gravest concern to those who, with Rhodes, were envisaging a common bond between the states of South Africa in trade, customs and railway matters – was the open and active participation of Dutchmen from Holland in the counsels of the Republic, and the more stealthy and insidious growth of a pro-German policy. The guiding force in both directions was Dr. Leyds, the State Attorney (i.e. legal adviser to the Government), an astute and not over-scrupulous young Hollander, who owed his appointment in the first instance to the Netherlands Railway group, and repaid his obligation by the most shameless jobbery in their interests. He displayed his hatred of all things British not only by pushing his own countrymen into government offices and posts in the railway, but by exerting a steady pressure upon the President to build up German connections. In commercial arrangements and in railway rates German houses acquired privileges which gave them an immense advantage over British and Cape colonial firms.

The only political organisation which the Uitlanders of Johannesburg possessed was the Transvaal National Union, originally formed in 1892. According to Sir Percy Fitzpatrick it was a body composed ' of men drawn from all classes, who felt that the conditions of life were becoming intolerable, and that something would have to be done by the community to bring about reforms which the Legislature showed no signs of voluntarily introducing '.[1] He goes on to explain that the capitalists, or ' big firms ', were not at first represented on the National Union, as they were loth to be associated with any definite anti-Government propaganda. It was only when they realised that the Government, so far from showing an inclination to redress grievances, were designing fresh burdens to be borne by the Uitlanders that they began to join in the agitation for reform – to whisper, first among themselves, and then cautiously and with bated breath to others outside, the suggestion of revolution.

Of these ' big firms ' the two foremost were the Eckstein group and the Goldfields group. The former was controlled by the London house of Wernher Beit & Co., of which Mr. Alfred Beit, a Director of the Chartered Company, was one of the principals, and was represented at Johannesburg by Mr. Lionel Phillips, who had lived for some years at Kimberley, and was well known to Rhodes and his friends there. In addition to managing Eckstein's he was President, in 1894, of the Transvaal Chamber of Mines, and therefore the spokesman for the whole of the mining industry on the Rand.

The Goldfields of South Africa, Ltd., generally known

[1] *The Transvaal From Within*, p. 94.

as 'The Goldfields', was controlled to a great extent by Rhodes, who was a large shareholder and one of the Managing Directors, but as he could seldom be in Johannesburg he was represented on the company by his brother, Captain Ernest Rhodes. Mr. J. H. Hammond, as already mentioned, was the consulting engineer.

The attitude of Lionel Phillips towards the Uitlander movement was at first extremely cautious. After the Raid his private letter-book was seized by the Boers and its contents explored for evidence against him. Certain letters from him to his principal, Mr. Alfred Beit, written in June 1894, were printed in the Transvaal Government Green Book, and their contents shed a good deal of light on the situation at that time. They are significant as containing the first suggestion on the part of one of the leaders of the mining interests of the possibility of a resort to arms. Phillips mentions the formation of a rifle association in Johannesburg, 'to which, however, I attach little importance, though I cannot be blind to the object'. But the most interesting passages in the letters are those relating to Rhodes. It appears that the 'Goldfields people' were urging Phillips, in view of the failure of all efforts to secure relief from the burdens borne by the gold industry, to go to Capetown and consult with Rhodes as to the position and the best line of action, but that he hesitated to take this course, partly because he was afraid of the effect on the Boer Government if it were known that he had approached Kruger's most dreaded enemy, and partly because he was not certain whether he could trust Rhodes. He put this plainly before Beit. 'If you trust Rhodes, and cable " See Rhodes ", I will run down.'

Phillips, at that time, obviously had no stomach for violent measures and preferred a policy of waiting and watching. Besides, it was rather a delicate matter to approach a man in the position of Rhodes, the Premier of a self-governing colony, and the head of the three most influential concerns in South Africa – De Beers, the Charter and the Goldfields – with suggestions that he should interfere in the affairs of a neighbouring friendly State. These considerations may also have weighed with Beit. At any rate, Beit cabled, 'Do not see Rhodes', and Phillips did nothing more at the time.[1]

There is strong ground for assuming, however, that the conversations which Hammond had, a few weeks later, with Rhodes in Matabeleland were prompted by the 'Goldfields people' – Hammond himself being one of them – who were not so shy as Phillips, and that they were of the nature of feelers to ascertain how far Rhodes's sympathy with a more active policy – possibly a revolutionary policy – could be counted on. Had Jameson not been present the result of the feelers might perhaps have been different.

[1] On 15th July, 1894. See Report of Cape Committee, Appendix, p. vii., No. 5.

CHAPTER IV

Germination

IN describing Jameson's reception in England after the Matabele war there has been an anticipation of a few weeks, and the story must now be resumed from the time when his conversations with Hammond in Rhodesia first put into his head the temptation to mix himself up in the troubles of the Transvaal. There is nothing to indicate that he at once elaborated a plan of action, but, on the other hand, it is clear, from his own evidence before the Parliamentary Committee, that the embryo of a plan was already forming in his fertile brain from the moment he left Rhodesia, and that it took a definite shape during the next few weeks.

Suppose we endeavour to reconstruct, from his movements at the time, aided by the admissions in his evidence, the line of thought he was pursuing, and trace the means he employed to turn, first the Colonial Office, then the Directors of the Chartered Company, and finally the hesitating leaders of the Johannesburg Uitlanders into instruments for his purpose.

The train of his ideas seems to have been somewhat as follows: 'If matters can be brought to a head in Johannesburg, and a resort to armed force is decided on, I and my Rhodesians must have a finger in the pie. Therefore I must first have an organised force ready in Rhodesia to give help. But Rhodesia is a long way from the Rand, and the whole thing might be over before I could get there. A better striking position is indispensable. There is only one frontage where troops could be of any use – the border of the Bechuanaland Protectorate, which marches for some hundreds of miles with the Transvaal, and just north of Mafeking is only 200 miles from Johannesburg. We must get a foothold there from the Imperial Government. The extension of the railway from Mafeking will be the card to play. That will give us an excuse for placing troops close to the border.'

The organisation of a revolutionary movement in Johannesburg was not his job, but it is probable that the desirability of inducing Rhodes and Beit to lend financial and other support to the agitators on the spot had occurred to Jameson – had perhaps even been suggested – though nothing was actually done in this direction until some months later.

Now let us see how Jameson's actions fit in with this image of his thoughts.

On leaving Rhodesia with Rhodes in October 1894, he went to Pretoria and Johannesburg, where he occupied himself in verifying, by direct communication with the miners and working classes, the information he had gleaned from Hammond. Apparently he was satisfied that Hammond's forebodings were well-founded, for he arranged with Rhodes, who had been making independent enquiries among the mine managers and leading men in the industry, that the Chartered Company's police and volunteers – the latter did not, in fact, exist, but I am quoting from Jameson's own statement – 'should be made as efficient as possible, in order to be prepared for eventualities, so that if a revolt did occur in Johannesburg, and help were required, I should be in a position to use my discretion as to how, when and where, if at all, the police and volunteers should be utilised.'[1]

[1] Select Committee Report: question No. 4513. Note that the Chartered Company, whose paid servants the police were, equally with Jameson, were not to be consulted.

This was as far as he had got before he left Africa, but it was not a bad beginning.

Rhodes and Jameson, with Willoughby and Rutherfoord Harris in attendance, reached England on the 16th December, and the two former at once, before going near the Chartered Company, opened discussions at the Colonial Office with three objects in view, all of which have a bearing on our story: first, an extension of the Company's sphere of action over the vast area north of the Zambesi, i.e. between that river and the Belgian, German and Portuguese colonies; secondly, permission for the continuation of the railway system northwards from Mafeking towards Bulawayo, and lastly – and this is the one that most directly concerned Jameson's plans – the grant to the Chartered Company of administrative powers over the Bechuanaland Protectorate, through which the new railway line would have to pass. They were successful in regard to the first, and the railway proposals also received Lord Ripon's blessing. He was only too glad to see private capital employed for the development of a country which, so far, had been no more than an expensive incubus to the Government.

As regards the administration of the Protectorate, it was not the first time that the subject had been brought forward. The value of this territory to Rhodes had always been as a corridor to the regions further north – 'the Suez Canal to the Interior', he used to call it – and he was now ready and anxious to carry the railway through it for the benefit of Rhodesia. He had mapped out a vast scheme of railway construction of which the section from Mafeking to Bulawayo was to be the first stage. It was essential therefore that he should acquire a strip of land for the purpose. That was a small matter, and could have been arranged without incurring administrative responsibilities. There was no special reason for saddling the Company, on the top of the other heavy burdens which it was now shouldering, with the duty of governing an immense tract of country containing huge waterless stretches, sparsely inhabited, and offering no inducements to settlers. It is true that Rhodes had acquired mineral concessions over a large part of the Protectorate from various native chiefs, but there was little indication of mineral wealth in Bechuanaland – no sign of gold reefs, or even of coal or base metals. Besides, the country was safe from outside interference, and, though under the dead hand of Downing Street, it could not run away. However, the Colonial Office was not disinclined to be relieved of the expense of maintaining the Protectorate, and Rhodes and Jameson had their own motives for wanting it. Their success in settling Matabeleland and Mashonaland was a strong point in their favour, and they had little difficulty in obtaining a promise that the transfer should take place, though without any specific date being fixed.[1] There the matter was left for the time being.

Their next proceeding was to get the Board of the Chartered Company to sanction a rather sensational increase in the military forces of Rhodesia – then amounting to about 350 mounted police. Neither Rhodes nor Jameson disclosed the real object of this increase. They employed the argument that ' in view of the extension of the Company's responsibilities *north* of the Zambesi and the necessity for maintaining a properly equipped force in its territories ' it was desirable to raise a volunteer corps with divisions in Matabeleland and Mashonaland.[2] Put in that way, the proposal seemed a reasonable one,

---
[1] Select Committee: Dr. Harris, No. 6220; Mr. J. Chamberlain, No. 6223.
[2] Select Committee: Duke of Abercorn, No. 7472.

and it was warmly taken up by the Directors, who were in the mood to accept any recommendation, however extravagant, from those who had just added a province of 70,000 square miles to their estate. They authorised the immediate purchase of rifles and maxim guns of the latest pattern, with ammunition on a generous scale, and appointed a sub-committee to discuss details with Jameson and Willoughby, who now reappeared in his character of Military Adviser. Sufficient ordnance was ordered, in the first instance, for a force of 1,500 men, and buying was actually begun on the 17th January – a month from the date of Jameson's arrival.[1]

Apart from being a party to the concealment from his colleagues on the Chartered Board of the real purpose in raising a volunteer force, Rhodes had, so far, taken no step which he could not have defended to them, and even to the world, as a measure of precaution. In strengthening the military forces of Rhodesia, which was bordered by the Transvaal for some hundreds of miles, he was only following the example of the High Commissioner (Sir Henry Loch), who had taken similar action in July 1894, at the time when the commandeering of Uitlanders for service in the Malaboch campaign had provoked such excitement and resentment in Johannesburg that an outbreak was expected at any moment. Loch had then ordered the Bechuanaland Police to be collected and concentrated near Mafeking, and had given directions for other forces to be ready to move.[2] This was as far as Rhodes at this time intended to go –

[1] The purchase of arms and equipment, though done quietly, did not escape the vigilance of the Press, and there was a good deal of speculation as to its object. It is amusing to recall the general impression that these preparations were made for occupying Barotseland, a task which was accomplished in 1898 by a 'force' of less than a dozen civilians ! See, for instance, *South Africa*, for 6th April, 1895, where a full account of the projected expedition is given.

[2] Mr. J. Chamberlain, in the House of Commons, 12th Feb., 1896.

to have a body of troops in readiness on the border prepared to act in the Transvaal if the lives and property of British subjects there should be in jeopardy. He was certainly anticipating a crisis which can hardly be said to have become acute, but, whatever Jameson's ideas may have been, it is unlikely that Rhodes, even in his own mind, was inclined to do more than make ready for that crisis.

However, just as he was on the point of embarking, with Jameson, on his return voyage to the Cape, tidings reached him, from two quarters simultaneously, which struck at the very root of his aspirations for a united South Africa, and may have been partly instrumental in tempting him to assume a graver and more dangerous responsibility. President Kruger, whose pro-German tendencies had long caused misgivings in Rhodes's mind, came out into the open in a speech at a banquet given by the German club at Pretoria in honour of the Kaiser's birthday on January the 27th.

The following quotation from the report in the Johannesburg *Star* of the next day shows unmistakably the direction in which his thoughts were running. After speaking in effusive terms of the friendly feeling displayed towards the Transvaal by the German Emperor, he continued :

'The subjects of the German Empire who come into this Republic to stay . . . have always proved law-abiding citizens, and in our trouble with the blacks, not only the recent ones,[1] but in those of former years, they willingly came forward to assist us, and refrained from stirring up the burghers against the laws of the land. I know I may count on the Germans in future, and I hope Transvaalers will do their best to strengthen

[1] The war against the native chief Malaboch.

and foster the friendship that exists between them. Only lately, when the subjects of Her Majesty the Queen of Britain took shelter under their nationality,[1] four Germans came to my house and said, "We are subjects of the Kaiser of Germany and have not been naturalised, but we have come to live here, and if you wish us to assist in defending the land we are willing to do so. If you want us we will go," and they went.

'That is the spirit I admire, and they obeyed and respected the law.... When the convention with Her Majesty's Government was signed I regarded this Republic as a little child, and a little child has to wear small clothing. But as the child grows up it requires bigger clothes – the old ones will burst, and that is our position to-day. We are growing up and although we are young we feel that if one nation tries to kick us the other will try to stop it. When we asked Her Majesty's Government for bigger clothes they said, "Eh ? Eh ? What is this ?" and could not see that we were growing up. I am very pleased to see you Germans here . . . and I feel certain that when the time comes for the Republic to wear still larger clothes you will have done much to bring it about. It is my wish to continue those peaceful relations, and I wish also to give Germany all the support a little child can give to a grown-up man. The time is coming for our friendship to be more firmly established than ever.'

It can hardly be deemed a mere coincidence[2] that precisely at that moment a concerted attack was launched in the German Press on Rhodes, who had just before, in an interview given to a Berlin paper, expressed the belief that the racial differences in the Transvaal would adjust themselves normally and simply, and that the

[1] By resisting the efforts to commandeer them for service in the war on the grounds that they were not citizens of the Republic.

[2] It may be noted that Dr. Leyds, the Transvaal State Secretary, was in Germany just before (Basil Williams, *Life of Rhodes*, p. 254).

English would, by sheer weight of numbers, secure representation in the Volksraad. The tone of the Press campaign may be gathered from one example, quoted from the *Vossische Zeitung* :

' In Pretoria people count on German help against a possible aggressive policy on England's part, and they will not be deceived. There are German interests to defend in the Transvaal, and the determined attitude of the Imperial [German] Government will prevent the Cape Government from taking imprudent steps.'

In the same issue it was pointed out that there were two German ships of war at Delagoa Bay – Kruger's cherished outlet to the sea – which would soon veto any attempt to get this port into British possession.

This, and other German articles in the same vein, together with the cabled report of Kruger's speech, were handed to Rhodes and Jameson as they embarked at Southampton on February the 2nd, 1895, and gave them something to think about on the outward voyage. If Rhodes had previously felt qualms at interfering in the affairs of the Transvaal, the evidence of these German intrigues must have gone a long way towards dissipating them.

CHAPTER V

Getting Ready in Rhodesia

THE mail steamer *Athenian*, with Rhodes and Jameson on board,[1] reached Capetown on the 21st of February, 1895. On the very next day a sensation was caused when Sir Henry Loch, the Governor of Cape Colony and High Commissioner for South Africa, announced his intention of immediately retiring. Rhodes had by now become so well-known as the dominating force in South Africa that certain sections of the Press and public at once credited him with the responsibility for this decision. It was recalled that Loch had, more than once, acted as a restraining influence on the free hand which Rhodes claimed for his northern projects, and that he had ingratiated himself with President Kruger and the Transvaal Executive. It was hinted that differences had arisen between the Governor and his Prime Minister, and that the former had chosen the easiest way out of an impossible situation. As a matter of fact, there was not the barest foundation for any such suggestion. He left in the ordinary course, after a long career in the public service, and had expressed his desire to do so before Rhodes's visit to England.

On the other hand, there is good reason for thinking that Rhodes had a considerable voice in the somewhat surprising choice of Sir Hercules Robinson as Loch's successor, and that it had been discussed – if not absolutely settled – with Lord Ripon during his interviews at the Colonial Office. There were obvious objections to

[1] Rutherfoord Harris was prevented by illness from accompanying them, but sailed two months later. *South Africa*, 2nd Feb. and 6th April.

Sir Hercules. He was seventy years old and far from robust. Since his retirement in 1889 from the very post which he was now to re-assume he had been chiefly concerned in the direction of South African companies. He was a Director of the Standard Bank of South Africa and sat as Rhodes's colleague on the Board of De Beers. Although Rhodes warmly repudiated the charge that he had been 'intriguing against the late Governor', and denied that he was aware, before leaving England, of the definite appointment of his successor,[1] it can hardly be doubted that he had used his influence in high circles to secure the latter. For Sir Hercules, in his previous term of office, had been a sturdy champion of Rhodes's northern policy, and had helped him to obtain his Charter; he had openly stated his conviction that direct Imperial rule should disappear from South Africa,[2] and he was likely to be far more amenable than Loch, and better disposed towards the unfettered extension of the Chartered Company's interests. It would be going too far to suggest that Rhodes counted on him as a prospective ally in his schemes for interfering in the Transvaal, but it will be seen later that within six months of his arrival at the Cape he did actually propose to treat him as a sort of marionette, whose strings he could manipulate at will for his own political purposes.

Robinson did not arrive at Capetown till the end of May, and, in the meantime, Rhodes was immersed in the parliamentary and official work which had accumulated during his three months' absence; in touring Tembuland, the Transkei and other Kaffir districts; in developing his native policy, and in preparing for the approaching session of the House of Assembly. Jameson, though

---

[1] Speech at Queenstown, Cape Colony, 3rd April, 1895.
[2] Speech at Capetown, on relinquishing appointment, May 1889.

his presence was urgently needed in Matabeleland where there was a rush of new-comers and every promise of immense activity in mining and land settlement, could not resist the temptation of first paying a flying trip to the Rand to see for himself how the current of opinion had progressed since he had passed through in October. He could always find an excuse for such a visit, as his brother Sam, with whom he was on terms of the greatest affection, was in business at Johannesburg.

From his evidence before the Select Committee[1] we learn that he ' found the resentment against the Executive very high, and a rooted determination on the part of the general body of the people to insist upon and, if necessary, to enforce reforms. Rifle associations had been formed, and there were other indications that the inhabitants were preparing for emergencies '. How far he may, in conversation, have hinted at his secret purpose, either to his brother or to others, we have no means of knowing. From his own statement it must be inferred that he did not, on that occasion, suggest to any of the leading and influential residents of Johannesburg the idea of armed support from outside. But whatever he heard must have stiffened his resolution, for he now began to elaborate his preparations with a determination that points to his having satisfied himself that the simmering disaffection at Johannesburg could be brought up to boiling-point when the proper moment arrived.

On his arrival in Salisbury and resumption of duty in April 1895, he lost no time in unfolding to the settlers his proposal for a new Volunteer Corps, which seems to have been greeted locally as an agreeable surprise. In interviews given to the newspapers[2] he announced that

[1] Select Committee Report, question No. 4513.
[2] See *Bulawayo Chronicle* and *Rhodesia Herald* for April 1895.

GETTING READY IN RHODESIA

the force was to be a mounted one. It would be provided with Lee-Metfords, handsome uniforms and brass bands, and would have good pay when volunteering for active service. There were to be engineer and artillery troops, and everything would be found by the Chartered Company.[1] The proposals were enthusiastically received, especially at Bulawayo, where Captain H. M. Heyman,[2] the Civil Commissioner, made the announcement at a meeting of over 700 citizens. Sir John Willoughby, who had not yet returned from England, was gazetted to the command of the whole force, and Heyman, who had been an officer in the Pioneer column, and the hero of an encounter with the Portuguese on the border, besides serving in the Matabele war, was selected for the command of the Western, or Matabeleland Division. These were old and tried officers, and their appointments were accepted with satisfaction. Some surprise, however, was caused by the choice of the brothers Henry and Robert White for important positions in the new force. The ascendancy which these two, who were sons of the second Lord Annaly, rapidly acquired is, in truth, rather remarkable. They were comparatively recent arrivals in Rhodesia, but had been preceded by another brother, the Hon. Charles White, a Lieutenant in the Royal Fusiliers, who had been seconded for duty with the Company's Police in 1891, and in the following year had been promoted to be Chief Commissioner. Captain the Hon. H. F. White, of the Grenadier Guards, an elder brother, appeared shortly after the Matabele war. After holding two or three magisterial posts, he succeeded Charles as Chief Commissioner of Police in 1895, and was now given command of the Eastern Division of the Volunteers as well. Robert, the youngest of the three, a

---

[1] See *South Africa*, 18th May, 1895. [2] Now Sir Melville Heyman.

Captain in the Royal Welch Regiment, did not reach Rhodesia till 1895, but was at once seconded for the Company's service and gazetted as Chief Staff Officer.

Naturally there was much speculation in Rhodesia as to the why and wherefore of all this warlike preparation. There was no special ground for anticipating trouble from the local natives. The general opinion was that the Matabele had become resigned to the knock-out blow they had received eighteen months before and were content to settle down and become workers. A number of their young men had been formed into a smart and well-disciplined police corps, and there was no sign of disaffection among the remainder. As for the tribes in Mashonaland, nobody ever gave them a thought. They were outwardly a weak, craven lot and seemed of no account as fighters. It was clear therefore that there must be something else in the wind – something further afield – and to the Rhodesian pioneers, who had already tasted the joy of occupying new territories, and were by no means averse from other adventures of the same sort, the idea was a fascinating one. The first report was that the Company had in view an expedition to Barotseland and the unknown regions north of the Zambesi, and the magnitude of the preparations lent colour to the notion. This hare was started in February by a newspaper in Pretoria – the *Press* – and was followed up by several journals in England – among others by *South Africa*, which on 6th April published a circumstantial forecast of the Company's 'plan of campaign'. Then came another rumour – that a rising was expected among the Bechuanaland tribes of the Protectorate, who were said to be uneasy at the projected extension of the railway, and to be bent on resisting it, as some of them had once before resisted the erection of the telegraph line. This

GETTING READY IN RHODESIA 47

was nearer the mark and was allowed to go uncontradicted. It was not altogether unsatisfactory that the protection of the railway works should serve as a pretext for drafting troops down to the country immediately north of Mafeking. There were, however, further complications in the Protectorate which will be referred to presently.

The real motive behind all this military organisation was known, at least to Sir John Willoughby, from the start. Whether Jameson revealed it at this stage to any of the other officers mentioned, or, if so, how much he told them, it is difficult to say. In his own mind he had, without doubt, cast some of them for the plot in which they afterwards figured as *dramatis personæ*.

Early in April – within a few days of Jameson's return to Rhodesia – Captain the Hon. Robert White, the newly appointed Chief of Staff for the Rhodesian Volunteers, came south and on the 12th visited Rhodes at Groote Schuur, his house near Capetown. From his diary – which afterwards fell into the hands of the Boers, and was made public – it appears that a conversation took place about conditions in the Transvaal, and drifted on to the situation in Uganda, where, Rhodes thought, the policy of the British officers on the spot should have been to force the hands of their Government by vigorous, if unauthorised, action to check the French advance. In recording this conversation in his diary, White added the words '*verb. sap.*' When interrogated two years afterwards by the Select Committee, Rhodes appeared to have retained only a sketchy recollection of the talk, but repudiated the suggestion that his words had been meant to apply to action in the Transvaal.[1] Be that as it may, ten days later White was round about Pretoria, making

[1] Select Committee, questions 769–771.

notes on its position from a military point of view, the *northern* road leading to Bulawayo, and such like matters,[1] and Rhodes in his evidence admitted that he must have gone there by Jameson's orders, and as a result of previous discussions between himself and Jameson.[2] Captain White, long afterwards, informed Mr. Colvin that any notes he then made were in accordance with his habits as a soldier – he was a Staff College man – and without any thought or any knowledge of what was afterwards to happen.[3] He was accompanied during some of his investigations by Captain Charles Hyde Villiers, of the Royal Horse Guards, who, like himself, had just been seconded for service with the Chartered Company, and by Captain Holden, another of the Company's officers. (Incidentally, nothing in the story of those days is more surprising than the easy way in which Army officers succeeded in getting sent out for vague duties in Rhodesia, where, as far as the War Office knew, there was no reason to suppose that any military operations were likely to take place.) White's tour in the Transvaal included an inspection of the direct route between Pretoria and Bulawayo – the route *via* Nylstroom and Pienaar's River – and besides Villiers and Holden he met at this time Captain Ernest Rhodes – still at the Goldfields Company as representing his brother Cecil – and one Wolff – presumably Dr. Wolff, of whom we shall hear again in connection with routes into the Transvaal.

The significance of the simultaneous presence of White and Villiers in the Transvaal so soon after their appointment to posts in the Rhodesian forces is not entirely removed by the former's disavowal of an ulterior purpose. It is possible that Jameson may have given them to

---

[1] Select Committee, questions 777, 786, 794, 795, etc.
[2] Select Committee, questions 799–802, 941, 942, etc.
[3] Colvin, *Life of Jameson*, p. 31, footnote.

Elliott & Fry

COLONEL FRANK RHODES, D.S.O.

(*face page* 48)

understand that he wanted information for a new coach road between Bulawayo and Pretoria, or some such innocent and non-military object. *Credat Judæus Apella!* Knowing, as we do from his own admissions, what was in his mind, it is natural to deduce that he was envisaging not merely an advance from the Bechuanaland side, but a movement in support by the Rhodesian Volunteers from Bulawayo direct on Pretoria, and we shall see hereafter that this had actually become an essential development of his original plan.

After this excursion White fades, for a while, from the picture, as many of the actors in this curious drama seem to have had the faculty of doing.

During Jameson's absence his place had been kept warm for him by Colonel Francis William Rhodes, D.S.O., an elder brother of Cecil's. In training, habits and temperament the two brothers were wholly different. 'Frankie', as he was called by all his friends – no one would ever have dreamed of addressing the other as 'Cecil' – had been a noted cricketer at Eton, and when he passed into the 1st Dragoons became known as a thorough sportsman. He had seen active service in the Soudan and under Sir Gerald Portal in Uganda. He had also been Military Secretary to the Governor at Bombay, where his social charm won the affection of every man and woman with whom he came into contact. His light-hearted, boyish enjoyment of life and his inability to cherish a grudge, or to be glum under the most depressing circumstances, combined to make him one of the most popular officers in the army. But as a man of business and as an organiser he lacked both experience and capacity. He was too good-natured to drive a bargain, too pliant to maintain a purpose against opposition, and his appointment – first to act as Administrator of Rhodesia, and later to replace Ernest Rhodes as representative of the great Cecil on the management of the Goldfields Company – can only be explained by saying that in both cases he was a convenient and agreeable stopgap. His subsequent entanglement in the meshes of the Johannesburg plot was a catastrophe. Anybody less suited for a part in a revolutionary intrigue it would be difficult to imagine.

On being relieved of his temporary post, Frank Rhodes did not at once leave the country. It was arranged that he should remain as ' Military Member of the Council ' – an appointment created *ad hoc*, and quite unnecessary, except to provide an official who could keep the community in a good temper and relieve Jameson of interviews while he pursued his own strategy.

So far everything had progressed in a direction which suited Jameson. The Volunteer force was under way; the rifles and equipment were beginning to arrive, and the mood of the Johannesburg malcontents was daily ripening into active aggressiveness. In June, however, a new and rather serious cause for anxiety arose in the Bechuanaland Protectorate, and it required the united efforts of Rhodes, Jameson and Rutherfoord Harris to cope with it. The discussion of this must have a chapter to itself.

CHAPTER VI

The 'Jumping-Off Ground'

BEFORE going further it will be just as well to explain the position of the country known as Bechuanaland, which marched with the Transvaal on its eastern side and wasted away into the Kalahari Desert on the west.

Of this great expanse a relatively small portion in the south, extending from the Vaal River – some forty odd miles north of Kimberley – to the Ramathlabama – a small stream seventeen miles beyond Mafeking – was administered as a Crown Colony, and known as British Bechuanaland. Immediately to the north of it lay the 'Protectorate', which stretched to the confines of Matabeleland, and had a common boundary with the Transvaal for about 350 miles. The old trade route to the interior – roughly corresponding with the line of the modern railway, and originally formed to connect the towns of the principal native chiefs – ran for fifty miles or so quite close to the border, one of the nearest points being Pitsani Botluko[1] – twenty-six miles north of Mafeking, and less than four from the Transvaal.

Both the Crown Colony and the Protectorate had been rescued for British – as opposed to Boer – enterprise largely through the efforts of Rhodes himself in the early 'eighties, but whereas the former had always been regarded as the natural heritage of Cape Colony the Northern Territory was claimed by Rhodes as falling within the sphere of the Chartered Company. It was a

[1] For some unexplained reason constantly referred to as 'Pitsani Macklucke' in the correspondence at the time of the Raid. It was merely a wayside store and post station near a native *stad*, or village, on the road to the north.

vast, and for the most part inhospitable tract, sparsely inhabited by a number of tribes of common origin, the largest, and the closest to Rhodesia, being the ba-Mangwato, under a Christianised chief, Khama, a unique product of missionary influence, with one absorbing idea – the exclusion of drink from his country. The other tribes – proceeding southwards – were the ba-Kathla (Chief Linchwe); the ba-Kwena (Sebele); the ba-Maliti (Ikaning), and the ba-Ngwaketsi (Bathoen). In the extreme South, adjoining the Crown Colony, were the ba-Rolong, under Montsioa, in whose area the abovementioned station of Pitsani Botluko – destined to become famous in history – was situated. Most of the chiefs had, at some time or other, granted mineral concessions to various up-country traders and speculators, and these had gradually been secured by Rhodes on behalf of the Charter. The authority of the Crown was exercised by a 'Resident' Commissioner, who, however, resided not within the Protectorate, but at Mafeking, just outside it, and order was maintained by the Bechuanaland Border Police, a most efficient military corps, whose headquarters were also at Mafeking, though they were scattered in little detachments over a wide area reaching as far as the Rhodesian border-line.

Early in June 1895, Rhodes introduced in the House of Assembly a resolution for the absorption of British Bechuanaland by the Cape Colony, and, in speaking to his motion, let fall a broad hint that this step would be followed by the addition of the Protectorate to the territories of the Chartered Company, whose 'jurisdiction', as he called it, reached as far south as Mafeking.[1]

---

[1] Clause 1 of the Royal Charter (after the preamble) reads as follows: 'The principal field of the operations of the British South Africa Company shall be the region of South Africa lying immediately to the north of British Bechuanaland, and to the west of the Portuguese dominions.'

This came to the ears of Khama, who saw that, unless he bestirred himself, he, with the other chiefs, would have to exchange the benevolent – if somewhat listless – supervision of the Queen's Government for the red-hot activity of Rhodes, Jameson and their irrepressible pioneers. The fact that these same pioneers had recently brought about the downfall of his ancient enemy Lobengula did not probably weigh so much with him as the suspicion that the removal of native rulers might be part of the Company's policy, and that his own turn might come next. This would be the natural way in which the thoughts of a native – even of one so enlightened as Khama – would run. His uneasiness was kept alive by interested white men, and spread to the other chiefs. Some of them sent written protests to the Imperial authorities against being handed over to the mercy of men who, they feared, would cut up their country into farms, introduce strong drink, and treat their people as slaves.[1] It may be remarked that the implied abhorrence of drink, though genuine as far as Khama was concerned, was sheer hypocrisy in other cases, for several of the chiefs were notorious topers; but those who advised them knew it was an argument that would carry weight in England.

Before long a report reached Jameson that a deputation of chiefs, headed by Khama, was preparing to visit England to lay their case directly before the Queen. That of course would lead to endless difficulties, for they would be sure to obtain some public sympathy, and their representations, if unchallenged, would not only put obstacles in the way of the railway extension, but inevitably delay the transfer of the strip of country which

[1] See Blue Book C. 7962; petition of Bathoen to the Queen (p. 4), and of Linchwe (p. 6). See also letter to Colonial Office from Khama, Sebele and Bathoen (p. 13).

Jameson was so anxious to obtain for his own purpose. He therefore at once rushed off to Capetown to take counsel with Rhodes as to the best means to meet the emergency.

It happened that Khama was on bad terms with a refractory brother, who had a substantial following and had given him trouble for years. It was agreed that their quarrel should be employed to win Khama over. Jameson went back and visited the Chief at his own town with an offer to take the brother and his section of the tribe into Rhodesia, where sufficient land would be provided for them and they would cease to be a thorn in Khama's side. The proposal was received – if not with enthusiasm, at least with moderate approval, and Jameson was encouraged to lead up to the transfer of the Protectorate to the Company. He stated that this was bound to come sooner or later, but promised that the rights of the natives would be carefully safeguarded, and when he left the Chief he felt assured that his objections had been overcome and that he would consent to the change and induce the other chiefs to follow suit.[1]

In this he was mistaken, for a few weeks later Khama, and two other chiefs, Sebele and Bathoen, were in Capetown, expressing to the High Commissioner their rooted dislike for the Company and their determination to proceed at once to England to state their objections to the Government. There was a very real danger that the whole scheme of obtaining a foothold in the Protectorate would fall through, or, at any rate, be indefinitely postponed. A new Government (Lord Salisbury's) had just come into office, and Lord Ripon, who had approved of the cession to the Company, had been replaced at the Colonial Office by Mr. Joseph Chamberlain, an unknown

[1] Select Committee Report, evidence of Dr. Jameson, question 4513.

THE 'JUMPING-OFF' GROUND

quantity, who might not be so easily convinced of the Company's claims as his predecessor. Rapid action was called for to secure the position.

But Rhodes had not been blind to the danger. As soon as he learnt that the deputation was on the way, and before it had reached Capetown, he made plans to steal a march on them, and, as it was impossible for him to leave the Colony, he despatched Rutherfoord Harris to England to urge the Government to give immediate effect to the promise made six months before.

The selection of Harris for this diplomatic errand was by no means a happy one, for he was a man whose zeal was apt to outrun his discretion, and even to distort his vision. For the actual terms of Rhodes's instructions to him we have to rely on his evidence before the Select Committee, and it is surprising to learn from this that, in addition to urging the necessity of the cession for railway purposes, he might, if he thought fit, point out to the Colonial Secretary that ' in view of the grave situation in Johannesburg an immediate transfer would facilitate the placing of a colonial police force in a position to act should circumstances require it '.[1]

'Colonial police' could only mean the Company's police, and one would have thought that the possibility of military precautions becoming necessary would have appeared to the Colonial Secretary a strong reason for keeping the control of the border in the hands of the Imperial Government, which already had its own police on the spot. It was, in any case, a double-edged argument, and Harris would have been wise to have left it alone. When, at his first interview with Chamberlain on August 1st, he attempted to lead up to it, he did so in such a maladroit fashion as only to elicit a severe snub.

[1] Select Committee Report, evidence of Dr. Harris, question 6220.

But his indiscretion had further and more serious consequences. It supplied the starting-point of a chain of political intrigue leading eventually to the appointment of the Parliamentary Commission of Enquiry – the so-called 'Select Committee' – which was the outcome of determined attempts on the part of certain members of the Opposition to prove that the Colonial Secretary and members of his staff were aware beforehand of the secret aims of Rhodes, and that Chamberlain gave the control of the Protectorate to the Chartered Company with knowledge of the use which Rhodes intended to make of it. We shall see also that the supposed connivance of the Colonial Office was used in Capetown, in Johannesburg and at Pitsani to induce officials and others to act in a manner which they would ordinarily have shrunk from. For all of this Harris was responsible. Whether he had any justification can only be determined by a careful analysis of such evidence as is obtainable, and it is admittedly unsatisfactory.

At this meeting on 1st August there were present, besides Harris and Chamberlain, the Under-Secretary of State – Lord Selborne – and Mr. Fairfield, a senior official of the Department. The last named died before the Select Committee opened its enquiry, but the other three gave their recollection of what was said.

Harris came first. 'At that interview', he said, 'I entered, necessarily at great length and in minute detail, into all the questions of the late Government's promise, of Khama's opposition, the necessity for the railway ... and other matters pertinent to the transfer. Mr. Chamberlain expressed a keen interest in the policy of the railway extension, but regretted his inability to consider the question of an immediate transfer of the Protectorate. In addition to these complex and intricate questions it

THE 'JUMPING-OFF' GROUND

was present to my mind that in the event of a rising at Johannesburg, Mr. Rhodes wished to be in a position to render assistance with the police forces of the British South Africa Company should certain eventualities arise. I made no explicit statement to that effect, but I referred to the unrest at Johannesburg, and added a guarded allusion to the desirability of there being a police force near the border. Mr. Chamberlain at once demurred to the turn the conversation had taken.'[1]

Immediately on hearing this evidence, Mr. Chamberlain, himself a member of the Committee, interposed with the request that he might be allowed to give his version.

After confirming Harris's statement that the discussion had turned to the grievances of the British subjects in the Transvaal, he continued:

'It was in the course of this conversation that he made the remark, the exact words of which I could not possibly pledge my memory to at this distance of time, but it was to the effect: " I could tell you something in confidence", or " I could give you some confidential information." I stopped him at once. I said : " I do not want to hear any confidential information ; I am here in an official capacity. I can only hear information of which I can make official use " ; and I added, " I have Sir Hercules Robinson in South Africa ; I have entire confidence in him, and I am quite convinced that he will keep me informed of everything I ought to know." Dr. Harris says in his evidence that he had in his mind something which Mr. Rhodes had told him ; that he made no explicit statement to that effect, but that he referred to the unrest at Johannesburg (which is perfectly correct) ; and that he added a guarded allusion to the desirability of

[1] Select Committee Report, evidence of Dr. Harris, question 6220.

there being a police force near the border. Of course I do not wish to deny that, but all I have to say about it is that if such an allusion was made I did not understand it, at all events, as referring to anything which has subsequently taken place.'[1]

Lord Selborne generally confirmed this, and was most emphatic in asserting that none of those present had the least suspicion that Harris, when interrupted, intended to divulge anything more than private information as to the plans of the revolutionary leaders in Johannesburg, and he added that neither then or at any later date did the Colonial Office receive a warning or entertain a suspicion of what was on foot.[2]

It should be added that at a later stage Harris amplified his first statement by saying that the allusion he made was: 'We shall be here' – i.e. on the border – 'and if a rising takes place at Johannesburg of course we should not stand by and see them tightly pressed', or something to that effect, but he accepted Chamberlain's avowal that this allusion was not heard or understood.[3]

The combined result of the statements of these three witnesses is inconclusive, but there are certain points, common to them all, which stand out, and have never been explained. In the first place, why, when the business of the meeting was to discuss the cession of Bechuanaland, did Chamberlain allow Harris – an outsider, so to speak – to dilate on the grievances of the Johannesburg Uitlanders, a matter upon which Lord Selborne and other members of his own staff were fully informed?[4] That seems to have been the initial indiscretion, and if it gave

---

[1] Select Committee Report, Mr. Chamberlain, question 6223.
[2] Select Committee, evidence of Lord Selborne, question 9596.
[3] Select Committee, evidence of Dr. Harris, questions 8506–8512.
[4] Select Committee, evidence of Lord Selborne, question 9596.

THE 'JUMPING-OFF' GROUND

Harris a cue for attempting risky confidences the Colonial Secretary had only himself to blame.

Again, it seems amazing that a man so shrewd as Chamberlain should not have had his suspicion aroused by the half-statement which he admitted Harris did make. Having allowed the conversation to take a certain direction, it should have been obvious that Harris wanted to link up the transfer of the Protectorate with the revolutionary movement in the Transvaal, and it would not have required a great amount of perspicacity to detect that there was something behind the veiled hints and 'guarded allusions' which ought to be probed. But neither then, nor up to the very day of the Raid, did he or any member of his staff suspect!

The mystery of this conversation becomes still more involved when we study Harris's actions during the following months, and especially when we read the messages which he sent by cable to Rhodes at Capetown. These were not all produced, and such as were forthcoming were secured in face of strong opposition on the part of Harris and others concerned, but it was admitted by Chamberlain, who saw them all after the Raid, that the missing ones were of similar character. They contained passages calculated to convey to Rhodes the impression that what was called the 'Jameson plan' had been disclosed, if not actually to Chamberlain himself, at any rate to Fairfield, his confidential assistant; and, in fact, Harris, under pressure,[1] definitely said in his evidence that he had communicated to the latter Rhodes's intentions with regard to the force on the border. This is to some extent borne out by a letter from Fairfield to Chamberlain produced at the enquiry. It is a small clue but a significant one. On the 4th

[1] Select Committee, evidence of Harris, questions 8583–8586.

November Harris cabled to Rhodes : ' Chamberlain does not return London until to-morrow. I have spoken open E. Fairfield and I have accepted [i.e. accepted certain demands made by the Colonial Office as to the provision of land for the displaced natives] if Colonial Office will transfer to us balance of Protectorate with police. . . . Fairfield is anxious Johannesburg if they take steps in precedence of.'[1]

On the very same day Fairfield wrote to Chamberlain : ' Rhodes wants you to authorise the Bechuanaland Border Police to enlist with the Company. . . . He is urging a speedy settlement . . . in fact, Rhodes very naturally wants to get our people off the scene as this ugly row is pending with the Transvaal.'[2]

The last sentence was interpreted by Chamberlain as referring to the dispute with Kruger about the closing of the ' drifts ' at the railway terminus on the Vaal River, but a far more obvious explanation is that it refers to the impending rising at Johannesburg, for a little further on the letter continues : ' I do not think that there can be any doubt but that the Transvaal will give way on the immediate question of the drifts ; but that will not end the political unrest.'

It amounts to this. If the Colonial Office denials of foreknowledge are accepted unreservedly – as they were by the Select Committee[3] – no other conclusion is possible but that Harris deliberately and mischievously fabricated the suggestions conveyed to Rhodes in his cablegrams. It is difficult, however, to see what motives he could have had – except perhaps to magnify his own performance as a diplomatic agent.

[1] Select Committee, Appendix xiv., cablegram No. 7.
[2] Select Committee, letter read by Chamberlain, p. 449.
[3] Select Committee Report, p. xv., first sentence.

But unless we are to credit the Colonial Office officials – Chamberlain included – with almost incredible astigmatism, the solution would appear to lie midway between the two versions: that the high officials of the Department guessed that Rhodes had a plan of some sort to meet the impending crisis in the Transvaal, and that Bechuanaland had something to do with it; that they were anxious not to ask any questions or to know too much, lest they should seem to be accepting responsibility, but equally anxious to avoid putting obstacles in Rhodes's way, and that they therefore agreed, at the last moment, to his Bechuanaland proposals, which were capable of an innocent explanation; that Harris, for his part, assumed that the Colonial Office were as infatuated with the idea of Rhodes's omnipotence as he was himself, and that he exaggerated the effect of his arrested hints and half-uttered confidences; in plain words, that he mistook a nod for a wink.

CHAPTER VII

Underground Work

WE have not yet quite finished with Harris, who, whatever he may have lacked in discretion, was gifted with the most versatile and untiring energy. For our knowledge of what he was doing during his visit to England we have to rely on the evidence more or less dragged out of him by the Select Committee and on the few cablegrams brought to light, out of the many he undoubtedly sent and received, between his arrival on the 29th July and his departure four months later. Copies of thirty-three of these cables were reluctantly produced by the Managing Director of the Eastern Telegraph Company under great pressure from the Committee,[1] but they only cover the last four weeks of Harris's stay – those sent before the 1st November, 1895, having been destroyed in the ordinary course of the Company's routine. Included among those disclosed were about a dozen from Rhodes at Capetown, and it may be taken for granted that they contained his own words, a point which should be noted, because it is by no means certain that at a later stage – after Harris's return to the Cape – Rhodes was genuinely the author of all the telegrams sent in his name.[2] In addition to the messages from Rhodes actually forthcoming, the contents of others sent prior to November can be gleaned from Harris's own references to them. It is rather like attempting a jig-saw puzzle with only half the pieces, but it is

[1] Select Committee, Mr. J. D. Pender, 7158–7160.
[2] Select Committee, Dr. Harris, 6376–6377. See also evidence of Miss F. Shaw, 9682–9683.

worth while as revealing Rhodes's difficulties in trying to reconcile his open and legitimate object of getting a portion of Bechuanaland for the railway extension with his secret purpose of using it for the 'Jameson plan'.

We learn from Mr. Chamberlain's evidence that when the subject of the transfer was broached to him by Harris at their first meeting on 1st August he was strongly opposed to the policy, and declined to consider it.[1] Something must have taken place in the next few weeks to cause him to alter his mind, for by the time the deputation of Bechuana Chiefs – Khama, Sebele and Bathoen – with two missionaries in attendance reached England he had taken up an entirely different attitude, and at an interview with them on 11th September he informed them of the ultimate destiny of the Protectorate (i.e. that it would be handed to the Chartered Company) and recommended them to make terms with the Company.[2] At the interview, he says in his evidence, he found them 'not strongly hostile' to the transfer[3]; but this makes strange reading beside the words used by the Chiefs themselves in a joint letter which they afterwards addressed to him, and in which, in impassioned language, they voiced their alarm at the threatened change, and implored him at least to postpone it for ten years, to give them time to watch the course of the Company's rule in Rhodesia.[4] This appeal fell on unresponsive ears, for Chamberlain had made up his mind. He replied that the matter was as good as settled, and repeated his advice that they should try to get the best terms they could from the Company.[5]

[1] Select Committee, evidence of Mr. Chamberlain, 6223.
[2] Blue Book C 7962, cablegram to Sir H. Robinson, p. 13, No. 21.
[3] Select Committee, evidence of Mr. Chamberlain, 6223.
[4] Blue Book C 7962, No. 22.
[5] Blue Book C 7962, No. 26.

While these conversations and changes of mind were going on at home Rhodes was quick to see that the absence from Bechuanaland of three of its principal chiefs offered a good opportunity for making separate terms with those that remained, and, with the concurrence of Sir Hercules Robinson, he despatched his brother, Colonel Frank Rhodes, on 15th September, to try and persuade Ikaning and Montsioa, the two at the southern end where the railway was going to start, to cede jurisdiction over their respective territories to the Company. The Colonel was accompanied by Sir Sidney Shippard, the Administrator of British Bechuanaland, who received a clear hint from Robinson to throw his weight on to the side of the Company.[1] Within a few days the cession was agreed to, and Rhodes had the satisfaction of knowing that the thin end of the wedge had been inserted. Three weeks later (on 18th October) Sir Hercules issued a proclamation handing over the Southern Protectorate to the Company. This was accompanied by a notice appointing Dr. Jameson to be Resident Commissioner of the ceded area, and at the same time Major the Hon. Robert White (the Staff Officer of the Rhodesian Volunteers) was gazetted 'Magistrate of the Territories of the Chiefs Montsioa and Ikaning'.

Jameson lost no time in exercising his authority. On the day following the proclamation he gave orders for detachments of the Rhodesian Police to move down from Bulawayo to the Southern Protectorate, and the first troop, of eighty men with two maxim guns under Inspector Straker, started on 20th October, followed by others at short intervals. White went off in the Mafeking coach to assume his new duties on the 22nd. Whether he at any time exercised judicial functions is not recorded,

[1] Blue Book C 7962, No. 24, enclosure No. 2.

UNDERGROUND WORK

but his diary[1] tells us that on 29th October he arranged to take over from a relative of the Chief Montsioa a farm called Maliet, near Pitsani, in exchange for another promised by Shippard; that he contracted with a local merchant for the erection of a store, and that he interviewed Montsioa himself with regard to the establishment of a police camp, the site of which was inspected and approved by Jameson in person a day or two afterwards.

The three Chiefs at home kept up a stout fight till the last, but the forces against them were too strong. Chamberlain saw them again on 6th November and delivered his decision. Each of them was required to give up a strip of country along the Transvaal border; the line of the proposed railway was roughly mapped out, and all to the east of it passed into the hands of the Chartered Company. On 7th November the decision was cabled to Robinson, who was authorised to allow any members of the Imperial police force who wished to transfer their services to the Company to do so.[2]

The despatch in which Chamberlain confirmed this

---

[1] Major Robert White, who acted as senior Staff Officer to Jameson's force in the Raid, took with him into the Transvaal a despatch-box, which fell into the hands of the Boers after the surrender at Doornkop. In this he had carefully locked up his own diary – beginning on 'Good Friday, 12th April, 1895', and breaking off, in the middle of a sentence, on the 21st December – together with a number of compromising letters, telegrams and notes bearing on the conspiracy. Many of the telegrams were in cipher or code, but he had thoughtfully packed the code books as well!

How far this proceeding was justified by Staff College principles is immaterial. How far it was in accordance with ordinary common sense any layman can judge for himself. To the Boers the contents of the *trommel*, as they called it, were a veritable godsend, for they provided damning links in the chain of evidence used by the State Attorney in his prosecution of the Reform Leaders for treason.

The documents, a good many of which were printed in the Transvaal Green Book on the Raid, and subsequently by the Cape Committee in the appendix to their report, will be referred to in their proper sequence in the course of the story.

[2] Blue Book C 7962, No. 36.

cablegram contained a sentence which is worth quoting in view of what happened afterwards : ' It is also to be borne in mind . . . that the whole strip forms a frontier against an independent State, and that the Chartered Company now becomes charged with the responsibility of maintaining the integrity of that frontier, and performing all police and other similar duties in connection with it ; and that it may claim to be given the means of discharging such duties.'[1] It is easy to be wise after the event, but when it is remembered that, less than a week before, the British Government had sent an ultimatum to the President of this independent State in regard to his action in closing the drifts over the Vaal River against oversea goods, so as to steal the traffic of the Cape railway and divert it to his Pretoria-Delagoa Bay route, and that war with the Transvaal had only been averted by a hair's breadth ; when it is remembered too that Johannesburg was seething with threats of revolution, and that the feeling of the Uitlanders there was well known to the Government, the decision to surrender military control of the border to a commercial company appears – to put it mildly – to have been risky and premature. But it is a striking tribute to the reputation for infallibility which Rhodes had acquired in the eyes of Downing Street.

Chamberlain's cabled message to Sir Hercules Robinson announcing the cession of the border strip to the Company, and authorising the transfer of the police, was sent off on 7th November, and we see from one of Harris's cables that he had received repeated instructions from Rhodes that 7th November was to be the latest date for the acquisition of the police.[2] From another cable it appears that Rhodes had told him that the ' Jameson

---

[1] Blue Book C 7962, No. 39.
[2] Select Committee, Appendix 14, No. 18.

plan' was the principal object to be worked for.[1] He had allowed these instructions to outweigh all other considerations, and had fulfilled them to the letter. There was some excuse therefore for the note of triumph in the cable in which he announced to Rhodes the result of his diplomacy: 'There is no native administration between you and the Transvaal, and you are the border authority.'[2] But in his anxiety to smooth the way for the 'Jameson plan' he had been tempted to agree to sacrifices in other directions – to concede, for instance, large tracts of land for native reserves which Rhodes had hoped to secure for the Charter. When Rhodes learnt the actual details of the boundaries he was very bitter, and sent several petulant messages by cable describing the settlement as a scandal, and expressing his chagrin at having been outmanœuvred by the Chiefs.[3]

So far as it concerned the 'Jameson plan', however, Harris's mission had been a complete success.

What were the Directors of the Chartered Company doing while all this plotting and scheming was being carried on by their paid Secretary under their very noses?

Although Rhodes was preparing to use the resources of the Company to aid the revolution in Johannesburg 'in certain eventualities', it was no part of his plan to involve his colleagues on the Board in the affair. They had given him the fullest power to take any action he deemed advisable without consulting them,[4] but he knew, of course, that his discretion had certain bounds, and that revolutions were outside them. With two

[1] Select Committee, Appendix 14, No. 22.
[2] Select Committee, Appendix 14, No. 15.
[3] Select Committee Report, Appendix 14, Nos. 20 and 26. The latter reads : ' I do object to being beaten by three canting natives, especially on score of temperance, when two of them, Sebele and Bathoen, are known to be utter drunkards. The whole thing makes me ashamed of my own people.'
[4] Select Committee, Duke of Abercorn, 7529–7531.
FR

exceptions, none of the Directors could be regarded as on terms of confidential intimacy with him. The Dukes of Abercorn and Fife, with Earl Grey, had been put on the Board by the Government at the time when the Charter was granted. Sir Horace Farquhar had been added through the influence of the Duke of Fife. Lord Gifford and Mr. Cawston owed their directorships to the necessity of absorbing the rival interests which they represented. The remaining two were Mr. Rochfort Maguire, who had helped to gain the Matabele concession, was a close personal friend of Rhodes, and now sat on the Board as his proxy or 'alternate', and Mr. Alfred Beit, Rhodes's partner in some of his larger financial schemes and the controller of the powerful firm of Eckstein on the Rand. These two were in his complete confidence, and to them alone was Harris permitted to disclose his underground activities. The cablegrams which passed between him and Rhodes were shown to and discussed with them, and, in fact, were transmitted through Beit's London office. It was obviously out of the question that they should be seen by the staff of the Chartered Company.[1] All that Harris's other Directors were allowed to know was that he was negotiating to acquire the Protectorate strip for railway purposes, and that an increase in the orders for arms and ammunition, already large, was necessary to equip the additional force required to police it. The Board was content with this explanation and asked no questions. Their tranquil complacency seems astonishing, but there is no reason to suspect that it was assumed or unreal. It is difficult perhaps nowadays to realise that passive acquiescence was the usual attitude of people who allowed themselves to be led by Rhodes.

The purchase of arms was carried on vigorously under

[1] Select Committee, Dr. Harris, 6599–6603.

Harris's supervision. In addition to what had been ordered earlier in the year for the Rhodesian Volunteers he arranged to buy 4,000 Lee-Metford rifles, three maxim guns and from 200,000 to 300,000 rounds of ammunition. They were all consigned by him to the Chartered Company's agents at Capetown, but he was well aware that there was an intention of diverting some of them to Johannesburg for the use of those who were engineering the rising.[1]

Before leaving England, Harris made a final arrangement of an interesting and remarkable nature which brought into the plot the only woman whose name has been mentioned in connection with it. He secured the assistance of Miss Flora Shaw (the late Lady Lugard) to act as a go-between with the Press – what we should to-day call an agent for propaganda. It is not clear whether this was part of a pre-arranged plan made at Rhodes's suggestion, or was the outcome of an accident. She was a journalist of very exceptional attainments, and was regularly employed in the Colonial department of the London *Times*. In that capacity she appears to have enjoyed a privileged position with the Colonial Office, where she was in the habit of seeking information on any subject which the officials judged proper to communicate to the Press.[2] She was also a personal friend of Rhodes, and had visited South Africa, where she formed the acquaintance of the political leaders, and made a careful study on the spot of the special problems of the country. As a journalist whose business it was to keep her eyes open, and being, apparently, a person of greater discernment than the heads of the Colonial Office or the Directors of the Chartered Company, she scented, in the

---

[1] Select Committee, Dr. Harris, No. 6628, etc.
[2] Select Committee, Miss Shaw, No. 8870.

autumn of 1895, a connection between the military activity in Rhodesia and the development of unrest in Johannesburg, and made up her mind to probe it.[1] A meeting with Harris gave her the opportunity. She put her suspicions plainly before him, and, after some hesitation, he confided to her the 'Jameson plan'. Finding her sympathetic, and realising that she would be a valuable ally, he arranged that after his departure she should be informed of the developments in the situation, and handed her the private telegraph code of the Chartered Company, so that she could communicate freely with Rhodes and keep him posted as to the attitude of the Press in England and Europe towards the Uitlander movement in the Transvaal.[2]

In December, Miss Shaw sent several cablegrams which were later exhumed, like those of Rhodes and Harris, from the files of the Eastern Telegraph Company, and when interrogated by the Parliamentary Committee as to the meaning of certain suggestive passages in them she gave elaborate explanations – she was by far the most voluble witness examined – which will be dealt with in a future page.

Harris had now done all he could and was anxious to get back to South Africa, so as to have a front seat when the curtain went up for the last act, which, he was assured, was to be before the end of the year.[3] He sailed on the 29th November in company with Alfred Beit, who was in poor health, but undertook the journey on Rhodes's representations that his presence was essential. We will leave them on their voyage while we take up the story again from the South African end.

---

[1] Select Committee, Miss Shaw, Nos. 8874 and 9314.
[2] Select Committee, Miss Shaw, No. 8830 and Appendix 14, No. 33.
[3] Select Committee, Appendix 14, Nos. 14 and 16.

CHAPTER VIII

Johannesburg Comes In

UNTIL the possession of the Protectorate and his own appointment as Resident Commissioner were accomplished facts, Jameson was not in a position to approach the Uitlanders in Johannesburg with direct proposals. He was nevertheless working away at his programme on the assumption that these essential points would be gained, and it must be recorded to his credit that throughout 1895, while many of those involved were hesitating and half-hearted, or at best allowing themselves to be swept along by the tide of events without settled intentions of their own, he never swerved from his original design or abandoned his resolve to force others into it.

It was not until his military arrangements were fairly advanced that the people most concerned – the heads of the National Union – had any knowledge of the plot which was being hatched to help them from outside. The first hint came to them from Alfred Beit.[1] In May and June of the year he was in South Africa, and had many talks with Rhodes at Capetown as to the situation on the Rand. At that time the Uitlanders were engaged on a last effort to get redress of their grievances by constitutional means. They were preparing a petition to the Volksraad, praying for the right to the franchise. Rhodes had no great faith in the result, and was sure that, sooner or later, there would be a rising; and Beit held the same view. Both were afraid that it might take place before Johannesburg was in any way prepared, in

[1] Select Committee, Mr. Beit, 8973.

which case it would peter out and the Uitlanders would be left in a worse plight than before. Then one day Rhodes came out with the proposal which Jameson had already convinced him must be adopted – that there must be a force on the border – not, however (as Jameson had in mind), to stimulate a rising, but to be in readiness in case Johannesburg should need support.[1] With this too Beit agreed, and he went off to Johannesburg to get closer to the situation. There he sounded his representative, Lionel Phillips, President of the Chamber of Mines, and Charles Leonard, Chairman of the National Union. Circumstances had forced these two into leading positions among the Uitlanders, but neither of them was cast in the mould of a conspirator. Phillips was probably the ablest business man on the Rand ; a naturally gifted financier and a tactful mediator, who had acquired considerable influence even in Government circles. His instinct was to keep aloof from politics, especially those of a militant character. No one ever thought that he embarked on a revolution for the love of the thing, and although the suggestion was made in certain quarters that he did so for gain, it was indignantly repudiated by him and dismissed by everyone who knew him.[2] Leonard was a talented young solicitor of South African birth whose professional earnings were in the neighbourhood of £10,000 a year. He was fired with a burning sense of the injustice which he and his countrymen were suffering at the hands of the Transvaal Boers, and took an active part in voicing their wrongs. He owed his position to his brilliant platform eloquence, but he had no qualifications for heading a revolution.

However, these two were the most influential men on

[1] Select Committee, evidence of Mr. Beit, 8967–8969.
[2] Select Committee, Mr. Phillips, 7307, 7448, 7451–7452.

the gold-fields, and to them Beit imparted the purport of his conversations with Rhodes. He found them as apprehensive as himself of the danger of a rising before Johannesburg was prepared.[1] They were anxious also that the conflict, if it came, should be as short and decisive as possible, and they realised that a display of force on the border might contribute to this by its moral effect on Kruger and his burghers.[2] No details were discussed, and Phillips and Leonard committed themselves to nothing, but they were left with the general understanding that both Rhodes and Beit were ready to help an organised revolt with their purses, and, somehow or other, if matters came to a head, to furnish armed support.

Close on Beit's heels came Jameson, who spent a few days in Johannesburg on his way to the north after his attempt to induce Khama to agree to the cession of the Protectorate. He too had talks about the position with Phillips and Leonard, and interviewed many others, including Ewald Esselen, an ex-judge of the Transvaal High Court, who had fallen foul of Kruger on account of his progressive views, and had been jockeyed out of his seat on the Volksraad by an election trick on the part of the President's satellites.

Jameson was not quite ready to show his hand. He says himself that no plans were discussed.[3] He was not yet certain of the Protectorate, and his only military force was in Rhodesia – too far off to be of any real use. He was really feeling his way, and trying to find out how far the leaders were in earnest in their threats and revolutionary talk, and to what lengths they were prepared to go if they failed to get the concessions they demanded.

But matters now began to move more rapidly. In

---

[1] Select Committee, Mr. Beit, 8968.   [2] Select Committee, Mr. Beit, 9014.
[3] Select Committee, Dr. Jameson, 4513.

August the great petition for the franchise was presented to the Volksraad. It was signed by 38,000 Uitlanders, who urged that, as contributing the bulk of the taxation, they were entitled to admission within a reasonable time to the ordinary rights of citizens. It was debated at a full meeting of the Raad on the 16th August, to the accompaniment of much heated and violent language. Some of the more moderate members were in favour of a certain extension of the franchise. Lukas Meyer,[1] the Chairman of the Memorial Committee, considered the claims of the petitioners were just, and favoured their cause. Carl Jeppe, the member for Johannesburg, made a speech of great eloquence on behalf of the Uitlanders, and won over a few of those who were sitting on the fence. But these were voices in the wilderness, and were shouted down by the irreconcilables – Kruger himself among them. The signatures to the petition were characterised as forgeries; the petitioners as rebels. One excited member challenged them to come into the open and fight for their claims, and eventually, after a three days' debate, the memorial was rejected by sixteen votes to eight.[2]

From that moment the temper of the Johannesburg Uitlanders grew more sullen. Exclusion from the rights of citizenship – a matter which a year before had not perhaps weighed very heavily on them – now began to assume a tremendous importance, for they had the rankling feeling that they were being treated as naughty children. Even the capitalistic element, which had

---

[1] Lukas Meyer was the leader of the Progressive section of the Boers, and it afterwards leaked out that he had been selected by the Reform conspirators as the first President of the reconstituted Republic. An enormous man considerably over six feet high, he is chiefly remembered as the Commandant who, at the commencement of the Boer War, made a sudden swoop on Natal and invested Ladysmith.

[2] Johannesburg *Star*, 17th August, 1895.

hitherto kept clear of political agitation, was constrained to think, and talk, about having to resort to measures of force. All hope of gaining relief by constitutional means had fled with the rejection of the petition.[1]

Early in October Kruger heaped fresh fuel on the smouldering fire of indignation – not only at the Rand, but throughout South Africa – by closing the drifts at the end of the Cape railway, on the Vaal River, against oversea goods, thus preventing the Johannesburg importers from using road transport to avoid the heavy rates imposed on the section between the river and the Rand, for the purpose of diverting traffic to the Delagoa Bay route, in which the Transvaal Government was deeply interested.[2] The crisis, so long expected, seemed at hand.

Just when popular feeling was strung up to the highest pitch of exasperation Jameson paid another visit to the Rand. Although the cession of the Southern Protectorate had not actually been proclaimed he was now certain of getting it, and his military base was thus assured. He was quick to see that the leaders of the National Union were in a receptive mood – ready, in fact, for mischief, and he seized the opportunity to tell them openly of his willingness to help them with his Rhodesian troops – the armed support that Beit had hinted at in June.

They listened – played with the idea, and were hal convinced. But was this Jameson only, or were Rhodes and Beit really behind him? That had to be cleared up, and Phillips and Leonard were deputed to go at once to Capetown and make sure. They met Rhodes, and had

[1] Select Committee, C. Leonard, 7985.
[2] This action nearly led to war, but at the last moment Kruger gave way before a strong remonstrance – almost an ultimatum – from Mr. Chamberlain, and the drifts were re-opened in November.

two interviews with him, at the first of which his brother Frank and John Hays Hammond were also present. The conversations were fraught with far-reaching consequences, and I cannot do better than quote the account given by Sir Percy Fitzpatrick, who had first-hand knowledge of what transpired.[1]

The position of Mr. Rhodes in the matter was recognised by them (Messrs Phillips and Leonard) to be a difficult one. Whilst as the Managing Director of the Consolidated Goldfields he had as much right as any other man interested in the Transvaal would have to concern himself in a movement of this nature, his right to act in his capacity of Managing Director of the Chartered Company would depend entirely on the nature of the part which he professed to play ; but his position as Prime Minister of the Colony made the already difficult position much more complicated. Realising this, Leonard and Phillips, acting on behalf of the others, determined to have a perfectly clear understanding, and to ascertain from Mr. Rhodes definitely what were his objects in associating himself with the movement. The matter was discussed at Mr. Rhodes's house, and the report given by the two deputies to their colleagues on their return was that Mr. Rhodes frankly admitted that he had two objects in view : one was to obtain an amelioration of the conditions such as he was entitled to claim as representing an enormous amount of capital invested in the Transvaal ; the other object is best described by Mr. Leonard. 'We read to him,' said that gentleman when reporting to his comrades the result of his visit, ' the draft of our declaration of rights. He was leaning against the mantelpiece smoking a cigarette, and when it came to that part of the document in which we refer to free trade in South African products he turned round suddenly and said : " That is what I want. That is all I ask of you. The rest will come in time.

---

[1] Fitzpatrick gives the date of these meetings as in November, but this is at variance with Leonard's evidence before the Select Committee (q. 7877). Besides, Col. Frank Rhodes left for Johannesburg on 20th October, and did not return (see his evidence, q. 5102). It is probable that the meetings took place just before his departure.

We must have a beginning, and that will be the Convention, and other things will all come in time." He then added that we must take our own time about this movement, and that he would keep Jameson on the frontier as long as it was necessary as a moral support, and also to come to our assistance should we get ourselves into a tight place. We asked him how he hoped to recoup himself for his share of the expense in keeping Jameson's force on the border, which should be borne by us jointly. He said that, seeing the extent of his interests in the country, he would be amply repaid by the improvement in the conditions which it was intended to effect.'[1]

Now this account, which is confirmed in many particulars by Leonard's evidence before the Select Committee (given some months after Fitzpatrick's book was written, but before it was published),[2] besides supplying the key to Rhodes's real objects in associating himself with the Uitlander movement, reveals in the clearest possible way the limits to which, in October 1895, he was prepared to go in supporting it.

Jameson was to be on the frontier with a force – as a moral support; a threat, possibly – but not to move on Johannesburg unless the conspirators there were hard pressed. This was how he interpreted the ' Jameson plan ' then, and there is not a word in the telegrams which he sent to Harris – not a sign in any of his actions in the next couple of months – to show that he ever contemplated going beyond it. Whatever impressions to the contrary Jameson may have got from his own conversations with the Johannesburg leaders, or whatever causes may have operated to induce him to take an independent course of action, there is not the slightest doubt that Rhodes expected the revolt to begin in Johannesburg, and intended that any movement by

---
[1] *The Transvaal From Within*, p. 97.
[2] Questions 7989–7991 and 8141–8153. See also Phillips, 7314–7318.

Jameson should be secondary, and dependent on what took place there.

The effect on the two delegates of their interviews with Rhodes was completely to reassure them. They now knew for certain that he was with them, and so was Beit. And they had a new ally in the person of Colonel Frank Rhodes, who came up at once to Johannesburg to represent his brother on the Goldfields Company, with full authority to draw on him for whatever funds might be necessary for the purpose of the revolution, and with the understanding that he was to be in charge of the military preparations. On the financial side they were safe, and when the time came there would be Jameson on the border with his Rhodesian invincibles ready to come to their aid at a moment's notice.

All Phillips's hesitation vanished. A few days after his return, when presiding at the opening of the new premises of the Rand Chamber of Mines, he delivered a rousing speech, in which he solemnly warned the Government that the Uitlander community would not for ever allow their lives, their property and their liberty to be subject to its arbitrary will.[1]

[1] The full text of Mr. Phillips's speech is given in *South Africa*, 21st Dec., 1895.

CHAPTER IX

The Plan of Campaign

JAMESON left Pitsani on the 1st November for Cape Colony, and a few days after arrival learnt that the transfer of the Protectorate to the Company had received the sanction of the Secretary of State. In his eyes the main importance of this was that it involved the disbandment of that highly trained corps of seasoned frontiersmen, the Bechuanaland Border Police, and he was most anxious that they should, before dispersing, at once re-enrol under the Chartered Company. On his way down country he had stopped at Mafeking to make tentative enquiries on this point from their Commanding Officer, Major Raleigh Grey,[1] though without disclosing the use he intended to make of them. Had his meeting with Grey taken place three or four days later, by which time he would have seen Harris's cablegram of the 4th November giving Rhodes to understand that the Colonial Office was cognisant of the 'plan',[2] he might have felt free to speak openly to Grey. As it was, he was obliged to be careful of what he said to an Imperial officer.

Grey belonged to the Northumbrian family of that name which, in the last 150 years, has bred so many distinguished soldiers and statesmen for the Empire. His great-grandfather was the first Earl Grey, the hero of Martinique and Guadeloupe. As an officer of the Inniskilling Dragoons he had served in the Zulu war, and when, later, he was seconded to the B.B. Police he

---

[1] Now Sir Raleigh Grey, K.B.E., etc. The meeting took place, according to Major White's diary, on 1st November.
[2] See Chapter VI., p. 60.

had taken part in the operations which led to the occupation of Matabeleland. A cool, practical soldier, with rigid ideas of military discipline, he was not the sort of man to be attracted towards any such adventure as Jameson had in mind unless assured that it had official backing, and this is no doubt the reason why Jameson could not, until some time later, invite his personal co-operation. He left Mafeking with the impression, however, that he could count on about 200 of the B.B. Police as likely to volunteer for service under the Company, and he hoped to supplement these, and the troops he was bringing down from Rhodesia, by recruiting further men in the Cape Colony.

The engagement of these last and certain preparations for sending arms and ammunition into the Transvaal kept him busy at the Cape till the middle of the month, when he started for Johannesburg to complete his final arrangements with the leaders of the Reform party.[1]

A good many of the representative men in the professions and in mining and business circles were now, to a greater or less extent, 'in the know'. Jameson's brother Sam was one, and another was Sir Percy (then Mr.) Fitzpatrick, afterwards secretary of the Reform Committee, and the faithful historian, from their point of view, of the whole movement. Frederick Howard Hamilton, Editor of the *Star*, the principal organ of the Uitlanders, and George Farrar, a mine-owner and large employer of labour, also took a prominent part. But the responsibility of settling details was assumed by

[1] About the 17th November, according to a statement (printed in the report of the Cape Committee) by Mr. J. A. Stevens, who fixes the time because 'about that date' his brother, Sam Jameson, was seriously ill, and the Doctor made that the excuse for going there. Appendix to report, p. cxxix.

THE PLAN OF CAMPAIGN

Phillips, Leonard, Frank Rhodes and Hammond, who constituted themselves the executive of that amorphous body, the National Union.

The plan of campaign as agreed fell into two parts. There was the action to be taken by the people on the spot, and there was the help to be given by Jameson from outside.

To the Johannesburgers the internal plot was the nucleus of the venture, and although it ultimately failed to mature, no controversy has ever arisen as to its design. According to Fitzpatrick[1] the outbreak was to be opened by the seizure at night of the railway between Johannesburg and Pretoria, and of the fort at the latter town containing an arsenal or magazine in which were stored 10,000 rifles, 10 or 12 field pieces and 12,000,000 rounds of small arm ammunition. This was regarded as a simple matter as the fort was a flimsy structure and its capture made easier by the fact that one wall had been temporarily removed to effect some alterations. The garrison consisted of about 100 men, of whom not more than half-a-dozen were expected to be on night guard. It was thought that little difficulty would be encountered in overpowering so small a body and in seizing the stores of arms and ammunition, of which as much as possible would be carried off by train and the remainder destroyed. As far as this portion of the plot is concerned the intentions of the conspirators are quite clear.

When we turn to the subsidiary part of the scheme – that in which Jameson was to participate – we are at once faced by uncertainties and contradictions. It seems extraordinary that lawyers and company managers, accustomed in their daily business to commit their

---

[1] *The Transvaal From Within*, p. 98. See also Select Committee, Dr. Wolff, 5987–5990.

contracts and transactions to writing, should not, in a matter of such supreme importance, have taken the same precaution. But that does not seem to have occurred to anyone. The neglect is typical of the haphazard manner in which so much of the staff work on both sides was handled. It renders the task of the historian more difficult, but on the whole far more fascinating, for the writing of history would be shorn of much of its attractiveness if it could be contained in a dull straightforward chronicle of accepted facts.

The points on which doubts exist are as follows:

1. The general scheme in which Jameson was to co-operate;

2. The number of troops he was to have in readiness on the border to support the rising;

3. The smuggling into Johannesburg of additional arms and ammunition;

4. The question of whether Jameson was authorised to take independent action and to select his own time for marching into the Transvaal; and

5. The use to be made of the letter signed by the principal conspirators – the famous 'letter of invitation', or 'women and children' letter.

6. A further question arises as to whether Jameson had discretion to act without reference to Rhodes.

On all these matters there are grave discrepancies between the statements of the persons concerned, and against Jameson's account on the one hand we have a mass of contrary testimony. The points of difference can best be shown by placing the various stories side by side.

1. *The General Scheme*

Jameson's statement as given before the Select Committee	*Fitzpatrick's version as given in ' The Transvaal From Within '*
	Association with Jameson as the leader of an invading force is the one portion of their programme which the Reform leaders find it extremely difficult to justify....
The first proposal of the leaders was to act alone, but my troops to be in readiness on the border.... On further consideration they came to the conclusion that they could not hope to succeed without the co-operation of an armed force. ... They therefore invited my help, stating that unless they were assured of assistance in Johannesburg the rising would not succeed.... I agreed, and it was arranged that I should take my force to Johannesburg to maintain order and to bring pressure to bear on the Government while the redress of grievances was being enforced by the people....	The eventual intention of the Reformers was only to call upon Jameson in case they found themselves attacked and unable to cope with the Boers; but it is only fair to Jameson to add that this was a modification of the original arrangement by which both forces were to act simultaneously and in concert – when the signal should be given from Johannesburg....

Here, at the very outset, and in regard to a fundamental part of the programme, the parties were at cross-purposes. One is left with the impression that, while Jameson's ideas were clear-cut and definite, the Johannesburg leaders did not know their own mind, and allowed themselves to be persuaded to a course of which they afterwards repented.

Whether looked at from a military or a common-sense

standpoint, the first proposal, which Jameson says was rejected, but which, according to Fitzpatrick, was the 'eventual intention', appears to have been the sounder. The presence of a well-equipped body of trained men on the frontier – small though it was – would probably have carried more weight with Kruger and his Boers than the same men, after a forced march of 200 miles, in Johannesburg, where they would have been more or less merged in the general crowd of revolutionaries. But such a disposition would have meant that Jameson would be playing second fiddle – a part which he never had any thought of filling.

2. *The Number of Troops to be Provided*

Jameson's statement	*Statements by the Reformers*
It was intended that the force should be 800 strong but in fact it only mustered about 500 . . . (Select Committee, 4513).	It was agreed that he should maintain a force of some 1,500 mounted men, fully equipped, a number of maxims and some field artillery; that he was, in addition, to have with him 1,500 spare rifles and a quantity of spare ammunition. . . . On the occasion of Jameson's last visit it had been extracted from him that instead of 1,500 men he would probably start with from 800 to 1,000. These discrepancies and alterations caused the liveliest dissatisfaction in the minds of those who realised that they were entering upon a very serious undertaking (*Transvaal From Within*, p. 101). The basis of the compact with Mr. Rhodes was originally, I think, that 1,200 men were

THE PLAN OF CAMPAIGN

> to be on the border. That watered down until finally, just before Jameson came over the border, I think it was 750 (Leonard, Select Committee, 7998).
>
> The arrangement was that Jameson should be on the border with about 1,200 men . . . to come in when called upon (Phillips, Select Committee, 6815).

As to this, it may again be noted that Jameson was at no time in a position to put 1,500 troops, or even 800, on the border. Anything above 600 could only have been provided by the inclusion of further reinforcements from Rhodesia. But there were weighty reasons for avoiding such a step, as will be shown later.

3. *The Smuggling of Arms*

Jameson's evidence before the Select Committee

Q. 4563: With reference to the munitions of war – more particularly the maxims – that went into Johannesburg . . . you probably could give information as to the arrangements about that?

A: Yes, I made them all . . . at Kimberley and everywhere.

Q. 4564: With whom at Johannesburg did you arrange?

A: The leaders . . . about October 1895. . . .

Q. 4568: The arrangement was this: I ordered them through Capetown at home for

Fitzpatrick's account

It was agreed . . . that about 5,000 rifles, three maxim guns, and 1,000,000 rounds of ammunition were to be smuggled into Johannesburg (*Transvaal From Within*, p. 98). . . . During the weeks that followed the conclusion of the arrangement considerable dissatisfaction was felt at the very slow progress made in obtaining arms. The number originally agreed to was deemed to be sufficient but no more; and when it was found that it would not be possible to obtain this number, but that a my Volunteer force in Rhodesia, and then, with a view in my mind of what might occur in Johannesburg, I ordered an ample amount so that some could be diverted to Johannesburg if required.

Q. 4582–4588: I do not think any of the munitions of war were ordered while Dr. Harris was in England. . . . If they were it would be by my order.

few hundreds less would have to be accepted, doubts were freely expressed as to the wisdom of proceeding until a sufficient supply had been obtained. When on two subsequent occasions it was again notified that still a few hundreds less would have to be accepted, some members were very emphatic in their objections to proceeding any further until they should be satisfied that the undertakings upon the strength of which they had entered upon the arrangement would be faithfully adhered to . . . (*Transvaal From Within*, p. 101).

Note.—Dr. Harris was in England in October, when the arrangement between Jameson and the Johannesburg people was made, and did not leave till 29th November. He stated in his evidence that according to an understanding arrived at before he left South Africa in July he was buying arms for Rhodesia up to 4,000 rifles and 200,000 or 300,000 rounds, with the knowledge that some of them might be diverted (Eviddence of Harris, q. 6625–6650).

When Jameson did move there were only 3,000 rifles in the possession of the Uitlanders, and the maxim guns did not arrive till two days after the Raid started (*Transvaal From Within*, p. 113).

If Jameson gave the undertaking as to arms and

ammunition, as stated by Fitzpatrick, there was a lamentable break-down in his arrangements. Harris's evidence points to Jameson having anticipated the necessity for supplying *some* arms to Johannesburg several months before he made his agreement with the leaders, and we are left to infer that he sent no additional orders after that agreement. It is conceivable, and quite in keeping with Jameson's way, that, knowing considerable supplies were being ordered somewhere by someone, he may have said to the people in Johannesburg, " Oh, I'll see that you have all the arms you want", or given some vague assurance of that sort, and that when, at the eleventh hour, he found that the large amount required would not be forthcoming, he trusted to luck and dismissed the matter from his mind.

As he admitted responsibility for this part of the programme, it is astonishing to find that he did not know definitely of Harris being engaged in buying the necessary munitions, or make sure that the requisite amount would be obtained. Equally strange is it that, in so essential a matter, the Johannesburg executive did not depute a trustworthy agent to proceed to the Cape and supervise the process of smuggling them in. But, like actors in amateur theatricals, they seem to have cherished a happy confidence that everything would be 'all right on the day.'

4. *Was Jameson free to take independent action?*

Jameson's statement before the Select Committee	Statements by the Reformers
The time selected for the rising in Johannesburg was the end of December. It was agreed that simultaneously with the rising I was to start.	Various plans were discussed, and even dates were provisionally arranged. The first arrangement agreed to was that Jameson should start two days

My final arrangements with Johannesburg were that this date should be adhered to as far as possible, though it was thought an earlier date might prove necessary if the Transvaal Government gave signs of massing troops on the border. . . . *Of this necessity I was, with my troops on the border, to be the judge.*

before the intended outbreak in Johannesburg . . . but subsequent discussion convinced the leaders that there were the gravest objections to such a course, and it was therefore decided that Jameson should be notified to start from his camp on the same night as the outbreak in Johannesburg. The dates of 28th December and 4th January were in turn provisionally decided upon, but the primary condition of these arrangements was that *under no circumstances should Jameson move without receiving the word from the Johannesburg party* (Transvaal From Within, p. 100).

It was never left to Jameson to choose his own time (evidence of Colonel F. Rhodes, 5122).

It was always definitely arranged that he (Jameson) was to wait for instructions from Johannesburg (evidence of L. Phillips, 6816).

Q. 7370: Are you clear in your understanding that Dr. Jameson was not to come in until he had received an invitation from Johannesburg?

A.: Perfectly clear; that was arranged with Mr. Rhodes as well as with him (evidence of L. Phillips).

5. *The Letter of Invitation*

(The full text of this letter, which was handed to Jameson

THE PLAN OF CAMPAIGN

during his last visit to Johannesburg, towards the end of November, is printed in Appendix I.)

Jameson's statement as given before the Select Committee

They [the leaders] invited my help. . . .

I therefore obtained a letter signed by four representative leaders. . . . This letter was advisedly left undated, it being agreed I should insert the date when, in my judgment, the time for acting upon it arrived.

Statements by the Reformers

The letter was drafted by Mr. C. Leonard, and was signed then by four out of five signatories, the fifth signature [that of G. Farrar] being added some weeks later in Capetown. It was not dated, and was only to be used for the purpose of excusing Jameson to the Directors of the Chartered Company and the Imperial authorities in the course which it was intended to take (*Transvaal From Within*, p. 100).

Evidence of Colonel Rhodes (Select Committee)

Q. 5015: Was the letter solicited by Jameson for ulterior use or was it a spontaneous expressing of opinion and invitation of help coming from those who signed it?

A.: Oh, I think Jameson asked for it.

Q. 5122: Was it understood (I want to put this to you as one of the signatories to the letter) that the date was left open in order that Jameson might put it in when he thought the right time had come?

A.: No. We differ with Jameson there . . . (5123). Our point is . . . that he was absolutely not to use the letter until he heard from us.

Evidence of L. Phillips

Q. 6950: Were you aware that the date was to be shifted forward to the day when Dr. Jameson started?

A.: No, we always thought that the date was to be filled in according to advice from us. . . .

Q. 6951: . . . The letter was given for two reasons. One was that Dr. Jameson . . . wanted to have something to justify himself with his Board. . . . Another was that his men might raise some objection if he simply said: 'I want to go to Johannesburg', and he wanted to have something to show them if necessary.

Q. 6952: The phrases about danger to women and children were anticipatory?

A.: They were.

Q. 6953: And not actual facts?

A.: Certainly not.

Q. 7377: In your view that letter was never given as a justification to him to move without hearing from Johannesburg?

A.: No. I mean that it is so obvious that that could not have been the idea. How can a man from outside say when a revolution is to take place?

Evidence of C. Leonard

Q. 7945: The letter was given to Jameson at his request . . . for the simple alleged reason that it would be required to justify him with the Chartered Company's Directors afterwards, and under a solemn pledge that it was not to be used for any other purpose. . . . The letter had nothing to do really with the arrangements for his coming in.

The use made of the letter by Jameson, and afterwards by Harris and Miss Flora Shaw, will be described in a later page; for the present it is sufficient to say that the opening sentences are rhetorical in style and were clearly not intended for the information of Jameson, who was perfectly well acquainted with all the facts. The five men who signed it knew, at any rate, that he would not simply put it in his pocket and keep it there, and, having taken the responsibility of preparing a document which must have been intended for the edification of outsiders, they forfeited the right to complain at the construction which was placed on it by the world at large. Whatever their intentions were as to the use to be made of it, there are only two words to be applied to the letter itself. It was untruthful, and it was extremely foolish. Untruthful, because it foreshadowed a reign of terror which could only arise as a result of the plot which they themselves were hatching, and foolish, because it was of the nature of an uncrossed cheque payable to bearer. Harris became the bearer, as we shall see in due course.

6. Was Jameson responsible to Rhodes?

Jameson's statement as given before the Select Committee	Rhodes's statement as given before the Select Committee
I required no orders or	I placed upon the borders of

authority from Mr. Rhodes. ... My arrangements were made direct with the people in Johannesburg. ... I was not waiting for instructions from Capetown (q. 4513). the Transvaal a body of troops under Dr. Jameson, prepared to act in certain eventualities. ... With reference to the Jameson Raid, I may state that Dr. Jameson went in without my authority (q. 19).

In answer to another question (No. 4532) Jameson told the Committee: 'I was the evidence to Rhodes of what was going on in Johannesburg', and again (No. 4537): 'Colonel Rhodes was practically, you may say, my agent after he went up to Johannesburg. I was the sole communication with Mr. Cecil Rhodes.'

Many of the above quotations from Jameson's statements to the Committee reveal the characteristic – almost arrogant – attitude of mind in which he manipulated the crisis, and perhaps supply some explanation of his ultimate failure. The Chartered Company, whose resources he was using; Rhodes, under whose orders he was acting; the Uitlanders, whose cause he was supposed to be fighting, were all relegated to the background. It is 'My force', 'My judgment', 'My arrangements' throughout. In short, he had taken charge of the whole enterprise, as he intended to do from the outset.

It was this overweening self-confidence – this megalomania – which drove him, and with him those who trusted him, to disaster.

CHAPTER X

Pitsani and Mafeking

THE spot chosen for a police camp by Major White at the end of October was about a mile east of the native kraal of Pitsani Botluko, on the main road from Mafeking to the north. A more unattractive site for a prolonged stay it would be difficult to imagine. The country for miles round was flat and devoid of vegetation beyond a little thorn scrub, all timber trees having been cut down by contractors for the supply of fuel to the Kimberley mines. The coaches running between Mafeking and Bulawayo stopped at Pitsani to change teams and to enable the passengers to snatch a hasty meal, shared by myriads of pestering flies, at a wayside store, which, except for the mule stable, was the only building in the place.

The reason for fixing on this spot for a camping ground was obviously the fact that it was only three and a half miles from the Transvaal border and the first point within the Protectorate where a constant supply of water could be relied on. But it would have been impossible to keep troops for any length of time in such depressing surroundings, and when Jameson decided to bring the Rhodesian police there from Bulawayo he was counting on being able to move them into the Transvaal before the end of the year.

Although his avowed purpose in stationing troops at Pitsani was simply to have a base from which to police the Chartered Company's strip of territory, and to provide a guard for the railway works, preparations were put in hand for a camp for three or four hundred men, and contracts made with merchants in Mafeking for regular supplies in proportion. The contractors, in the belief that the force from Rhodesia would remain there for some time, erected stores for their own use at a cost of about £700, and were so unprepared for the possibility of an early evacuation that all through November and December they were pushing up waggon-loads of provisions, beer and the like for the use of the troops.[1]

The first contingent of the Mashonaland Mounted Police turned up on 30th November, having been six weeks on the road from Bulawayo. It was followed by further detachments during the next day or two, and supplemented by the arrival of about thirty men recruited at the Cape, bringing up the strength to about 280 of all ranks.[2] Simultaneously Jameson arrived from Johannesburg, having made a short stop on the way at Capetown, to report the result of his meetings with the Reform leaders. The impression made on Rhodes may be gathered from the message which he at once cabled to Harris in London:

' Jameson back from Johannesburg. Everything right. My judgment is it is certainty.'[3]

What could he have told Rhodes to justify this feeling of confidence?

It is difficult to follow the working of Jameson's mind at this period. In a letter written to Major R. White shortly after his arrival in Johannesburg he said he expected his force to be about 600, made up of the police from Rhodesia, 200 of the disbanded Bechuanaland

---

[1] Blue Book C 8063, despatch from Mr. Newton, p. 34.
[2] Blue Book C 8063, p. 46.
[3] Select Committee, Appendix XIV., No. 29.

police, and about 100 recruits from Stevens.[1] All that he was certain of at that date were the men coming down from Bulawayo, but if he had looked at their 'marching-out state' (which he must surely have received from White) he would have seen that they only amounted to about 250, to transfer whom he had denuded Rhodesia of five-sixths of its effective police strength. Even if his hopes were realised as to the B.B. Police and recruits the combined force would fall short of his figure of 600. Yet, almost in the same breath, he was, according to his own statement, promising the Reform leaders that he would have 800 men trained and equipped on the border, and ready to move on the 26th December (his own date); in fact, if we are to believe the leaders, he had, either then or on his previous visit, talked of 1,200 or 1,500.[2]

Unless therefore he was wilfully misleading the Johannesburg people, or trusting to a stroke of luck such as had carried him to victory two years before in Matabeleland, he must have had some expedient in his head for making up his numbers to the agreed total, and as there was certainly no other source in the south to which he could look, the inference is that he intended to use the Rhodesia Horse Volunteers. The point will be dealt with later in this chapter; for the present it need only be said that Willoughby, the commanding officer of the Rhodesia Horse, though destined to lead the force which Jameson was organising on the Transvaal border, was being kept back – much against his own inclination – in Bulawayo, where he was ostensibly engaged in the business of the important mining company of which he

[1] This letter, dated 19th Nov., is printed in Appendix A of the Cape Committee's Report.
[2] Fitzpatrick, p. 98. Select Committee, Phillips, 6815; Leonard, 7998. The actual strength of the force with which Jameson entered the Transvaal was 510; made up of Rhodesian police and recruits, 372; B.B. Police, 122; and staff, 16. See Appendix II.

was Managing Director, but was also making arrangements for mobilising the Volunteers.

In justice to Jameson it must be stated that there were sound reasons for avoiding a larger concentration of troops on the western border than actually took place. The essence of his whole scheme was secrecy, and had any further movement of men from Rhodesia been observed it is certain that suspicion would have been excited among the Boers – to say nothing of the Imperial authorities. As it was there had been rumours afloat. So many people in Johannesburg knew what was in the wind that it would have been remarkable if a certain amount of leakage had not occurred. One of the officers attached to Colonel Frank Rhodes was found to be 'talking too much' and was sent away to join the camp at Pitsani.[1] Even in Rhodesia there was gossip as to the purpose of the transfer of the police to the Protectorate. As early as 1st November a letter was sent by someone in Bulawayo to a correspondent in Ireland containing the following item:

'We hear some talk up here of the English taking the Transvaal. The Chartered Company's troops have gone south under secret orders. I saw them off about four in the morning. They took ten guns and a large number of waggons, so that it looks suspicious. . . .'[2]

The Boer authorities at Pretoria were aware that a plot of some kind was being hatched in Johannesburg, and they had their detective agencies at work. A story was current that the Secret Service department employed a well-known 'woman of the town', who managed to extract a good deal of information in confidential

---

[1] Undated letter from Jameson to White, found in the latter's despatch-box and published in the Transvaal Green Book.
[2] Letter published in *South Africa*, 4th Jan., 1896.

moments from a friend in the revolutionary camp. That the Government was not altogether asleep was shown also by a remark made by President Kruger a few days before the Raid at a meeting with some of his burghers at Bronkhorst Spruit, in connection with the prevalent rumours of a rising. 'Wait until the time comes', he said. 'Take a tortoise; if you want to kill it you must wait until it puts out its head, and then you cut it off.'[1]

It is clear, then, that if Jameson's concentration of troops at Pitsani had assumed much larger dimensions, the suspicion would have turned into alarm and would have led to counter-preparations on the Boer side. This danger was constantly present to him, and accounted for many actions – otherwise unaccountable – on his part. He had represented it to his colleagues at Capetown, who began to realise that it might cause him to act precipitately, and up to the last moment were doing their best to keep him calm.

It is strange that the same fear of creating suspicion by massing troops does not seem to have prevailed among the Johannesburg leaders, otherwise they could never have contemplated the placing of 1,500 men on the border. That would have been a fatal move, and would infallibly have brought their whole plot tumbling about their ears.

Still more strange is it that none of the current rumours seems to have disturbed the High Commissioner, or prompted him to direct a watchful eye on Jameson's proceedings. If the curiosity of Miss Flora Shaw, 6,000 miles away, was piqued by the presence of inflammable material on the border in such close proximity to the smouldering fires of sedition at Johannesburg, how was it that Sir Hercules Robinson, who was on the spot,

[1] Select Committee, Schreiner, No. 4117.

whose duty it was, in those troublous times, to look out for danger signals and, as Mr. Chamberlain put it, ' to keep the Colonial Office informed of everything they ought to know ', remained unobservant up to the very end ?

How was it, again, that Rhodes's colleagues in the Cape Ministry, whose jurisdiction extended to within ten miles of Pitsani and actually included Mafeking – the two points where the mischief was developing – asked no questions and scented nothing unusual ?[1]

Throughout the whole of November and December Jameson really acted as his own Chief of Staff. Rhodesia, of whose administration he was still nominally the head, was left to take care of itself, though an Acting Administrator (Mr. Justice Vintcent) was appointed to carry on the work of government. Among other matters which had to be attended to in connection with the Transvaal business were two of paramount importance, one of them affecting the preparations in Johannesburg and the other the supporting movement from the border. Jameson had to fulfil his promise to supply the insurgent party with arms and ammunition, and he had to arrange for the provision of victuals and remounts for his own force along the route of 180 miles between the border and their objective. The arms and ammunition were to be taken out of the supplies purchased by the Chartered Company – or rather by Harris on their account – in London. The necessary expenditure on the route was guaranteed by Rhodes, who had given his brother Frank *carte blanche* to draw on him, through the Company's office at Capetown, for such amounts as

---

[1] Select Committee, Schreiner, Nos. 3254 and 4104. It may be mentioned that the *Illustrated London News* was alive to the possibility of serious developments in the Transvaal, and at the end of October, 1895, despatched Melton Prior, the famous war-correspondent and artist, to the scene (*South Africa*, 19th Oct., 1895). The London *Times* also had a correspondent on the spot – Captain (now Sir Francis) Younghusband.

were needed for this and other requirements.[1] Additional funds were provided by Alfred Beit, through Lionel Phillips, his agent at Johannesburg.[2] The use made by Rhodes and his brother of the Chartered Company's accounts was unfortunate, and, not unnaturally, gave rise afterwards to suggestions that they, as a corporation, had been incurring expenditure in connection with the projected revolution.[3] But suspicions as to their connivance were completely dispelled during the enquiries that were instituted, and it was made clear that, while certain of their servants were implicated, the Directors at home were entirely in the dark as to the use that was being made of their property, their banking account and their credit. Rhodes accepted the whole responsibility for the drafts and made them good out of his private purse to the extent of over £60,000, while Beit's corresponding little bill was in the neighbourhood of £200,000.[4]

It is obvious that the arms could not be introduced into Johannesburg openly, and all sorts of roundabout and amusing devices were employed to smuggle them in under various disguises. Space will not permit a detailed account of these, but the main channels through which they were conveyed were the De Beers Company at Kimberley (of which Rhodes was of course Managing Director), and the Chartered Company's forwarding agents at Capetown and Port Elizabeth. The staff of De Beers had often been of assistance to the Charter in receiving and giving temporary house-room to munitions, horses and other military requirements, and there was nothing out of the way in the delivery to them of

[1] Select Committee, C. J. Rhodes, Nos. 57–58 ; Colonel Rhodes, 4956.
[2] Select Committee, A. Beit, 9032–9039.
[3] Select Committee, Rhodes, 35–69.
[4] Select Committee, Rhodes, 42 ; Beit, 9032–9039.

guns and cartridges *en route* for Rhodesia. But in order to divert any part of them to Johannesburg it was necessary that someone in authority at De Beers should be let into the secret. During November Jameson arranged, through Captain Holden, one of his officers, with Mr. Gardner Williams, the General Manager of the Company, for the gun-running business, and that gentleman appears to have entered into it with considerable zest.[1] Some of the rifles were concealed in trucks of coke, while others were packed in cases marked 'Mining Machinery', and consigned to the Simmer and Jack mine, controlled by George Farrar, one of the 'big five' in the conspiracy. A good deal of the ammunition, together with maxim guns, was hidden in oil drums cunningly devised with internal tubes of genuine oil in case of inspection. These were despatched by rail to Port Elizabeth, where they were received by the Chartered Company's shipping agent and sent forward to Johannesburg as if they had arrived by freight steamer.

In addition to arms a few trustworthy men – playfully referred to by Harris in one of his telegrams as 'eleven fine diamonds' – were selected by De Beers' officials, under instructions from Gardner Williams, and sent to Johannesburg with orders to report to Colonel Rhodes – for what object they were not told.[2]

The forwarding of arms was managed very thoroughly and with absolute secrecy on the part of all concerned, but it was done too late – too late, that is, for the date which Jameson had in mind for the rising – and some

---

[1] Select Committee, Rhodes, 80–90. Cape Committee, evidence of Gardner Williams, who when asked why he, an official of De Beers, took orders from an employee of the Chartered Company, became as mute as an oyster (1068–1071). Cf. also Jameson's letter to 'Bobby' (Major White), in Transvaal Green Book – 'Everything seems to be going right, especially the Gardner Williams part of it.'

[2] Cape Committee Report, evidence of R. G. Scott, 1754.

Elliott & Fry

SIR GEORGE FARRAR, D.S.O.

of the consignments did not reach their destination till after he had set the ball rolling. It may be noted also that the rifles were Lee-Metfords – at that time unfamiliar weapons to most South Africans. Rifles of the same pattern – they were of course part of the same order – were issued rather late in the day to Jameson's troopers, who had previously been armed with the Martini, and had to accustom themselves in a few weeks to a new arm requiring a long and special training.

Great ingenuity was displayed in the preparations along the road – which in most parts was little more than a waggon spoor, or track – between the border and the Rand. For this work Jameson secured the services of Mr. Henry Albert Wolff, whom he had known years before in Kimberley. Wolff was an active member of the Uitlander movement from the beginning, and in the latter part of 1895 had been entrusted with the 'Intelligence Department', for which his nationality and his profession – he was an American doctor practising in Johannesburg – gave him advantages. Early in November he was asked to put himself in touch with Jameson, at whose request he undertook the duty of organising stores for the troops along the proposed line of march. He eventually became one of Jameson's most trusted advisers and his chief source of information as to what was going on at the Rand and among the Boers.

In order to carry out his special work along the route he invented a sham company – the 'Rand Produce and Trading Syndicate' – whose professed business was to buy maize and other local produce with a view to resale at a profit in Johannesburg or elsewhere. With funds provided from Colonel Frank Rhodes's 'war chest' he then proceeded to run up galvanised iron sheds to serve as depots, at which he rapidly accumulated stores – not only of grain, but also corned beef and other rations for the troops.

His 'syndicate' also bought several hundred horses on the pretext of starting a coach service between Mafeking and the Rand. The majority of these were placed for grazing purposes on a farm midway on the road, owned and occupied by a Mr. Malan, who happened to be a member of the Transvaal Volksraad! The first of Wolff's food depots was at Malmani, forty miles from the border, near the junction of the roads from Pitsani and Mafeking. Four others were established at intervals of about thirty miles, the last being placed a short distance from Krugersdorp, a town eighteen miles from Johannesburg, at the extreme western end of the Rand mining area.[1] No suspicion was at first created among the local Boers by these activities, which bore the appearance of a genuine, if rather risky, speculation. The stores were stocked in good time, with ample supplies of mealies, bully-beef and biscuits. The remounts, however, were on the whole a poor lot, many of them being unbroken to the saddle, and therefore useless for their purpose.

The next matter tackled by Jameson was the engagement of the members of the Bechuanaland Border Police, who were about to take their discharge. In his letter to White of 19th November he had written that he counted on getting 200 men from this source, but his confidence may have been shaken by a telegram which he received at Capetown from that officer on the 27th, warning him that many of the men were taking civilian posts, and urging that he should come up at once and communicate the precise terms of re-engagement to their commanding officer, Major Raleigh Grey.[2]

[1] Select Committee, Dr. Wolff, 6190–6195.
[2] The telegram was found among White's papers, and printed in Appendix to Report of Cape Committee, p. xxx.

A few days earlier Rhodes had arranged with Sir Hercules Robinson that the B.B.P. should be assembled at Mafeking to await Jameson's arrival during the first week in December.[1] The main body was already there, but it took some time to recall the small outlying detachments scattered about in the remoter parts of the Protectorate, and Jameson was too impatient to delay matters for their arrival. On 3rd December he went with Major R. White to Mafeking to settle with the commanding officer the details of the transfer of the personnel and also of the surplus stores and equipment. Besides Major Grey he met Mr. F. J. Newton,[2] the newly appointed Resident Commissioner of what was left of the Protectorate. The strength of the B.B.P. was at that time about 300, and of these the Imperial Government had decided to retain sixty for ordinary police duties and a few men who had been specially trained as telegraphists and customs officers – in all about 100. The remainder Jameson hoped to secure for the Chartered Company, but he was disappointed to find that little more than half responded to his invitation.

At this meeting he decided on the bold course of communicating his plans, not only to Grey, but also to the Commissioner, Newton himself. He told them that there would shortly be a rising in Johannesburg against the Government, and that the force on the border was to be held in readiness to march across country when this took place to preserve order there, but that he did not think there would be a shot fired. Both Grey and Newton were invited to assist in different capacities.[3]

Although – apart from the evidence given by Newton

---
[1] Blue Book, C 7962, despatch No. 52, enclosure 5.
[2] Now Sir Francis Newton, K.C.M.G., etc.
[3] Major White's diary, 3rd Dec. Transvaal Green Book. See also Select Committee Report, Mr. Newton, Nos. 4629–4635.

to the Select Committee – no exact details of what Jameson said, either to him or Grey, have been forthcoming, it may be taken for granted that he hinted, if he did not actually state in plain language, that the Government at home were privy to the movement and would support it. This is what he probably believed – at any rate was justified in believing – on the strength of Harris's suggestive cablegram of the 4th November.[1] Making full allowance for Jameson's persuasive gifts, it was the only argument likely to carry weight with two Imperial officers of the calibre of Grey and Newton.

The former agreed to throw in his lot with Jameson as commander of his own men who were being transferred, and for the time being to keep them together at Mafeking, where he was, so to speak, at Jameson's elbow. Newton also was induced to fall in with the proposals, even to the extent of promising to accompany the force when the time arrived, though in what capacity, and with what further action in view, it is impossible to say. Jameson, however, regarded his assent as a point scored, for he telegraphed to Rhodes in the following terms:

'F. J. Newton will help you as much as possible. Has expressed a strong wish to go with us or by Capetown to Johannesburg races.'[2]

A few days later Newton had to go to Capetown on official business. As soon as he was free from the hypnotic influence which Jameson seemed to shed on all who came in contact with him he was seized with misgivings, and ultimately resolved to take no further part in the affair.[3] Jameson may also have had second

---

[1] 'I have spoken open to Fairfield,' etc., see p. 60, Chapter VI.
[2] Cape Committee Report, Appendix, p. xlvii.
[3] Select Committee, Newton, No. 4641.

thoughts as to the propriety of entangling him in the plot, for about the same time he telegraphed again to Rhodes:

'Raleigh Grey is going with us. Therefore will not require Newton. You may allow him to go to races.'[1]

It would almost appear as if the races were the real attraction in Newton's case!

The account of Jameson's military preparations would not be complete without reference to the Rhodesia Horse – the force which he had created with the express object of being ready for the crisis which was now at hand.[2] During the course of his evidence he stated that he never intended that they should be brought down,[3] but the information from other sources points clearly to his having made plans for using them in some way or other.

The Rhodesia Horse Volunteers consisted of two regiments under the general command of Sir John Willoughby. The regimental commanders were, in December, both absent from Rhodesia – nominally on leave, but in reality detached for special duties connected with the plot. Lieut.-Colonel the Hon. H. F. White, who had been appointed to the command of the Mashonaland Regiment, was at Pitsani in his other position as O.C. the Rhodesian police, while Lieut.-Colonel H. M. Heyman, the Civil Commissioner and Magistrate of Bulawayo, and also O.C. the Matabeleland Regiment of the Volunteers, was assisting Colonel Frank Rhodes and the Reformers' executive, in some vague military

[1] Cape Committee Report, Appendix, p. xlix., No. 51.
[2] Select Committee, Jameson, 4513, p. 259.
[3] Select Committee, Jameson, 5750.

capacity, at Johannesburg.[1] In their absence the senior officers in Rhodesia were Captains William Napier and John Anthony Spreckley, and it afterwards came to light that detailed instructions had been given by Willoughby to one or both of them as to the action to be taken if the Volunteers were required down country. A telegraphic code was arranged whereby either the Matabeleland Regiment alone, or the two regiments combined, could be called out, and an interesting item in the instructions was that, on receipt of a certain code word, with a date after it, Spreckley was to ' get Reuters and other news-agents to wire down country that the Rhodesia Horse are moving down country immediately '.[2]

Notes of these arrangements, together with a list of ten depots on the road between Bulawayo and Pitsani, where food and forage rations had been laid down for the use of troops proceeding southwards, were among the papers which fell into the hands of the Transvaal authorities after the Raid.

Towards the end of the month Jameson sent telegrams to Napier and Spreckley bidding them hold themselves in readiness to come to his assistance with as many men as they could raise.[3]

---

[1] Select Committee, Colonel Rhodes, 5429–5440.   Fitzpatrick, *The Transvaal From Within*, pp. 128–132.

[2] Cape Committee Report, Appendix, p. xli., No. 44.

[3] These telegrams were read at a mass meeting held at Bulawayo immediately after the news of Jameson's advance became known, when it was resolved that 1,000 men should at once be despatched (see *Bulawayo Chronicle*, 4th Jan., 1896). Corroborative evidence is furnished by the following telegrams unearthed by the Transvaal Government and printed in their Green Book, Appendix No. 89 :
(1) *From Napier, Bulawayo, to Jameson, Johannesburg. Dec. 31st.*
' Will strictly follow your instructions. There is considerable excitement. Keep us well posted. Write privately if action likely to take place in near future.'
(2) *From Spreckley, Bulawayo, to Jameson. Dec. 31st.*
' Much disappointed that I cannot participate. You have not behaved at all fairly to me. Can I leave by coach for Johannesburg to join Heany ? '

Similar if not quite such explicit instructions were given to Captain Gibbs, the adjutant of the Mashonaland Regiment. On 9th December Willoughby wrote telling him that 'he had to leave for England hurriedly on his company's business' and reminding him that Napier was the next senior officer in the country, and, failing him, Spreckley.[1] A fortnight later Gibbs was ordered to Bulawayo, where Jameson, who had run up for a day or two, told him that a 'camp of exercise' was probably to be held at Pitsani, and asked him to give an estimate of the number of men and horses he could put into the field, and to report how soon they could be mobilised after receiving orders. (Pitsani, be it remembered, was not less than 750 miles from Salisbury, and there was no railway.) Gibbs was then told to 'stand by' for further instructions. He left for Salisbury on the 26th December, but was held up on the road by heavy rains, and consequently missed a telegram sent to him with orders to move. This he found awaiting him on his arrival, when it was too late to act on it.[2]

The two divisions of the Rhodesia Horse might have given Jameson perhaps an additional 1,000 men, but it would have been impossible at that time of the year – the height of the wet season – to have brought them into the Transvaal, even by a direct march across the northern border, in less than two or three weeks. This disposes of the idea that they were to act simultaneously with Jameson's Pitsani force. It can only be concluded, therefore, that Jameson was absolutely confident of being able to reach Johannesburg or Pretoria with his own small column without trouble, and that he intended

---

[1] Transvaal Green Book, Appendix No. xliv.
[2] Information supplied by the late Colonel J. A. C. Gibbs, C.B., who, in 1895 and 1896, was adjutant of the Mashonaland Regiment of the Rhodesia Horse, in which the present writer was then serving as a trooper.

then to call upon the remaining forces in Rhodesia to come down from the north[1] and complete the triumphant *coup d'état* which he had arranged in his own mind. This, of course, was very far from what was contemplated by those who had sought his co-operation, but it was consistent with the boldness of imagination which inspired everything he undertook.

Providentially the Volunteers were restrained by the course of events from leaving their own territory. Had they done so the native rising which came suddenly upon Rhodesia three months later would have found the white settlers absolutely without protection and at the mercy of the rebels.

Jameson's preparations were now complete. He sent for Willoughby on 9th December, and with such patience as he could muster – though patience was never one of his outstanding qualities – he sat down to wait for the day he had himself appointed.

[1] Possibly by the route through Nylstroom and Pienaar's River, which Major R. White had reconnoitred in April. See Chapter V., p. 48.

CHAPTER XI

Cross-Purposes

THUS far we have been dealing with evidence which, disjointed as it is, and dependent to some extent on the blurred recollections of individuals, can, nevertheless, be pieced together to form a fairly coherent story. When we try to find out what was going on in Johannesburg during the crucial period just before the Raid we become involved in a bewildering tangle of side issues, with no documentary evidence to help us except a number of more or less obscure telegrams.

When Jameson left Johannesburg in November, having made, as he thought, final arrangements with his principals in the Reform movement, they had less than six weeks to complete their preparations if they meant business before the end of the year. It was all too short a time for the choosing of lieutenants and allocation of their duties, the setting up of machinery for the distribution of arms, the storage of provisions and the multitude of other details involved in their project. But instead of being free to concentrate on these matters, they were chiefly engaged in smoothing over differences in their own ranks. Much of those precious weeks was taken up in talk. Even their apologist, Sir Percy Fitzpatrick, has failed to disclose that any very thorough organisation was effected. They had 'plans', but no clear-cut programme. Worst of all, they had no one with sufficient confidence to take control – no master mind.

Rhodes and Beit, who were financing the movement, were both too far off to make their influence fully felt. Beit, in fact, only arrived in South Africa from England towards the end of December, and was in such poor health that he could not undertake the journey to Johannesburg. Charles Leonard, the nominal head of the Executive, though in public a firebrand of a somewhat demagogic type, lacked the determination to carry into practice the heroic methods which he advocated on the platform and in the Press. Lionel Phillips had been drawn in by stress of circumstances, and against his own inclinations, which were towards diplomacy rather than force. Though held in great respect by his associates in financial circles, he was little known to the general body of the Uitlanders. Hammond was a staunch supporter of the cause, inspired by a sincere conviction that the mining industry would never prosper until the corrupt Government of Kruger was displaced. He did not, however, come much into the open, possibly from a feeling that his views were not shared by the majority of his fellow-countrymen on the Rand, who were there as sojourners, and, as long as they were making money, did not trouble themselves about politics or reforms. Either Farrar or Fitzpatrick would have made an admirable commander, for both had the necessary qualities of experience and resolution. They were also more directly in touch than the others with the miners, who were expected to form the main body of the army of revolution – Farrar as a large employer and Fitzpatrick as having himself worked on the Barberton diggings. But they did not assume leading parts until it was too late to shape the course of events.

Finally there was that pathetic figure, Colonel Frank Rhodes, who had been sent up specially to take charge of the military side of the preparations. Unfortunately he was never able to assimilate the ways of thinking of the men into whose midst he had suddenly been cast – company men, stockbrokers and mining engineers – all equally strange to his experience; nor could he grapple with the irresolution which, as the moment for action drew near, crept over the conspirators like a palsy. Had Jameson and he changed places – had the former been at Johannesburg to engineer the insurrection, and Colonel Rhodes been put in command of the force on the border – the result might have been different, for Jameson would certainly have taken a grip of the situation and galvanised the plotters into decided action, while Rhodes, with his sense of military discipline, would have adhered conscientiously to his orders and never attempted to force the pace. The revolution in the Transvaal might have succeeded, and the entry of British troops, if it had ever taken place, would not have been a 'Raid'.

History tells us that revolts against established governments have in most cases started spontaneously, or have originated in some sudden incident which has come as a climax to a series of acts of oppression, and provoked a stampede. This revolution in Johannesburg was to be different. It was to be 'organised', and no appeal to mob impulse was ever contemplated. Herein lay pitfalls. They fixed a date for their rising. It was timed to begin on a day between Christmas and the New Year. In South Africa, especially where the British element predominates, no business is transacted during that week; all devote themselves to holiday-making and sport, combined as a rule in a race meeting. The Johannesburg Turf Club had arranged to hold a meeting which was to open on 26th December, and it was inevitable that a large number of people would flock into the town from the outlying mines, and even from Kimberley and Capetown. However ripe for forcible action the community might be, it would be difficult to work up the necessary enthusiasm at a time when it was absorbed in sport and diluted by the presence of unusual numbers of visitors.

Again, at Christmas time it was the custom in the Dutch Church to hold 'Nachtmaal', the sacramental service of Communion, to attend which all respectable Boers trekked with their families from the countryside into the nearest towns in their great tented waggons, and spent a few days in fraternising and social gatherings. This meant that the population of Pretoria, the capital, would be swelled by a crowd of burghers, all of whom, in accordance with their invariable rule, would be armed.

In the hurry of their negotiations with Jameson the Reform leaders had overlooked both these points, but when left to themselves they soon realised that their choice of a date had been unfortunate.

Another matter that exercised them was the delay in the arrival of the promised rifles, and still more, as already mentioned, the intimation that there would be a considerable shortage in the number delivered.[1] But even had they arrived it is not easy to see how they could have been utilised until the last moment, for it would have been impossible to issue them without letting hundreds of people into the plot, and thereby destroying all hope of preserving secrecy. As it was, the number of prominent Uitlanders who had inside knowledge of what was afoot was growing daily. They were not all of the same nationality, and by no means of one mind; the original four or five leaders may have been in agreement, but each new adherent introduced fresh ideas, and team work became increasingly hard to maintain. It was this lack of cohesion during the period of preparation which proved fatal to the development of a definite course of action. The members of the central executive were

[1] *The Transvaal From Within*, p. 100.

constantly unsettled by the rumours, hesitations and currents of changing opinion which the others brought with them. The councils of the conspirators began at the end to resemble the meetings of a debating society.

Still, out of this somewhat chaotic state of affairs, there emerged the semblance of a programme. The first step was to be the announcement by the National Union of their intention to hold a public meeting at Johannesburg, to ventilate grievances and formulate demands. This, according to Fitzpatrick,[1] was at a later date intended to be employed as a 'blind', to divert the Government from the real proceeding in view – the seizure of the Pretoria arsenal – which was to be accomplished a day or two before the date fixed for the meeting, and simultaneously with the rising in Johannesburg. Originally the meeting was arranged for the 27th December, and another 'manifesto' was drafted by Leonard – much on the same lines as that which he had prepared for Rhodes in October[2] – which was to be made public in advance. But before the date advertised for the meeting they counted on having the Pretoria arms and ammunition in their possession. They could then throw aside all disguise; dictate terms to Kruger and his Ministers, and establish some form of provisional government at Johannesburg.

The next step agreed upon was that as soon as the outbreak occurred Rhodes, the Prime Minister of Cape Colony, should represent to Sir Hercules Robinson, the Governor, the danger inherent in a racial feud in a neighbouring State, and should press him at once to go up, in his other capacity as High Commissioner of South Africa, to mediate between the Uitlanders and the Government. It was understood that Rhodes would

[1] *The Transvaal From Within*, p. 102.   [2] See Chapter VIII.

come as well, though in what special rôle is not very clear.

In committing himself to this part of the Reformers' programme Rhodes was not taking a leap entirely in the dark. He had already had many conversations about the growing trouble in the Transvaal with Sir Hercules, who had, in fact, sounded him as to the best course to take in the event of a rising.[1] Rhodes's advice was that he should proceed at once to the spot and intervene, and he satisfied himself that this was the course which Sir Hercules would adopt. Jameson, who, as Administrator of Rhodesia, occupied a very responsible post in the territories of the High Commission, had also discussed the Transvaal question with Sir Hercules and had been informed of his intentions.[2] It is hardly necessary to say that in these conversations neither he nor Rhodes had given the slightest hint of their own connection with the revolutionary movement, or of the real object of the police force on the border, and Sir Hercules remained entirely unaware of the conspirators' design that, at a moment selected by them, he should appear on the scene as a *deus ex machina*. He would have been indignant if he had realised that Rhodes had made any sort of a bargain with them about it, and still more scandalised if he had known of their secret intention to put a pistol – so to speak – in his hip-pocket in the shape of Jameson and his troopers, who when he arrived would either be on the spot or within striking distance.

It should be mentioned that there was one member of the High Commissioner's staff to whom Rhodes had confided, under the seal of secrecy, a portion of his plans – Sir Graham Bower, the Imperial Secretary, who was made aware in October that the police force in the

[1] Select Committee, Rhodes, 261.   [2] Select Committee, Jameson, 4513.

Protectorate was to be used if trouble arose in Johannesburg. But Bower did not regard the threatened rising as a very imminent contingency; he felt sure that Rhodes would himself tell the High Commissioner before the troops were moved, and though the revelation had certainly placed him in an embarrassing position he did not feel at liberty to break the confidence by communicating it to his Chief.[1]

Although they did not at first seem to be conscious of it – in fact, they professed to attach great importance to this part of their programme – the decision of the Reformers to appeal to the High Commissioner carried with it serious implications. Their avowed intention was not to seek re-annexation to Great Britain, but to maintain the Republic as a purged republic – a 'true republic', as Leonard expressed it in his 'manifesto', by which presumably was meant one in which all white residents should have equal political rights irrespective of race. But the moment the Imperial factor was introduced there was likely to arise a condition inconsistent with the continuance of a republic in any form. Sir Hercules Robinson was in South Africa as the representative of Great Britain, which claimed to be the Suzerain Power in the Transvaal,[2] and it would have been impossible for him to have acted as if he were a mere disinterested arbitrator, or, in the event of constitutional changes becoming necessary, to have taken part in any discussion which should ignore Great Britain's right to lay down terms for the future government of the Transvaal. At a later stage the Reformers had this possibility brought home to them in another connection, as will presently be seen.

Just a fortnight after Jameson had concluded his arrangements with the Johannesburg people he received

---

[1] Select Committee, Bower, 2516–2524.   [2] See Appendix III.

IR

the first hint that they were wavering. It came in the shape of a telegram from Colonel Rhodes to Major Robert White at Mafeking on 7th December, reading as follows:

'Dr. Wolff leaves Capetown for Kimberley to-night. Tell Dr. Jameson the polo tournament here is postponed for one week or it would clash with race week. Please acknowledge this as soon as possible.'[1]

'Polo tournament' was a characteristic metaphor adopted by Colonel Rhodes for the rising.[2] The excuse

[1] Report of Cape Committee, Appendix, p. xxxvi. This telegram was probably handed in on 6th Dec. for Wolff was with Jameson at Mafeking on the 8th, and must therefore have left Capetown on the 6th.

[2] As this is the first of a series of telegrams in which code words, metaphors and other modes of concealment were employed by the three sets of conspirators – those at Capetown, Johannesburg and Pitsani – it may not be out of place to explain the system followed.

Messages between Cecil Rhodes, Harris and Jameson were usually sent in the Chartered Company's private code, which was designed for economy rather than secrecy. In this code German words, or words of German origin, were assigned to English phrases and sentences in the ordinary way, a large number being left blank to be filled up according to special requirements. They were used by inserting the names of prominent officials and places, or for such expressions as 'Mr. Rhodes says . . .,' 'communicate the following to Dr. Jameson . . .,' and so on. There was also a number of elaborate tables for expressing in one code-word (Latin) various amounts of money, dates of letters, numbers of troops and similar phrases involving figures. The code was a complicated one, and in those offices which had a copy there were clerks specially trained to use it. Consequently messages sent by Rhodes, who always had clerks within reach, were properly coded and easy to decipher; but those from others like Harris, who attempted to code their own messages without understanding the method, were often confused and ambiguous.

Many of the Company's principal officers had registered telegraphic addresses. Rhodes, for example was 'Veldschoen,' and Harris 'Cactus'; and these were sometimes used in the body of a message instead of the appropriate code-word.

In addition there grew up among the conspirators – Rhodes excepted – a habit of using a sort of 'thieves' patter' in which innocent terms used in sport or company business were borrowed to disguise words which might create suspicion. Thus the proposed rising in Johannesburg was referred to as 'the polo tournament', or 'the flotation'; the High Commissioner became 'the Chairman'; Jameson was the 'contractor', and those in the plot 'the subscribers'.

When the telegrams were afterwards dragged to light these contrivances to put post-office officials and others off the scent proved rather mystifying, and they sometimes puzzled even those to whom they were addressed (Select Committee, evidence of Dr. Wolff, 'distant cutting', 6057; Fitzpatrick, p. 109, 'Godolphin', etc.). The method was, in fact, amateurish, and such as might have been expected from schoolboys 'playing Indians'. The necessary secrecy could have been better attained by a pre-arranged private code, as was done by many British officers – notably Colonel Baden-Powell – in the Boer War. But Harris and some of the others seemed to revel in such abstrusities.

for postponement was, as already shown, a sound one, though it must have been exceedingly irritating to Jameson to hear of it so late in the day.

White replied on the 8th as follows:

' Hope delay do not alter unless obliged according to original understanding considerable suspicion already therefore any delay would be most injurious.'[1]

Whether because this, as worded, was unintelligible or because in the meantime Wolff had arrived and had reported indecision in the Johannesburg camp, Jameson deemed it wise to supplement his staff officer's message by a personal one to Colonel Rhodes:

' Have everything ready here. Hope your telegram received yesterday Bobby White does not imply any delay, because any delay would be most injurious. Wolff leaves to-morrow [and] will explain.'[2]

A further telegram sent by him on the next day to the Chartered office makes no reference to the excuse about the races, from which it may be assumed that he still felt confident that the day originally selected – 26th December – would be adhered to. But uneasiness was again aroused when, on the 11th, White received from Colonel Rhodes another message, which, though its general terms were ambiguous, contained one significant word:

' Inform Dr. Jameson. – Do not send any more heroes before January. No room for them. Am sending Heyman to Grahamstown for next fourteen days.'[3]

[1] Cape Report, Appendix, p. xxxvi.
[2] Cape Report, minutes of evidence, p. 15, No. 168.
[3] Cape Report, Appendix, p. xlviii.

There has been some doubt among those who have told the story as to the meaning of the word 'heroes', but Colonel Rhodes fully explained it in his evidence before the Select Committee.[1] It referred to two officers sent by Jameson to help in the military organisation at Johannesburg, one of them being Lieut.-Colonel H. M. Heyman, the Commanding Officer of the Matabeleland Regiment of the Rhodesia Horse. The other, although not named by Colonel Rhodes, was no doubt Major Maurice Heany, also of the Rhodesian Volunteer force, a pioneer of Mashonaland and a close personal friend of Jameson, who had taken him into his complete confidence, and had asked him to go to Johannesburg to assist in raising a corps of miners and others.[2] He had not actually arrived on the 11th December, but Colonel Rhodes must have known that he was coming. It was quite natural that the introduction of Rhodesian officers into their councils should have created a certain amount of feeling among the Johannesburg plotters; at all events, they took an early opportunity of getting rid of both of them, as well as of a third, Captain Holden.

But to Jameson the ominous word in the above-quoted telegram was 'January', clearly indicating that they were still playing for delay. Before January, if all went according to plan, he expected the rising to be an accomplished fact; the fort at Pretoria would have been seized and looted, and his own force would have made a triumphant entry into Johannesburg. Thoroughly roused to the urgent need for checking any tendency to weaken, he despatched on 12th December a strong telegram to Stevens of the Chartered Company at Capetown :

[1] Select Committee, Colonel Rhodes, 5423-5440.
[2] Select Committee, Heany, 5858-5859.

'Send following message to Colonel F. Rhodes: begins: Grave suspicion has been aroused. Surely in your estimation do you consider that races is of the utmost importance compared to immense risks of discovery daily expected, by which under these circumstances it will be necessary to act prematurely. Let J. H. Hammond inform weak partners more delay more danger. Dr. Wolff will explain fully reasons to anticipate rather than postpone action. Do all you can to hasten the completion of works.'[1]

This was transmitted by Stevens (Harris's deputy) to Colonel Rhodes in a message which must also be quoted, because it provided another 'mystery':

'Dr. Jameson wires most strongly to urge no postponement of shareholders' meeting, and let Hammond inform weak partners any delay most injurious. Dr. Wolff will explain fully reasons at Directors' meeting. The London *Times* also cables confidentially to effect that postponement of meeting would be a most unwise course.'[2]

The reference to the London *Times* is at first sight rather puzzling, for *The Times* had sent no such telegram. But Rhodes, giving evidence before the Select Committee, supplied the clue.[3] Simultaneously with Jameson's impatient telegram of the 12th a private cablegram, addressed to him personally, had been received from Miss Flora Shaw, the *Times* correspondent:

'Delay dangerous. Sympathy now complete, but will depend very much upon action before European Powers given time to enter a protest, which, as European situation considered serious, might paralyse Government. General feeling in Stock Market very suspicious.'[4]

[1] Cape Report, Appendix, p. xlviii.   [2] Cape Report, Appendix, p. l.
[3] Select Committee, 208.   [4] Select Committee, Appendix 16, 164.

This had been seen by Stevens, who, in transmitting Jameson's message to Colonel Rhodes, not only tried to turn it into polite and intelligible English – thereby robbing it of much of its 'punch' – but reinforced it by adding the little item about *The Times*. Throughout his evidence before the Cape Committee he took up the attitude that in the Chartered Company's office he was a mere machine [1] – just three initials and a rubber stamp, so to speak – but when questioned on this particular message he could not be sure whether he had sent it under Rhodes's instructions or not, and he admitted that he had no right to use the words 'London *Times*'.[2] This was an important admission, for although Rhodes, when examined by the Select Committee in London, made no attempt to shirk responsibility for the telegram,[3] it enables us to acquit him of any deliberate intention to throw dust in the eyes of the Reform leaders.

Whatever Stevens's motive was, the telegram must have given the Johannesburg people something to think about, for a few days later – on the 18th – Wolff telegraphed to Jameson:

'There is not likely to be any postponement.'[4]

No sooner was the difficulty about the races disposed of than a new one was discovered. Alfred Beit, with Harris as fellow-passenger (and also, it may be mentioned, with two prominent Reformers, Messrs. Wools Sampson and Abe Bailey) arrived in Capetown from England on the 17th December. Beit, it will be remembered, had guaranteed, through Lionel Phillips, an

---

[1] Cape Report, Stevens, 142.   [2] Cape Report, Stevens, 214.
[3] Select Committee, Rhodes, 208.   [4] Cape Report, paragraph 22.

CROSS-PURPOSES 121

unlimited credit for the revolutionary war chest, while Rhodes had done the same through his brother, who represented him on the Goldfields Company. Some trouble may have arisen as to the allocation of their respective contributions. This would appear to be the only reasonable explanation of a telegram which, on the 18th December, Hammond, of the Goldfields, sent to Rhodes at his private house, Groote Schuur, near Capetown:

> 'Cannot arrange respective interests without Beit. Flotation must be delayed until his arrival. How soon can he come?'[1]

Postponement again! 'Flotation' this time, but the same thing of course as the 'polo tournament' of Colonel Rhodes's message. It is becoming apparent that they were ready to clutch at any excuse to gain time. Beit was ill and unable to travel, but he made it clear to Phillips that the 'flotation' must not be delayed for any trumped up excuse about funds; that if they once let the opportunity slip they might never get another chance; that Jameson was ready and could give no extension of time, and that 'our foreign supporters', whoever they might be, were urging immediate action.[2] He repeated this in several telegrams, and Harris also kept the telegraph office busy with messages to Jameson – reassuring him – and to Colonel Rhodes – urging that nothing should be allowed to interfere with the original plan.[3]

The fertility of the Johannesburg Reformers in conjuring up bogies was not by any means exhausted. On 21st December Colonel Rhodes, who, as a man of action,

---
[1] Cape Report, Appendix, p. lii.
[2] Cape Report, Appendix, pp. lii. and lvi., No. 63.
[3] Cape Report, Appendix, p. ccxxx.

must by this time have been sick to death of the whole business, sent this telegram to the Capetown office:

> 'Please inform C. J. Rhodes: It is stated that Chairman will not leave unless special letter inviting him. Definite assurance has been given by all of us that on day of flotation you and he will leave. There must absolutely be no departure from this, as many subscribers have agreed to take shares on this assurance. If letter necessary it can still be sent, but it was agreed that document left with J. A. Stevens was sufficient, and that you are responsible for Chairman's departure. It is very important to put this right. Reply to Lionel Phillips.'[1]

This telegram requires some comment. 'Chairman', it transpired, meant the High Commissioner, but what was the 'document'? Phillips and Leonard said later that it was the 'Declaration of Rights' drawn up by the latter for Rhodes on his visit to Capetown – the paper which has elsewhere been called the 'Manifesto'.[2] If so, it was hardly sufficient for its purpose. It was an impassioned appeal to the civilised world for sympathy in the grievances of the Uitlanders, but beyond one sentence – 'Driven to despair of ever getting justice, we have determined to strike for it' – it contained no hint of an intention to resort to force – nothing that would in itself have justified the High Commissioner in taking the serious step of rushing, uninvited, up to the Transvaal, still less of taking with him the Prime Minister of Cape Colony. The only justification for such a course would have been an actual outbreak of violence, and as soon as that occurred the manifesto would be superfluous. Until it occurred any 'special letter inviting him' would have carried little or

---

[1] Cape Report, Appendix, p. lvii., No. 64.
[2] Select Committee, evidence of Philips, 6999; Leonard, 7877.

no weight. The letter given by the Reform leaders to Jameson would have been a far more cogent inducement to the High Commissioner to take action, as it stated explicitly that the lives of British subjects, including women and children, were in danger. It is difficult to follow the reasoning of the Johannesburg leaders in sending this telegram – unless we fall back on the supposition that it was just another effort to gain time.

However, Beit sent a reply to Phillips solemnly assuring him – presumably on Rhodes's authority – that no request or letter was necessary, and that it had been arranged that the High Commissioner would come up – he might almost have said 'the goods would be delivered' – immediately on 'flotation',[1] and there the matter ended.

[1] Cape Report, Appendix, p. ccxxxii.

CHAPTER XII

Union Jack or Vierkleur

At this date – 23rd December – it seemed to those in Capetown that all doubts and hesitations were at an end. Only a few days remained before the time for 'flotation', and everything was ready at Pitsani. Harris had telegraphed to Colonel Rhodes on the 21st:

' Reply when you can float in your opinion so that I can advise Dr. Jameson ',[1]

and although no telegraphic answer to this has come to light it appears that a special messenger was sent to Rhodes from the leaders at Johannesburg to say that the rising was timed for 28th December at midnight.[2] This news Harris communicated to Jameson on the 23rd in the following terms:

' Company will be floated next Saturday 12 o'clock at night. They are very anxious you must not start before 8 o'clock, and secure telegraph silence. We suspect Transvaal is getting aware slightly.'[3]

' Secure telegraph silence ' is presumed to mean ' cut the wires between Mafeking and Pretoria '. This, as will be seen later, was to be done by the Bechuanaland Police,

---

[1] Cape Report, Appendix, p. lvii.
[2] Select Committee, evidence of Harris, 6392–6393, 6713–6717. Harris declined to give the name of the messenger, on the ground that he still lived in the Transvaal, and might get into trouble. C. J. Rhodes disclaimed knowledge of the incident (273), and Colonel Rhodes seemed doubtful about it (5041). Is it possible that the messenger and the fixture were flights of fancy on the part of Harris?
[3] Cape Report, Appendix, p. lix., No. 68.

UNION JACK OR VIERKLEUR

or arranged by Dr. Wolff. The 28th meant a postponement of two days only – the date originally fixed having been the 26th – but Jameson still showed signs of uneasiness. On the 24th he replied:

> 'Dr. Wolff informs me plans Johannesburg too unsettled. Probably they would be quite afraid to act if I start before Saturday, although meeting held Zeerust and southerly town. Will endeavour to delay till Saturday. If you can by cable do all you can to hasten it. Every day is of the utmost importance. On receipt of telegram am quite prepared to move on date of delivery. Colonel Rhodes, etc., intolerable.'[1]

'Meeting' must mean a gathering of Boer burghers. Zeerust was a small town in the Transvaal 35 miles north-east of Mafeking, and the 'southerly town' is no doubt Lichtenburg, about the same distance away on the south-east, for which there was probably no word in the code book. Jameson was very apprehensive that the burghers of these two districts, which lay north and south of his prepared route to Johannesburg, were on the *qui vive*, and might concentrate in front of him so as to block the road. On the previous day a certain Mr. A. Bates, a civil servant who had just been posted to Mafeking, was granted a fortnight's leave which, by arrangement with Major R. White, he employed in spying out the movements of these Boers of the western Tranvsaal as far as Rustenburg, a biggish town, half-way between Mafeking and Pretoria. For this purpose he was provided with funds by White and with a horse by Major Grey. He was authorised to cut the telegraph wire between Rustenburg and Pretoria if he could find an opportunity of doing so at the last moment without detection, but he did

[1] Cape Report, Appendix, p. ccxxxii.

nothing of this sort, and does not seem to have gathered any information of value.¹

It was clear from his telegram of the 24th that Jameson was in a dangerous mood and might act precipitately, and Harris had to face the delicate task of holding him in check, while doing his best to whip up the Reformers to prevent them from lagging. To the former he telegraphed on the same day:

> 'You must not move before Saturday night. We are feeling confident it will take place Saturday night. Since Dr. Wolff left feeling our subscribers greatly improved.'²

Wolff, it should be explained, had gone across country to inspect his food depots, and on Tuesday, the 24th, was with Jameson at Mafeking, leaving on the return journey on the same day.

To Colonel Rhodes Harris telegraphed on the 24th:

> 'Jameson says he cannot give extension of refusal for flotation beyond December, as Transvaal Boers opposition shareholders hold meeting on Limpopo at Pitsani Macklucke.'³

Even for Harris, with his inveterate dislike of plain speaking, this was a surprising achievement in obscurity! All that can be said is that it does not tally with the message he had received from Jameson, and was not calculated to enlighten the people at Johannesburg.

In the meantime, however, the Johannesburg executive were busy with another scare – the last and, as it turned

---

¹ Cape Report, Bates, 2308–2415. ² Cape Report, Appendix, p. ccxxxiii.
³ Cape Report, Appendix, p. ccxxxiii.

out, the fatal one. It rested on what has been called the 'flag question,' a most precise account of which has been given by Sir Percy Fitzpatrick,[1] though he offers no explanation of what led up to it. An attempt will be made here to supply that deficiency.

The inner ring of the conspirators, like the general body of the Uitlanders, was composed of men of several nationalities.[2] To some of them – whom we may regard as the extreme right – the idea of revolution was inseparable from the re-conquest of the Transvaal and its rehabilitation as a colony under the British Crown. It was fairly well known that Mr. (afterwards Sir Aubrey) Wools Sampson and Mr. Karri Davis – possibly also Colonel Rhodes himself – had this idea at the back of their minds. There were others, among them Home-born men as well as British Colonials, who were definitely opposed to direct Imperial rule. What they wanted was to expel the corrupt Government of Kruger and to free the country from the insidious influence of Germans and Hollanders, and provided this was achieved they preferred to keep the constitution and flag of the Transvaal. Phillips and Leonard and many of the rank and file, including all the Americans and most of the Afrikanders, were of this way of thinking. Finally there was an intermediate section which had probably not given much thought to the question of the future constitution. They would have welcomed any form of government which guaranteed them free institutions, an abatement of the iniquitous taxation and their 'civil rights', and the question of a flag had never occurred to them.

[1] *The Transvaal from Within*, pp. 101–3.
[2] The Reform Committee, formed a few days later, was composed of 34 British; 17 Afrikanders; 8 Americans; 2 Germans; and one each of Australian, Swiss, Holland, Turkish and Boer nationality (Select Committee, Phillips, 6928).

Outside Johannesburg there were similar strata of opinion. Rhodes was chiefly concerned in securing for the Transvaal a form of government which would have enabled it to become a unit in a federated South Africa. He was not anxious to see it return to the inelastic clutch of Downing Street, which would only have acted as a sort of tourniquet, but, as an Englishman himself, he recognised that a constitution on British lines was the only one which would give South Africa its opportunity. He certainly had no attachment to the Vierkleur – the flag of the existing Republic – which, if retained, would be a constant reminder of the reactionary Kruger regime. The Union Jack was the symbol of his ideals, and he believed in it as a precious emblem, but, at the moment, he was alive to the danger of injudicious flag-wagging, which would only have the effect of alienating the sympathy of his Dutch supporters in Cape Colony. For these reasons he was content to leave the question in abeyance. It could be decided later when the people had settled down and could have a plebiscite to determine their future constitution. Let them keep their local flag by all means, and even their republic for local matters, provided it was one sufficiently plastic to be moulded into the general scheme of South African union, under the British flag, for railway purposes, customs tariffs and defence. These were the things that really mattered.[1]

Jameson, if he had taken the trouble to think about the question at all, would probably have adopted the same line of reasoning, but his immediate plans were absorbing his mind to the exclusion of all constitutional problems. His job was to get his men as quickly as possible into the forefront. Commissariat and transport, horses and ammunition, were for the time being of far

[1] Select Committee, Rhodes, 290–292.

UNION JACK OR VIERKLEUR 129

more importance than the particular flag under which the crowd at Johannesburg elected to start their revolt.[1]

In this, as in other cases, it is probably on Rutherfoord Harris that the initial responsibility for raising a controversy rests. Some time before he left England he must have sent a cablegram to Rhodes suggesting that public sympathy at home would be alienated unless it was made clear that the object of the revolution in the Transvaal was to strengthen the British position in South Africa, and that there were rumours current that Rhodes's own ideas were not whole-heartedly British. The cablegram has not come to light, but its purport is fairly certain from Rhodes's reply of the 6th November:

> 'As to English flag they must very much misunderstand me at home. I of course would not risk everything as I am doing excepting for British flag.'[2]

To this Harris sent an incoherent reply in which, however, there stands out one intelligible and illuminating sentence, worthy of study, as it supplies a key to a good deal of the misunderstanding which ensued:

> 'From information received know there is great danger Phillips and Leonard may do business without assistance from British South Africa Company and also independently of British flag. It would have serious effect your position here.'[3]

This lets the cat out of the bag. Harris had made up his mind that the revolution in the Transvaal should be regarded as an achievement by Rhodes and the Chartered

[1] Select Committee, Rhodes, 1351.
[2] Select Committee, Appendix 14, No. 9.
[3] Select Committee, Appendix 14, No. 32.

Company on behalf of Great Britain, and no doubt he cherished the thought that a full share of the honour and glory of bringing it about would come to himself as one of the most active organisers. It was a fantastic idea, and one which Rhodes must be acquitted of entertaining, but there is ground for believing that Harris was not alone in his delusion.

It has already been mentioned that among the passengers on the mail steamer which took Harris to the Cape in December were two well-known gentlemen connected with the reform movement – Messrs. Bailey and Wools Sampson, both on their way back to Johannesburg. What is more likely than that Harris, in discussing with them the position in the Transvaal, as he is bound to have done, showed them Rhodes's cable of the 6th November, which, taken by itself, certainly gives the impression that his support for the coming revolution was conditional on its being conducted under the Union Jack. Immediately on landing Messrs. Bailey and Sampson went up to Johannesburg, and we have Fitzpatrick's authority for saying that certain remarks let fall by one or both of them started the report which so seriously disturbed the republican advocates among the reformers. The news soon got round and was probably embroidered. The Executive realised that until the question was disposed of there could be no unanimity, and their enterprise would be doomed. One of their friends, whose name they seemed afterwards reluctant to disclose, happened to be going to Capetown on business and was asked to get the matter cleared up.[1] He returned on Christmas Day and reported that from

---

[1] Select Committee, Phillips, 6836. Mr. Basil Williams, in his *Life of Rhodes* (p. 267), makes no secret of the matter. It was Captain (afterwards Sir Francis) Younghusband, the special correspondent of *The Times*.

Rhodes himself he had received satisfactory assurances about the flag, and as to his intention faithfully to carry out the terms of his agreement with Leonard, but that from other sources he had gathered an impression that the rumour as to the British flag was well founded, and that Rhodes's word could not be depended on. According to the evidence these suspicions were created by a conversation with Harris, who had hinted, if he did not actually affirm in plain words, that it was Jameson's intention, on reaching Johannesburg, to hoist the Union Jack.[1]

It may be that Harris, who, as we have seen, was inclined at times to let his enthusiasm betray him into indiscretion, had repeated his suggestion that the Colonial Office was aware of the use to be made of Jameson's force, and that when it moved it would do so with the approval of the Imperial Government. It was common knowledge that the force was composed almost exclusively of young Englishmen, and was commanded by officers of whom many had held, or were still holding, Her Majesty's commission. They would be loth to run the risk of taking part in an invasion of the Transvaal unless convinced that the Government was behind it. This is tantamount to saying that they would be marching under the British flag. It was only a step further for the Johannesburg Reformers to infer that when the outbreak occurred the Imperial Government would take complete charge of the situation. They – the reform leaders – would be relegated to the background; Jameson would be the man in possession; the Transvaal would be placed under the Chartered Company, and so on, and so on.

On Christmas morning a meeting of the Executive was

[1] Fitzpatrick, pp. 101-2; Select Committee, Phillips, 6827-6834; Leonard, 7936, 7958-7959.

held at Colonel Rhodes's office in the Goldfields building, which had become the revolutionary headquarters, and the flag question was excitedly discussed. In the end it was resolved that Leonard himself, as President of the National Union, should proceed at once to Capetown to thrash the matter out with Rhodes, and that he should be accompanied by Mr. F. H. Hamilton, the Editor of the *Star*, the principal organ of the Uitlanders. It was also resolved that the meeting of the National Union should be postponed till the 6th January, and that all action should be suspended until a positive assurance was obtained that the authority of the Imperial Government would not be insisted on. It is rather interesting to remember that four days earlier the same people were insisting that their plans depended on the intervention, at the critical moment, of the Imperial Government's chief representative in South Africa ! No stronger proof is wanted of the confusion of thought and vacillation which pervaded their councils.

Jameson was apprised of the new turn in the situation by telegrams from his brother Sam, and from Harris, both of which contained once more the odious phrase 'postponement of flotation'. The first read as follows :

> '26th December. It is absolutely necessary to postpone flotation through unforeseen circumstances here altogether unexpected, and until we have C. J. Rhodes's absolute pledge that authority of Imperial Government will not be insisted on. C. Leonard left last night to interview Rhodes. We will endeavour to meet your wishes as regards December, but you must not move until you have received instructions to. Please confirm.'[1]

[1] Cape Report, Appendix, p. ccxxxiv.

Harris's telegram was to the same effect, and concluded with these words :

'C. Leonard will therefore arrive Capetown Saturday morning. You must not move till you hear from us again. Too awful! Very sorry.'[1]

It is not difficult to picture Jameson's disgust. All his preparations were complete. His troops were keyed up by the sense that some excitement was at hand, and, though not certain of the objective, were eager for the moment to arrive. Every day the danger of Boers massing in front of him grew more serious. He knew nothing of the flag business. All he knew was that the Johannesburg people, at the last moment – two days before the date which they had given him – had shown themselves 'infirm of purpose'.

Small wonder then that his thought at this moment was, 'Give me the daggers !'

[1] Cape Report, Appendix, p. ccxxxiv., No. 73.

CHAPTER XIII

The Damp Squib

THE Reformers were by this time well aware that Jameson was a difficult person to restrain, and, in fact, were desperately afraid of him. They knew that he was champing his bit at Pitsani and seem to have sensed the possibility that, in spite of their postponement messages, he might actually start on the day first agreed and force their hands. To guard against this terrifying prospect there was only one course to pursue; messengers must be sent direct to stop him. There was just time, and fortunately the very men – as they thought – for the purpose were ready to hand – the two Rhodesian officers, Major Heany and Captain Holden, Jameson's own men, who were not required in Johannesburg and would surely carry more weight with him than any of their own number. It was decided to despatch both at once – Heany by rail and Holden across country along the route which Wolff had so carefully prepared, and on which he could obtain relays of horses. Their instructions were to explain the position and to give Jameson peremptory orders on no account to move without further advice. Heany was furnished with full particulars of the arms and other ordnance in possession of the Boers at Pretoria, as well as of those which were held by the Reformers, and he took these and other details down in his pocket-book. He had an interview with the committee, at which half a dozen, including Hammond and Phillips, were present, and was asked his opinion as to what Jameson would do when he got the message to stop. He replied, 'He will come in as sure as fate.' Holden also expressed the same opinion, but both agreed to go.¹ They left on the 26th December, and both actually arrived in time and faithfully delivered their messages. Their subsequent action will be referred to later.

The position in which the Reformers found themselves at this juncture was, in very truth, an anxious one. They had not received the arms they expected, and in other respects were hopelessly unready; they were by no means sure that their messengers would arrive in time to stop Jameson from moving, and they were haunted by Heany's ominous warning that he would ignore their orders. Added to this, their conspiracy was no longer a secret. It was being discussed openly in the clubs and in the streets. They could not be sure that the Government had not already heard of it and was only waiting, as Kruger had sardonically phrased it, 'for the tortoise to put out its head'. And yet they were paralysed by their own actions, for they could do nothing until they heard from Leonard and Hamilton, who had not yet reached Capetown. That their plot was more or less public property is shown by the following telegram, sent to Rhodes on the 27th December by a great friend of his – Mr. J. A. Faure,² a member of the Cape Legislative Council, who was visiting Johannesburg for the races:

> 'It is publicly stated by members of the National Union that you are inciting rebellion here and have 800 police stationed near border. Your friends strongly advise your official denial.'³

We do not know whether Rhodes replied to this, but he saw the danger of the growing rumours and realised the effect they might have if they reached Jameson's

---
¹ Select Committee, Heany, 5875, 5915-5918.
² Select Committee, Rhodes, 356.   ³ Cape Report Minutes, p. 76.

ears. He at once sent a telegram to him to allay apprehension:

> 'Do not be alarmed at our having 600 men at Pitsani Macklucke [*sic*]; we have the right to have them. You know we are sorting the B.S.A. Co.'s police for eventual distribution, and if people are so foolish as to think you are threatening Transvaal we cannot help that. Police at Mafeking will cost half what they do in Matabeleland and horses do not die. At same time, as you know, we must keep up a certain police force for the country as per our agreement with the Imperial Government.'[1]

Now, so far from curbing Jameson's impatience, this advice was calculated to increase it, for it indicated that Rhodes had failed to grasp what was causing him concern. Jameson saw the futility of trying, by specious excuses, to justify the presence of his force so close to the Transvaal. What he feared was that the Boers would soon mass in sufficient strength to make it impossible for him to break through. If he was to move at all it must be at once, and this telegram implied that he might have to wait indefinitely (which was precisely what Rhodes meant). The fact is, of course, that he and Rhodes were at cross-purposes. He was for instant action, while Rhodes was for keeping him there for future action. Therein lay the essence of the misunderstanding which was to bring disaster upon both of them.

On receipt of Rhodes's 'reassuring' telegram Jameson began to force the pace. In quick succession he sent off several telegrams to Harris. On the 27th:

> 'I am afraid of Bechuanaland Police for cutting wire. They have now all gone forward, but will

[1] Cape Report, Appendix, p. ccxxxvi. Select Committee, Rhodes, 305.

endeavour to put a stop to it. Therefore expect to receive a telegram from you nine to-morrow morning authorising movement. Surely Colonel Rhodes advisable to come to terms at once. Give guarantee or you can telegraph before Leonard arrives.'[1]

The 'guarantee' presumably refers to the 'absolute pledge' which his brother Sam had told him must be given that the authority of the British Government would not be insisted on. The arrangements made for cutting the wire were disclosed in notes found in the captured despatch-box, afterwards printed in the Appendix to the report of the Cape Committee. Two junior officers (named) of the B.B.P. were detailed to go to Malmani Oog, on the Krugersdorp road, where they were to break the connection at two places between Malmani and Zeerust at 3 p.m. on the 28th December, rejoining their troop at 5 a.m. on the following morning. They were to be in civilian clothes, and were on no account to carry 'anything regimental'. Another officer and a N.C.O. were to proceed to Zeerust at 8 a.m. on the 28th to destroy the line at a couple of points, five or six miles apart, between there and Rustenburg. They were then to ride across the veld to certain lead mines, seventy miles along the road, and await the arrival of the column, or catch it up. These instructions are in accordance with Jameson's original intention of starting on the 28th. There were other notes as to wire cutting between points indicated as 'V' and 'K', which may mean Vryburg and Kimberley – or possibly Krugersdorp.

On the same day Jameson sent a further telegram to Harris:

'If I cannot as I expect communicate with B.B. Police cutting then we must carry into effect original

[1] Cape Report, Appendix, p. ccxxxvii.

plans. They will then have two days for flotation. If they do not we will make our own flotation with help of letter which I will publish. Inform Hammond, Wolff, A. L. Lawley whom you may rely on to co-operate.'[1]

This is an instructive communication, for it shows that he expected the initial movement to come from Johannesburg, and therefore stultifies his statement to the Select Committee that the discretion was left in his hands. In fact, it proves that Jameson's anxiety to move was not because that was in accordance with the original plan, but because he had found out that the Reformers were disinclined to move themselves.

His next telegram – also sent on the 27th – was to his brother in Johannesburg:

> 'Dr. Wolff will understand distant cutting British Bechuanaland Police have already gone forward guarantee already given therefore let Hammond telegraph instantly all right.'[2]

(Stops are purposely omitted, as it is not clear where they should be inserted.)

Dr. Wolff did *not*, however, understand, though there seems to be a reference to some additional arrangement for destroying the telegraph line nearer Pretoria, which he was expected to carry out. Hammond, so far from telegraphing 'all right', sent a strong reply to the contrary through Harris on the afternoon of the same day:

> 'Wire just received. Experts' report decidedly adverse. I absolutely condemn further developments at present.'[3]

---

[1] Cape Report, Appendix, p. ccxxxvii.
[2] Cape Report, Appendix, p. ccxxxviii.
[3] Cape Report, Appendix, p. ccxxxviii., No. 76.

And Phillips telegraphed to Beit in the same sense:

> 'It is absolutely necessary to delay floating. If foreign subscribers insist on floating without delay anticipate complete failure.'[1]

In face of the above telegrams, which were despatched after Heany and Holden had left hot foot with their messages for Jameson, it is absurd to think that the Committee at Johannesburg had not considered the possibility of his acting in defiance of these messages; they were not, in fact, so much taken by surprise as Fitzpatrick's account suggests. Moreover, they had good ground for fearing some such action. A message from Harris telling him that the 'shareholders' meeting' had been postponed to the 6th January; that Leonard's manifesto had been published, and there was nothing for it but patiently to await the result of his interview with Rhodes, only added fresh fuel to Jameson's burning impatience.[2] His frame of mind is well illustrated by the next telegram, sent off on Saturday the 28th:

> 'There will be no flotation if left to themselves. First delay was races which did not exist. Second policies, already arranged. All means fear. You had better go as quickly as possible and report fully or tell Rhodes to allow me. I stand to lose 50 good B.S.A. Co.'s police – time expires next week, and so on, as can tell them nothing.'[3]

---

[1] Cape Report, Appendix, p. lxiv., No. 80. 'Foreign subscribers' here seems to mean Jameson and his men. 'Foreign supporters' had perhaps the same meaning in Beit's telegram to Phillips of 19th Dec. (p. 121). Rhodes, however, in his evidence (310) seemed to think it applied to Mr. Beit and himself. On the other hand, Harris, in a later message to Jameson (28th Dec., page 141), used the term 'our foreign friends' to mean the Reformers. One is forcibly reminded of Mr. Punch's 'puzzles for historians'!
[2] Cape Report, Appendix, p. lxii., No. 67.
[3] Cape Report, Appendix, p. ccxxxvii.

Other telegrams sent by Harris on that critical day may be quoted in order of despatch, without comment, as they explain themselves :

To Jameson :

'It is all right if you will only wait. Heany comes to you from Colonel Rhodes by special train to-day.'[1]

Another to Jameson :

'You are quite right with regard to cause of delay of flotation, but Charles Leonard of *Star* informs us movement not popular in Johannesburg. When you have seen Heany let us know by wire what he says. We cannot have fiasco.'[2]

To Colonel Rhodes :

'Leonard says flotation not popular and England's bunting will be resisted by public. Is it true? Consult all our friends and let me know, as Jameson is quite ready to move and is only waiting for Heany's arrival.'[3]

To Heany, *en route* :

'Your special train arranged. Lose no time or you will be late.'[4]

A final telegram to Jameson :

'Goold Adams arrives Mafeking Monday, and Heany, I think, to-night. After seeing him you and

[1] Cape Report, Appendix, p. ccxxxix., No. 81.
[2] Cape Report, Appendix, p. ccxl., No. 79.
[3] Cape Report, Appendix, p. ccxli.
[4] Cape Report, Appendix, p. ccxxxix. Heany acknowledged this, and telegraphed back, 'If late shall follow'.

THE DAMP SQUIB 141

we must judge regarding flotation, but all our foreign friends are now dead against it and say public will not subscribe one penny towards it even with you as a director. Ichabod!'[1]

We can understand that Harris, seeing the wreck of the scheme on which he had been working night and day for six months, wanted, in the bitterness of his heart, to get away for a quiet week-end, but knowing, as he must have known, that it was touch and go whether Heany could reach Jameson in time to stop him – uncertain, as he must have been, whether, even if Heany did reach him in time, he would be able to stop him, it seems incredible that, when he left his office that Saturday afternoon, he did not detail from his staff of clerks one or two to be on the spot in case further news came in the evening or on Sunday morning. Neither he nor Rhodes lived in Capetown. Rhodes was at his own house at Rondebosch, five miles out, and Harris lived two miles on the other side. A striking feature of all the arrangements connected with the Transvaal plot was the wretched 'staff work' and disregard of elementary precautions. When Harris closed his office on the 28th December he made up his mind – God knows why! – that there was nothing more to be done.[2]

Leonard and Hamilton, after their interview with Rhodes, also felt fairly easy in their minds, and on Saturday afternoon sent off the following joint telegram to their Committee in Johannesburg:

'We have received perfectly satisfactory assurance from Rhodes, but a misunderstanding undoubtedly

[1] Cape Report, Appendix, p. ccxi., No. 82.
[2] Select Committee, Harris, 6695.

exists somewhere. In our opinion continue preparations, but carefully and without any sort of hurry, as entirely fresh departure will be necessary. In view of changed conditions Jameson has been advised accordingly.'[1]

Rhodes, who had no doubt taken Leonard's measure, saw that, for the time being at any rate, no active movement could take place. He sent for Graham Bower, the Imperial Secretary, and informed him that the revolution at Johannesburg 'had fizzled out like a damp squib' and authorised him to tell the Governor.[2]

Sir Hercules Robinson promptly sent a cablegram to Mr. Chamberlain – with what relief is betrayed by its spluttering tautology:

'I learn on good authority movement at Johannesburg has collapsed. Internal divisions have led to the complete collapse of the movement, and leaders of the National Union will now probably make the best terms they can with President Kruger.'[3]

But apparently Mr. Chamberlain had other and, as we shall see, better sources of information.

[1] *The Transvaal From Within*, p. 104.
[2] Select Committee, Bower, 2561–2562.   [3] Blue Book C 7933, No. 3.

CHAPTER XIV

Ready to Bolt

WHEN Rhodes was questioned, long afterwards, by members of the Select Committee in London, as to the various telegrams that were sent from the Chartered Company's Capetown office to Jameson and others during December 1895, he made no attempt to shirk responsibility for them. Nevertheless, the most cursory study of his evidence shows that, except in one or two cases, he knew very little about them.[1] This ignorance became more marked when the Committee dealt with the telegraphic correspondence after 17th December, which was the date of Harris's arrival from England. But even without Rhodes's evidence it is quite obvious that the phrases used – the jargon about 'foreign subscribers' and 'opposition shareholders', and the conciliatory appeals to Jameson to 'wait patiently' – were not his. When Rhodes wanted to say a thing he said it outright, without taking refuge in vague paraphrase. Contrast, for example, the language of the authentic Rhodes cablegram to Harris about the flag – 'I would not risk everything, as I am doing, except for the British flag' – with that of the one purporting to be sent by his authority to Johannesburg later – 'Leonard says England's bunting will be resisted by public; is it true?'

The present writer had charge, under Harris, of the correspondence in the Chartered Company's South African office in 1890 and 1891, and can assert positively that Rhodes, though constantly on the spot giving

[1] Select Committee, Rhodes, 230–245, etc.

general instructions, never saw a letter or a telegram that was despatched. Occasionally he would read an important communication received, but in no case one that went out. Yet Harris, no doubt with excellent intentions, and perhaps almost unconsciously, quoted Rhodes as his authority for practically everything he wrote at that time.

This habit, though encouraged by Rhodes's well-known aversion from letter-writing, was a dangerous one in the present crisis. If, instead of sending temporising messages which were really his own, Harris had gone to Rhodes and persuaded him to despatch a personal telegram to Jameson ordering him point blank to stay where he was, it is probable that much of the trouble that ensued would have been prevented. In his mood at the end of December, Jameson was impervious to anything short of a direct 'No' from the only man whose authority he still recognised. To Harris, whose idiosyncrasies he knew intimately, he paid very little attention. Even Hammond's very definite condemnation of an immediate movement made no impression on him.

On Saturday afternoon he sent off the following to Harris :

'Received your telegram Ichabod re Captain Heany. Have no further news. I require to know. Unless I hear definitely to the contrary shall leave to-morrow evening and carry into effect my second telegram of yesterday to you, and it will be all right.'[1]

The wording seems to show that it was intended for Rhodes himself, but did Jameson reflect when he sent off

[1] Cape Report, p. ccxiii. The second telegram referred to is the one in which he had used the expression 'we will make our own flotation.' See p. 138.

READY TO BOLT

such a critical message that, on a Saturday afternoon, there was a risk of its failing to reach its mark, or was he counting on Harris having sufficient sense to order someone to stand by – at the telegraph office if necessary – to look out for further communications?

Later in the same day his resolution seems to have stiffened, for we find him sending a still more definite message to his brother at Johannesburg:

> 'I shall start without fail to-morrow night. Inform Wolff distant cutting. He will understand.'[1]

Now what had happened to cause him to make this positive statement before the arrival of Heany, who, according to his information, was hurrying to Pitsani with an urgent communication from Colonel Rhodes as to a change of plan?

The answer is that he had just seen a sensational telegram from Reuter's South African agency which had been exhibited at Mafeking and Pitsani – a telegram which, if we accept his own statement, made him forget all about Heany – he knew nothing about Holden – and jump to the conclusion that the ball had been opened at Johannesburg. It was as follows:

> '*Johannesburg*, 28th December. Position becoming acute and persistent rumours afloat secret arming mines and warlike preparations. Women children leaving Rand. Americans passed resolution siding Transvaal, and Mercantile Association considers [in] case [of] trouble everything [to] lose and appointed committee investigate position. Market lifeless, no business, everything politics. *Volkslied* and God save Queen loudly cheered theatre.

[1] Quoted from Fitzpatrick, *The Transvaal From Within*, p. 105. It does not appear in the Cape Committee's Report.

'*Pretoria.* President and General Joubert returned. Political situation talk [of] town and opinion expressed by leading men *modus vivendi* will be arrived at and wiser counsels prevail in Johannesburg.'[1]

This Jameson chose to regard as conclusive evidence of two things – that the Transvaal authorities knew what was brewing, and that matters in Johannesburg had come to a head.

Of the two men now racing towards him with orders from the Reformers that he should hold his hand, Holden was the first to arrive. He reached Pitsani that evening, having covered the 170 miles from Johannesburg on horseback in just over seventy hours – a performance which shows that he had conscientiously carried out his undertaking to the Committee. He at once delivered his message to Jameson, who therefore had the night to think it over. But Holden was a comparative stranger to him, and not one to whom he would turn for advice.

The other – Heany – arrived early the following morning (Sunday). To reach Mafeking from Johannesburg by rail it was necessary in those days to travel towards Capetown as far as De Aar junction, and then north again through Kimberley.[2] Harris had arranged for him to have a special engine and coach from Kimberley so as to enable him to catch the Mafeking mail train, which was kept waiting for him at Vryburg for nearly two hours. On this there happened to be Mr. Newton, the Resident Commissioner, returning from his visit to

---

[1] Quoted from Jameson's statement before Select Committee, with certain corrections in the punctuation where it was obviously wrong (evidence, No. 4513).

[2] Heany was delayed at Kimberley for about three hours waiting for his special, and this fact gave rise to a suspicion that he had received certain instructions from Rhodes, or someone at the Capetown end. Mr. Rawlinson, a barrister sent out by the Home Government in Feb. 1896, to collect evidence for the impending trial of Jameson and his officers, instituted minute enquiries into this point, with entirely negative results (Cape Report, Appendix).

the Cape, but the two men were unacquainted, and had no conversation. On reaching Mafeking in the small hours of Sunday morning Heany could learn nothing of Jameson's movements, or even his whereabouts, and, thinking it possible that he might have already started, he routed out the manager of a store with which he had business connections, one Emmanuel Isaacs, and bought a pair of riding-boots and a kit-bag, in case he should have to follow. He also obtained a saddle horse. By 8.30 a.m.[1] he had covered the twenty-six miles to Pitsani camp, and at once sought Jameson, whom he found sitting in his bell tent. He read from his pocket-book the message he had taken down at the Reformers' headquarters, and gave him the information about their armament and what he had been told about that of the Boers at Pretoria. That was all. He had discharged his task. The two men were old and close friends, and had shared together many adventures and two campaigns, but in this affair the one felt that the other was not in the mood for seeking advice, and would settle the matter for himself.

Jameson got up and left his tent, and for twenty minutes paced up and down alone. The moment for final decision had arrived. He was not the man to shirk a decision, but his faculty of detached and collected reasoning may have become obscured by the dread that, at the eleventh hour, he might be robbed of his long-cherished, long-prepared enterprise. Even without his own admissions eighteen months later,[2] we may comprehend something of the tumult in his mind, and, comprehending, may be inclined to be tolerant – perhaps to condone.

The incidents of the past few weeks – and especially

[1] Cape Report, paragraph 33 ; Select Committee, 384. Heany, however, said 'about mid-day,' which must have been a mistake (see his evidence, 5845–5956).
[2] Select Committee, Jameson, 4513, 4594–4596.
LR

the last four or five days – had all combined to unbalance him – the pinpricks of the delays in Johannesburg, which seemed to him so trivial as he was not on the spot to know what had prompted them; the directions and counter-directions from the wire-puller at Capetown – Harris, who treated him as a clumsy rider would a restive horse, now patting him on the shoulder, and the next moment jerking at the bridle.

All round him in the camp the atmosphere was tense with expectation. There was no one near who could give him sane counsel. Had Rhodes been there, or Hammond, or even his brother Sam, he might have listened to them and kept his impulsiveness in check, but he was surrounded by inflammable material – firebrands like Willoughby and the Whites, whose presence only tended to increase the risk of explosion.

Behind him stretched the dreary background of Bechuanaland; in front the one clear outlet – the eastern horizon, and beyond it the goal on which he had kept his eyes fixed for months. And now, between him and that goal, his imagination pictured Boer commandos massing – threatening to cut him off. His plans seemed on the verge of crumbling.

There was that letter of invitation. Nobody knew better than he that it had been manufactured for an emergency which had not at the time arisen, but he saw that it could now be used to justify immediate action. He had intended, in any case, to use it. It said, 'Come to our aid if a disturbance arises here'. Well, Reuter's telegram provided the excuse. It spoke of secret arming, warlike preparations and women and children fleeing. Heany's message had been to postpone – not to abandon; but further postponement would be fatal. It must be now – or never. It should be now.

LEANDER STARR JAMESON
In 1895

He turned back to his tent, where Heany still waited. 'I am going in', he said, 'and you – what will you do?'

'Go in with you', replied Heany promptly, and that was the whole of the conversation.[1]

His mind once made up, Jameson lost no time in making his final arrangements. Within half an hour of his conversation with Heany he was at the camp telegraph office sending over the wires a number of messages consequent on his decision. One was to Napier and Spreckley, telling them to be ready to move with the Rhodesia Horse. This, as already mentioned, was read at a mass meeting at Bulawayo on the following day. Then there was a curious telegram, sent under his second Christian name, 'Starr', to Wolff:

> 'Meet me as arranged before you left on Tuesday night which will enable us to decide which is the best destination. Make J. W. Leonard speak. Make cutting to-night without fail. Have great faith in Hammond, A. L. Lawley, and miners with Lee-Metford rifles.'[2]

When this telegram was delivered at Johannesburg on Monday morning Wolff could not be found. Like the others in the movement, he had assumed that nothing could happen for a week and had gone out of town. But Sam Jameson, to whose care it had been addressed, opened and decoded it. Of the effect on him and those to whom he showed it mention will be made in a later chapter, but the explanation afterwards supplied by Wolff of the reference to 'best destination' may as well be stated at once. It appeared that before the flag question

---

[1] Select Committee, Heany, 5872, 5949–5951.
[2] Report of Cape Committee, Appendix, p. ccxliv.

had arisen to upset the Committee there had been a proposal that Jameson, instead of taking his troops to Johannesburg, should march direct on Pretoria, where, if their original programme had been carried out, the fort would be in the possession of the conspirators. On Wolff's last visit to Mafeking, on Christmas Eve, it had been agreed between him and Jameson that if this plan was adopted by the Committee he should come out to meet the column at Boon's Store (about 20 miles west of Krugersdorp, where the roads for Pretoria and Johannesburg branched) to let Jameson know.[1] But since Wolff left Mafeking the position had completely changed. All reasons for marching on Pretoria vanished when the rising was postponed. Jameson must have known this, and the suggestion in his telegram reveals the utter recklessness of his attitude. Had he, in the existing circumstances, made a knight's move by swerving to the Boer capital, he would have forfeited the only shred of justification he could claim for entering at all – the plea that he was hurrying to 'aid his fellow men in their extremity'.[2] His invasion would have been an act of aggression, pure and simple. More than ever he would have put himself out of court.

As regards the 'cutting', this can only refer to the telegraph line between Johannesburg (or Pretoria) and Mafeking, as to which, from Jameson's repeated allusions to it, there must have been some understanding with Wolff. But the latter, who had made such admirable arrangements for commissariat along the road, seems to have failed in this part of the programme – probably because he was confused by the last-moment change of

---

[1] Select Committee, Willoughby, 5595. Wolff, 6058.

[2] Jameson's letter to Sir Jacobus de Wet, 1st Jan. See Select Committee, evidence, No. 5712.

READY TO BOLT

plans. It may be added that the J. W. Leonard mentioned in the telegram was a leading barrister in Johannesburg, a brother of Charles, and, like him, a clever orator and an active member of the Reform party. Lawley was the railway contractor, of the firm of Pauling & Co., well known for his remarkable capacity for handling men.

The above details do not, however, entirely explain what Jameson meant to convey by the telegram, which bears evidence of having been written under the influence of strong excitement.

There was one more telegram to go, and it was to be the last sent by Jameson for many a long month. Addressed to Harris, it announced, with somewhat laboured attempts at justification, the final break-away – the decision to take the step from which retreat was impossible:

> 'Shall leave to-night for the Transvaal. My reason is the final arrangement with writers of letter was that without further reference to them, in case I should hear at some future time that suspicions have been aroused as to their intentions amongst the Transvaal authorities I was to start immediately to prevent loss of lives as letter states. Reuter only just received, even without my own information of meeting in the Transvaal, compel immediate move to fulfil promise made. We are simply going to protect everybody while they change the present dishonest government, and take vote from whole country as to form of government required by the whole.'[1]

This time Jameson hardly gave a chance for any countermanding order to reach him. It is true that the message was handed in at 9.5 a.m., and reached Capetown

[1] Report of Cape Committee, Appendix, p. ccxiii.

at 10.30, but it was highly improbable that at so early an hour on a Sunday morning any official would be found at the Capetown end of sufficient responsibility to deal with so critical a matter. But other obstacles were created. The Mafeking telegraph office was closed at 11.30 a.m., up to which time the line was in working order. During the afternoon it was cut at two points. About three miles south of Pitsani a couple of poles were broken and a length of fifty yards of wire removed; three miles south of Mafeking one pole was broken and both wires severed with pliers and torn from the insulators. The two camps were cut off from communication with the Cape until mid-day on Monday.[1] We have seen that plans were made for tampering with the lines in the Transvaal also, both at Malmani and nearer Pretoria, but the work was done too late, and the 'distant cutting', which was to be carried out by Wolff, seems to have been bungled. There is a commonly repeated story of a trooper detailed for the duty getting drunk and cutting the wire fence of somebody's farm, but this must be accepted with caution. It is clear from the notes found in the captured despatch-box that the task at the Mafeking end was not left in the hands of a trooper[2] and most probably the arrangement with Wolff was upset by the change of date.

[1] Evidence of Flowers, postmaster of Mafeking, at Jameson's trial in London, 23rd July, 1896. The line was open from Capetown to Kimberley and Bulawayo up to 1.30 p.m. See Cape Report, evidence of Tasker, Controller of central telegraph office, 2750-2768.

[2] See p. 137. Captain (now Sir Edward) Garraway, who was Medical Officer to the B.B.P. at the time, has kindly placed at the disposal of the writer a journal kept by him during the advance of the column. In this, under the date 30th December, he recorded that 'the three officers who had been sent on ahead to cut the telegraph lines rejoined the column at 8 a.m.' (i.e. about two hours after it had passed Malmani). The names of the officers are given and correspond with those mentioned in Major White's notes.

CHAPTER XV

They're Off!

AT 3 p.m. the usual Sabbath monotony of the camp at Pitsani was broken by an order for a dismounted parade of all ranks. The troops, having been formed up in square, were first addressed by Jameson. As to what he said, and how it was received, accounts vary slightly, but all agree that he read out at least a portion of the famous letter of invitation which he had obtained from the Reform leaders.[1] In all probability he omitted the wordy and ponderous opening sentences, which dealt with the political grievances of the Uitlanders, and only gave his men the vital part which immediately concerned them. The text of this was as follows:

'What will be the condition of things here [Johannesburg] in the event of a conflict? Thousands of unarmed men, women and children of our race, will be at the mercy of well-armed Boers, while property of enormous value will be in the greatest peril. We cannot contemplate the future without the gravest apprehensions. All feel that we are justified in taking any steps to prevent the shedding of blood, and to insure the protection of our rights.

'It is under these circumstances that we feel constrained to call upon you to come to our aid should a disturbance arise here. The circumstances are so

[1] See report to War Office by Sir John Willoughby (printed in the Appendix to Sir Percy Fitzpatrick's book). See also the evidence given at the trial of Jameson and his officers in England by Captain Gerald Ellis, Sergeant A. B. Cumming, Lance-Corporal W. H. Smith and Trooper P. L. Hill, and before the Select Committee by Major Heany (5898).

extreme that we cannot but believe that you and the men under you will not fail to come to the rescue of people that will be so situated. We guarantee any expense that may reasonably be incurred by you in helping us, and ask you to believe that nothing but the sternest necessity has prompted this appeal.'

Jameson went on to say that the crisis foreshadowed in this letter had now arrived, and he called upon them to march forthwith to the relief of their countrymen who were in such peril. The Bechuanaland police would march simultaneously from Mafeking and would join them at Malmani; they would find that remounts, rations and forage had been provided along the route, and troops would come out from Johannesburg to meet them. Neither the persons nor the property of the Boers would be interfered with; the sole object in view was to help their fellow-men in their extremity. He emphatically believed that there would be no fighting – no red blood spilt, as he put it – but if they were attacked on the march they would of course defend themselves. He concluded by saying that, while no compulsion would be exercised, he was confident that all would respond to the call.

According to Willoughby, Jameson's speech was received with the greatest enthusiasm, and the troops gave hearty cheers,[1] while Heany says they sang 'God save the Queen'.[2] At any rate, there were no hangers-back.

The parade was then dismissed and ordered to reassemble at sundown – mounted and in full marching order. We can picture the scene of excitement in the camp now that the men had at last learnt definitely that

[1] *The Transvaal From Within*, p. 327.   [2] Select Committee, Heany, 5898.

the moment for action had come. But there was little time for discussion. The next few hours were occupied in rapid preparations for the march. Rations for one day were issued to all, and each man carried 120 rounds of ammunition – ten in the rifle magazine, sixty in his bandolier and fifty in his saddle wallets, which also held fifty pounds of grain. Tents and stores were left behind, but one $12\frac{1}{2}$-pounder field gun and six maxim guns were taken, the ammunition for which was loaded on Scotch carts.

Shortly after sunset the column moved off – 356 strong, exclusive of staff – and took the road leading over the border to Malmani.

Now, all the above is common property – vouched for, in the main, by a number of credible witnesses. What is not so certain is whether the whole truth has come out as to the motives which impelled a body of over three hundred Englishmen to throw themselves, without any hanging-back, into this dare-devil adventure, for a moment's sober reflection would have told them it was utterly crazy and wrong. It is not perhaps so difficult to understand that the rank and file, and possibly some of the junior officers too, who heard of this extraordinary departure for the first time on that Sunday parade, were carried away by Jameson's eloquence, and followed him blindly, as the children in the legend did the Pied Piper. They did not stop to think – had no time really to think – whether everything was above board. There were a few there, however, and among them several officers who held commissions in the Regular Army or Militia, who had for some days heard rumours of the possibility of an invasion of the Transvaal, and they were, not unnaturally, anxious to know what their position would be if they took part in a hostile movement into a country with which Great Britain was – nominally, at any rate – at peace.

At the cost of interrupting the thread of the story an attempt must be made to discover why British officers, with service traditions behind them, should have allowed themselves to be inveigled into this act of folly. A number of Jameson's officers had afterwards to stand their trial on a criminal charge, and to face also the bar of public opinion. In some instances they were convicted, and, besides undergoing the humiliation of imprisonment, were deprived of their commissions. They took their punishment without flinching. With a solitary exception no one of them ever tried to exculpate himself by laying the blame on others. In justice to them some effort to get at the truth is called for.

It appears that either on the 29th December, when they knew definitely that they were required to invade the Transvaal, or perhaps a day or two earlier, in consequence of reports that had got about, several of the officers went to their Commanding Officer, Willoughby, and put their position before him – their anxiety about their commissions. When giving evidence on this point before the Select Committee, Willoughby shuffled and prevaricated, but in the end it was extracted from him that he had given them certain assurances – told one officer that his commission 'would be perfectly safe', and said to others that they ' would not be bothered by anybody – War Office, Imperial authorities, Chartered Company or Directors'.[1]

When pressed as to his authority for giving these assurances he fenced, and when asked point blank if the communications to his subordinate officers had been made on the authority of Jameson he declined to reply,

---
[1] Select Committee, Willoughby, 5517, 5518, 5525.

on the ground that any conversations he had had on the subject with Jameson were private. This, of course, sounded very discreet and loyal, but unfortunately Willoughby was one of those men whose discretion was intermittent. In September 1896, when smarting under the indignity of his conviction, he had written a confidential letter to the Adjutant-General (Sir Redvers Buller) in which occurred the following grave statement:

> 'I took part in the preparation of the military expedition and went into the Transvaal in pursuance of orders received from the Administrator of Matabeleland, and in the honest and *bona fide* belief that the steps were taken with the knowledge and assent of the Imperial authorities. I was informed by Dr. Jameson that this was the fact. It was in these circumstances, and on these statements, that I took in the other officers with me, namely Major H. F. White and Captains R. Grey and R. White, and the foregoing explanations apply to them also.'[1]

At a later stage in the enquiry this communication was produced, and both Willoughby and Jameson were recalled and cross-questioned about it. The latter was placed in a very embarrassing position. He was confronted with the alternative of giving the lie to his friend or of admitting that the statements attributed to himself were correct. If there was a third line he did not avail himself of it, but took the frank and honourable course of admitting that he had sanctioned such a letter in the hope that it might save his officers from losing their commissions, which he knew had in some cases been 'guaranteed' by Willoughby. He did not seek to

[1] Select Committee, Welby (a War Office official), 5622.

evade the implications of the letter (which he had not actually seen before despatch), but he did not entirely agree with the phraseology, which he thought went too far in suggesting that he had told Willoughby – and authorised him to pass the information on – that he had 'Her Majesty's Government at his back'. That he denied emphatically.[1]

There the matter must be left, for it is impossible to arrive at a conclusion which does not impugn the veracity of one or other of the two men. But there is no reason why a general inference should not be drawn, and perhaps the following is not far from the truth. In December 1895, Jameson felt assured that if his expedition was successful – and as to this he was perfectly confident – the Imperial authorities would find it impossible to repudiate him.[2] It may have been a delusion, but his whole attitude proved that it was an honest one. Doubtless also he had expressed this view to Willoughby in the careless camp-fire conversations which they must frequently have held, and in which, it is not unlikely, the High Commissioner's name and others had been freely introduced. At the last moment Willoughby, confronted with awkward questions from his subordinate officers, was reckless enough to guarantee that their commissions would be safe – the only logical deduction from which was that he had Imperial authority for saying so. Whether his *ipse dixit* was all they had to reassure them we shall probably never know, but it is quite certain that they went into the affair secure in the conviction that the Government was behind them, and that they were not jeopardising their careers in Her Majesty's Service by so doing.

---

[1] Select Committee, Jameson, 4605 and 5656–5693.
[2] Select Committee, Jameson, 4546.

This matter has been dealt with at some length because, far from being a side issue, it lies close to the very root of the reasons for the Raid.

The position at Mafeking was different from that at Pitsani, where Jameson and his troops had the place to themselves. Mafeking was in the Cape Colony, and the police there, though in process of re-organisation and partial disbandment, were very much under the eye of colonial officials, including the Resident Magistrate (who, however, appears to have had, up to the last moment, no inkling of what was going on). A portion of the corps – a little over a hundred altogether – had already been told off as definitely retained for the service of the Colony, and was to be placed under the command of one of the B.B.P. officers, Captain J. W. Fuller. A further 110 or so had decided to throw in their lot with the Chartered Company, while the remaining fifty or sixty were awaiting their discharge at the end of the year. It was generally understood that the Company's men would in due course be moved north, but for the time being they were kept at Mafeking, and formed into two troops, 'G' and 'K', under Captain the Hon. Charles Coventry. Those awaiting discharge were also formed into a temporary troop, known as 'F', and Major Raleigh Grey was still in command of the whole.

Jameson had, of course, communicated to Grey his decision to move, and, as at Pitsani, a parade was held on Sunday evening, 'F' troop forming up in rear. A last effort seems to have been made to induce members of this troop to reconsider their decision to take their discharge. They were addressed first by Coventry and then by Grey himself, and were informed of the proposed advance into the Transvaal. One of the men asked whether they would be marching under the orders of the Queen or of the Company, to which Grey is said to have replied that they were 'going to fight for the supremacy of the British flag in South Africa'.[1] Upon this about a dozen signified their willingness to go and were marched off to join the Company's squadron. At about 10 p.m. the little column, now numbering 122 of all ranks, under the command of Major Grey, and accompanied by Major R. White, moved out along the Protectorate road to the north. As soon as they were clear of the township they wheeled to the right and trotted across the *veld* to join the track to Malmani. They had with them two 7-pounder guns and two maxims.

As the troops were moving off Captain Fuller, who had only arrived in Mafeking that morning, but had already formed a shrewd idea that there was some secret and unusual business on foot, and thought it his duty to find out what he could about it, exchanged a few words with Major R. White, who bade him 'good-bye'. Fuller asked where they were off to, but got no direct reply. He said he would have to report the matter, at which White laughed, and said, 'You can do what you like. The wires are cut'. Thereupon Fuller detailed a junior officer to go after the column and make observations.[2]

One more local detail must be mentioned before we also follow its movements.

The fact that they were going into the Transvaal was made known to the officers of the B.B. Police definitely on Sunday morning. In a little town like Mafeking, where all the residents knew one another, and foregathered daily at the Club or for lunch or drinks at one

---

[1] Evidence of Sergeant Drummond Hay, at trial of Dr. Jameson, 22nd July, 1896.
[2] Evidence of Captain J. W. Fuller, at trial of Dr. Jameson, 22nd July, 1896.

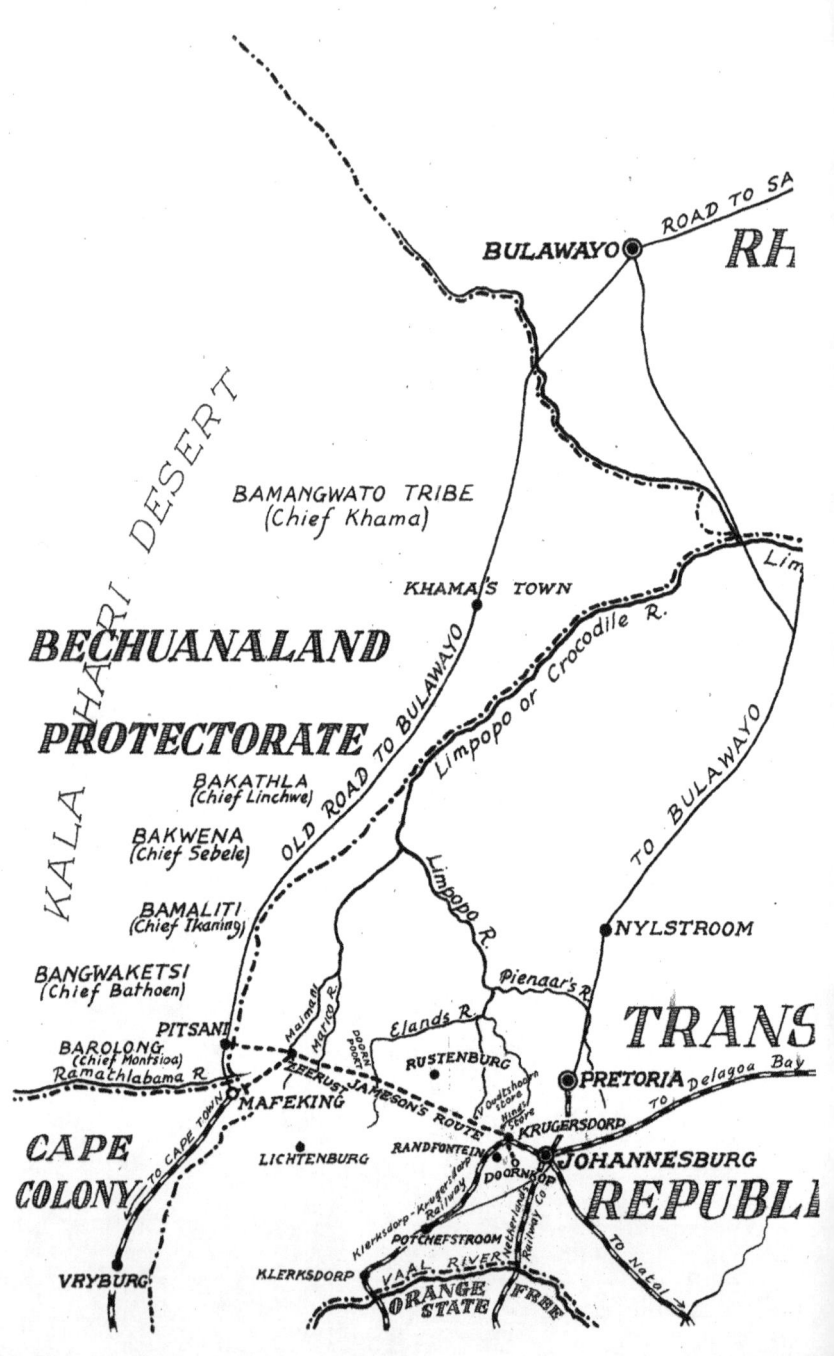

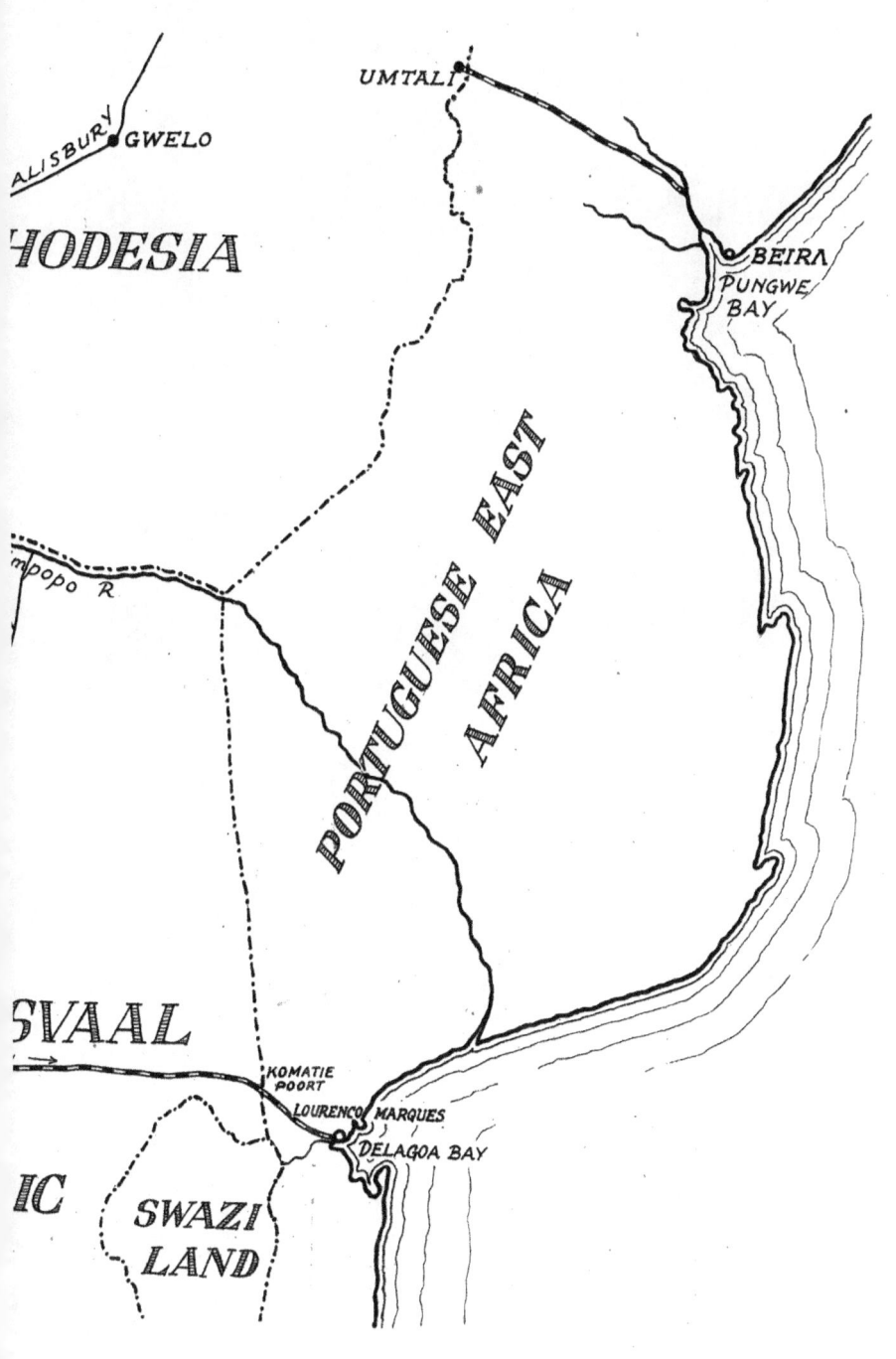

or other of the two hotels, news of this kind soon became public property, and by the afternoon there was hardly a soul in the place who had not heard it.[1] The telegraph office, as we know, was shut, but there were Boer transport-riders about and others in touch with the Transvaal, and it is quite likely that someone slipped over the border and sent a warning to Pretoria from the nearest telegraph office on the Transvaal side before the line was interfered with. In fact, as we shall see later, this is what undoubtedly occurred.

But there was at least one person in Mafeking who heard nothing of what was being so eagerly discussed that day or of the rumours that had been floating about for some days previously. This was Mr. G. J. Boyes, the Civil Commissioner and Resident Magistrate. It is rather hard to understand this, but as the principal Government official he may have preserved a slight social detachment, or perhaps he stopped at home that Sunday. He had only returned from leave three weeks before, but in that time had seen a good deal of Robert White, to whom he had expressed some curiosity as to the presence of so many of the Company's police at Pitsani camp, but White gave him a 'reasonable explanation', and apparently he thought no more of the matter. The only other hint that might have aroused his suspicion occurred in a chance conversation on the Saturday with a clergyman from Zeerust, who told him about the stores along the Transvaal road – Wolff's depots – and said there had been local gossip about their being stocked with 'bully beef' and that sort of thing.

On the evening of the 29th, after church, while sitting with his wife on the *stoep* of his house, Boyes heard the sound of cheering at the police camp a few hundred yards

[1] Cape Report, evidence of Emmanuel Isaacs, 1925.

away – an unusual occurrence on a Sunday. A little later someone on horseback clattered past in the dark and pulled up at a neighbouring bungalow, in which Raleigh Grey lived, and Boyes heard a voice, which he recognised as Grey's, calling out to a servant to bring out a pair of gauntlets, which he had left on the veranda, and after a minute or two the same voice saying to someone else, 'Good-bye. I'm just off'. Boyes said to his wife, 'I wonder where Grey's off to. I'll go and see what's up,' and walked down to the Club, where he heard for the first time, to his great amazement, that the police had started for the Transvaal, and were to be joined by Jameson's force.

Early next morning he tried to report the matter to Capetown by telegraph, but found, of course, that he could not get through. He happened to meet Sir Charles Metcalfe, the consulting engineer of the northern railway construction, and asked him if he knew what was going on. 'Well', said Metcalfe, 'I think the police have gone out to meet Jameson at Malmani'. He next interrogated Fuller, who could only tell him what he had seen, but added that he had tried to send an express message through to Vryburg the night before from the nearest open office, Maribogo. It was not till after midday that communication with the south was restored, and Boyes at once telegraphed to the head of his department reporting the facts. This was the first official news that reached the Cape Government of Jameson's action.[1]

[1] Cape Committee Report, Boyes, 809–888; Graham, 667, 668. The text of Boyes's message is given in the Report of the Select Committee; Schreiner, 3255.

CHAPTER XVI

The Raid

THE majority of the Rhodesian force – the Mashonaland Mounted Police, to give them their official title – had not done any previous campaigning, unless their 600-mile trek from Bulawayo can be regarded as such. Many of them were little more than recruits, and over 100, who had been brought up from the Cape Colony within the preceding few weeks, had never been in Rhodesia at all. For all that, they were a well-selected lot of men, especially as regards physique; otherwise they could never have borne the severe strain of the forced march which they were now about to undertake. Their discipline and morale were excellent, and the credit for this is due to the quality of the troop-officers and senior N.C.O.s, most of whom had already seen active service. Chief Inspector (Major) William Bodle, the second-in-command, had served in the Zulu and Basuto Wars, the Warren expedition and the Matabele campaign, and there were others who had a record nearly as good. These veterans were of the real Rhodesian metal, and to their campaign experience added that special quality known as 'veld-craft', which was developed to its highest perfection among the burghers of the Boer Republics.

The rank and file of the Bechuanaland Border Police, under Major Raleigh Grey, 123 of whom, on disbandment at Mafeking, had signed on for service with the Chartered Company, were a more seasoned body of men. So far from being recruits, most of them had served for a year or more in the Protectorate – often at distant stations and in isolated detachments under conditions well calculated to develop their faculties of self-reliance.

Taken as a whole, the five hundred who accompanied Jameson were good stuff, led by as fine a group of officers as could have been picked out of the army, and, however much we may condemn the motives that inspired the raid, the story of the actual march is one that reflects the utmost credit on all concerned.[1]

For the incidents of the eighty-four hours between their departure from British territory and the final *débâcle* at Doornkop our main authority is a report written to the War Office by Sir John Willoughby, immediately after he had been taken prisoner, and while the events were fresh in his memory. This report has never officially been made public, but it is printed in an appendix to Sir Percy Fitzpatrick's book, with a statement that it was supplied to the author by a journalist, and the authenticity of this copy is established by certain quotations made from the actual document during Willoughby's examination before the Select Committee, in whose possession it was during their enquiry. These are identical with passages in the report as Fitzpatrick prints it.

It goes outside the ground usually covered by a statement of this kind, as may be gathered from its heading, which reads as follows:

> *Official report of the expedition that left the Protectorate at the urgent request of the leading citizens of Johannesburg with the object of standing by them and maintaining law and order whilst they were demanding justice from the Transvaal authorities.*
>
> *By Sir John Willoughby, Bart., Lieutenant-Colonel Commanding Dr. Jameson's forces.*

[1] Details of the composition of Dr. Jameson's force are given in Appendix II.

THE RAID

So far as the actual incidents of the march are concerned the report is fairly well corroborated by such evidence as was given at the trial in England of Jameson and his officers, and by information supplied by friends of the writer who took part in the Raid.[1] If Willoughby had stuck to a plain narrative we could have no quarrel with him. It is when he begins explaining and justifying that he becomes trying to our patience, and one can only feel relieved that in this respect he stands alone.

The Pitsani contingent left their camp at 6.30 p.m. on Sunday, the 29th December, and marched through the night thirty-nine miles to Malmani, which they reached at 5.15 on Monday morning. Malmani was merely a small *dorp* in the fertile Marico valley. It had once been the centre of a certain amount of gold-digging, but at the time we are speaking of was deserted except by a few farmers. Major Grey and his B.B. Police, who had left Mafeking a little later, arrived at the same moment, and the two forces thereafter went forward as one. A member of the M.M. Police stated that on passing through Malmani he noticed that the telegraph wires were cut, and saw one of the Bechuanaland troopers coming from the *veld* with an axe.[2] If the work had been deferred till that moment it was a belated and useless effort, for the line must have been clear all night and during the previous day. The news of the movement of Jameson's troops across the border did, in fact, reach the Government at Pretoria at an early hour on Monday morning.[3]

At Malmani there was a halt of an hour or two while the horses were watered and the men snatched a hasty meal at the first of the stores provided by Wolff. The route of the column now lay for some distance across

[1] Including Sir Edward Garraway's Journal, previously referred to.
[2] Trial of Jameson, evidence of Lawlor.
[3] *The Transvaal From Within*, p. 110.

flat, open country. Hardly a human being was encountered, and the only signs of life were an occasional farm homestead with a patch of ploughed land, and a few sparse herds of sheep and goats. Willoughby had been informed by Robert White, who had gone over the route two months earlier, that thirty miles ahead, at some lead mines, there was a dangerous defile, and he was anxious to get through this before nightfall. It was afterwards ascertained that a force of several hundred Boers had been sent from Lichtenburg to intercept the column at this very spot, but arrived three hours after it had passed.

About midday the column was overtaken by a messenger from Zeerust, with a letter from J. D. L. Botha, the Commandant of the Marico district, who wrote in the name of the Commandant-General of the Republic, and addressed it to the ' Head Officer of the Expedition at Malmani Oog [eye] '. It was opened by Jameson, and proved to be a warning that his action was in conflict with the law of the land, and a breach of international convention.[1] Jameson's reply is given below. It will be seen that it makes no reference to the supposed critical position of the Uitlanders, or of the danger to women and children, and if it was intended to explain his presence with an armed force in the Transvaal it was singularly unconvincing; but we may suppose he had no time to waste on such small fry as a district commandant.

'*December 30th*, 1895.

' SIR,—I am in receipt of your protest of the above date, and have to inform you that I intend proceeding with my original plans, which have no hostile intention against the people of the Transvaal; but we are here

[1] Cape Report, Appendix, p. lxviii., No. 87.

in reply to an invitation from the principal residents of the Rand to assist them in their demand for justice and the ordinary rights of every citizen of a civilised State.

'Yours faithfully,
'L. S. Jameson.'[1]

The Lead Mines, seventy-one miles from Pitsani, were safely passed just before sundown on Monday evening, and at the next ' off-saddle ', two or three miles farther on, at McArthur's store, Willoughby relates :

' Dr. Jameson received a letter from the Commandant-General of the Transvaal [General Piet Joubert] demanding to know the reason of our advance, and ordering us to return immediately. A reply was sent to this explaining Dr. Jameson's reasons in the same terms as those used to the force at Pitsani.'

One wonders if this was literally correct, for it implies an avowal that the object of the invasion was ' to help their fellow-men in their extremity ' – a pretext which it is difficult to believe he would have used to one in General Joubert's position. One wonders also how a messenger could have covered the distance between Pretoria and McArthur's – not much less than 100 miles – within twenty-four hours of Jameson's departure from Pitsani. There are two possible explanations. One is that Joubert had a very efficient intelligence officer at or near the latter camp, who notified Pretoria by wire within a few minutes of the start – perhaps even before the start, on the strength of orders which he had heard – and the other, and more likely, explanation is that Willoughby was mistaken about this letter, of which no record has ever appeared elsewhere, and was thinking of

[1] Cape Report, Appendix, p. lxix., No. 88.

the letter from Zeerust, which he does not mention. He was writing from memory and it was an easy mistake to make.

The column marched during Monday night another twenty miles, and early on the morning of the 31st December reached Doornpoort, the farm of the worthy burgher and member of the Volksraad, Malan, where the horses bought by Wolff for his bogus ' coach-service ' had been running. Malan's indignation at discovering that he had unwittingly been aiding the invasion may well be imagined. The horses, however, were a poor lot and only a few were taken on, the men preferring to stick to those they started with – tired as they were. Malan may therefore have had some compensation for his wounded feelings.

Events now began to follow one another in quick succession. A few miles east of Eland's River the column was caught up by a mounted messenger, unarmed, but in the uniform of the B.B. Police, who had ridden hard to overtake it – Lance-Sergeant J. T. White, who brought despatches which he handed to Colonel Grey, saying that they were from the Resident Commissioner (Newton) at Mafeking. Grey must have had a pretty shrewd idea of their contents, but he directed White to Willoughby, who in turn sent him to Jameson. None of them seemed inclined to open the packet, but in the end Willoughby did so, and found in it letters addressed to himself, Jameson, Coventry and Captain Munro of the B.B. Police.[1] They were in identical terms, and contained orders from the High Commissioner directing the immediate return of the force. In repeating the message Newton requested the Commanding Officer to circulate

[1] There were originally five letters, but one, addressed to Captain Gosling, of the B.B.P., had been kept back by the Boer officials who arrested White at Malmani.

THE RAID

it among all his subordinate officers.[1] (To avoid breaking the continuity of the story of the march an account òf the circumstances leading up to Sergeant White's errand, and of his adventures on the way, is held over to another chapter.)

White waited half an hour while the contents of his packet were discussed, and was then ordered by Willoughby to go back with a verbal message that 'the despatches would be attended to'. As an intelligent N.C.O., who had ridden hard through the night in order to carry out a dangerous errand and knew perfectly well what was going on, this must have been galling to him, but he had no alternative but to obey.[2] Willoughby, in his report, gives elaborate reasons for not complying with the High Commissioner's orders to turn back. The force had exhausted the food supplies in rear; the horses were jaded with the forced march, and they had already covered almost two-thirds of the total distance – not correct, by the way, as, if their destination was Johannesburg, they had only travelled 91 miles out of 170; in fact, according to White himself, the point at which he caught up the column was only 80 miles from Mafeking, or less than half the total distance. But the most astounding reason given by Willoughby was that 'it appeared impossible to turn back in view of the fact that we had been urgently called in to avert a massacre, which we had been assured would be imminent in the event of a crisis such as had now occurred'. It is hardly necessary to comment on this. Even in the so-called 'letter of invitation' (written, as Willoughby must have known six weeks before, and therefore absolutely irrelevant to

---

[1] Fitzpatrick tells us that the letter from the Commandant of the Marico district reached Jameson *after* the receipt of Newton's despatch (p. 140). In this he is apparently mistaken, as Jameson's reply to Botha is dated 30th Jan. – Monday – and Sergt. White only left Mafeking on the afternoon of that day.

[2] Trial of Dr. Jameson, 22nd July, 1896, evidence of White.

the present situation, which had been created by Jameson and himself) there was no suggestion of a 'massacre'. The only chance of such a calamity was that the Boers might be provoked to violence by the invasion, and the only way to avert the evil consequences of this was to turn back. But turning back would have made Jameson and Willoughby the laughing-stock of the world, and that they could not face.

Later in the afternoon of the same day (31st), as the column neared Mrs. Boon's store, where Jameson expected to meet Wolff,[1] the first Transvaal official was encountered in the person of Lieutenant Saul Johannes Eloff of the Krugersdorp police, a grandson of President Kruger, who had ridden out with a small detachment of his men to pick up information as to the movements of the column. He was arrested by an advanced patrol, deprived of his arms and taken before Jameson, his men being sent back to Krugersdorp. The object of the expedition was explained to him and on giving an undertaking to remain where he was for two hours he was released, while the troops again moved on.

The passing of the old year found the column still pressing forward through broken and hilly country, and just after midnight, while approaching a rocky *krantz* which ran athwart the road, the scouts came under fire from a party of Boers who had been lying in wait for them behind cover. The advanced guard went forward and succeeded in driving them back, one of the M.M. Police being wounded – the first casualty on Jameson's side. The engagement was not a serious one, but it was a warning to Jameson that he was not going to have the walk-over he professed to expect.

[1] But Wolff was not there. After writing a letter to Jameson he managed somehow to disappear, and the next we hear of him is that Stevens was helping him shortly afterwards to get a passage by mail steamer from the Cape!

Early on the morning of New Year's Day, while the troops were halted at van Oudtshoorn's farm,[1] where another of Wolff's food depots had been established, they were met by two mounted Boers – one of them Daniel Bouwer, a member of General Joubert's civilian staff – who were the bearers of a sealed letter from Sir Jacobus de Wet, the agent of the British Government at Pretoria. It contained the following message transmitted from Sir Hercules Robinson:

'Her Majesty's Government entirely disapprove your conduct in invading Transvaal with armed force; your action has been repudiated. You are ordered to retire at once from country, and will be held personally responsible for the consequences of your unauthorised and most improper proceeding.'[2]

Bouwer said that his instructions were to carry back an answer at once. "All right," said Jameson, "I'll give you an answer," and a little later handed one to him. These were its terms:

'1st January, 1896.

'DEAR SIR,—I am in receipt of the message you sent from His Excellency the High Commissioner, and beg to reply, for His Excellency's information, that I should, of course, desire to obey his instructions, but, as I have a very large force of both men and horses to feed, and having finished all my supplies in the rear, must perforce proceed to Krugersdorp or Johannesburg this morning for this purpose. At the same time I must acknowledge I am anxious to

---

[1] In giving evidence at Jameson's trial Bouwer called it 'Van Uithout's *Winkel*' (store).
[2] Blue Book C 7933, No. 8.

fulfil my promise on the petition of the principal residents on the Rand to come to the aid of my fellow-men in their extremity. I have molested no one, and have explained to all Dutchmen met that the above is my sole object, and that I shall desire at once to return to the Protectorate.

'I am, &c.
'L. S. JAMESON.'[1]

One must confess to a slight feeling of weariness at this constant repetition of the phrase 'fellow-men in their extremity', the insincerity of which was better appreciated by those acquainted with the facts than Jameson seemed to realise.

At this time Willoughby was made aware that the column was being dogged by a small force of Boers who were keeping about a mile in rear, and he sent back an additional maxim gun and strengthened the rear-guard.

Five miles farther on, when clear of the hills, and marching in open country about thirteen miles west of Krugersdorp, the force was met by two men on bicycles, who had left Johannesburg that morning with letters from the 'Reform Committee', of which Jameson now heard for the first time. Their names were Rowland and Celliers, and they were members of an emergency corps of cyclists organised a few days before in Johannesburg for despatch-riding. Celliers, who was a Dutchman, had cunningly volunteered to convey a despatch to one of the Boer Commandants hovering around Krugersdorp on the look-out for Jameson, and had by this means obtained a 'safe-conduct', which enabled both men to pass

---

[1] Blue Book C 7933, No. 29. Willoughby, in his report, dismisses this incident with the following words: 'Early on the following morning Dr. Jameson received a second letter from the High Commissioner, to which he replied in writing.'

through the Boer lines and to reach the column. Rowland, having first read the letters in case of capture, concealed them in the tube under the saddle of his bicycle and now produced them.

Willoughby says in his report:

> 'These letters expressed the liveliest approval and delight at our speedy approach, and finally contained a renewal of their promise to meet the column with a force at Krugersdorp.'

How far this glowing statement was justified must to some extent be a matter of conjecture – not altogether, however, for although one of the letters disappeared, and the other only survived in a mutilated condition, enough remained of the latter to throw some light on its original contents, and, as it afterwards gave rise to one of the most acute controversies of any document connected with the Raid, while both letters had an important bearing on the subsequent actions of Jameson, they demand close attention.

One of the letters was from Wolff, who, in his evidence before the Select Committee,[1] explained that, on hearing that the Reform Committee were sending out messages to Jameson, he hurriedly wrote in pencil a short note telling him of the state of affairs in Johannesburg, and saying that if the Krugersdorp Boers decided to oppose the advance of his column the position they would take up would be on a ridge running across the road about three miles west of the town – a fairly strong defensive situation. He also told Jameson that it was impossible for the column to avoid passing through Krugersdorp, as the surrounding country was broken

[1] Select Committee, Wolff, 6060.

and hilly, and there was no road fit for waggons and artillery on either side of the place. According to Willoughby,[1] Wolff added that there were only 300 armed Boers in the town itself.

Jameson's account is that the letter was one of three pages, giving detailed instructions as to the best way for his force to reach Johannesburg and recommending him to take the road through Krugersdorp, and that it was in consequence of this advice, and against the wish of Willoughby, who wanted for tactical reasons to avoid the place, that he insisted on attacking it.[2] Willoughby admits that he was anxious to avoid Krugersdorp 'on the military grounds of the possibility of there being opposition in the town', but says that Jameson overruled him and said, 'No, we must go to Krugersdorp because we shall meet our friends there; as I have arranged with them'.[3] This would indicate that there was something in Wolff's letter about a force being sent out from Johannesburg to effect a junction with the column.

Now it is this question of a relief force from Johannesburg that has provoked so much bitterness, Jameson and some of his officers asserting positively that it was promised, that the promise made him change his plans, and that had the support been forthcoming he would have got through – in plain words that he was left in the lurch; while the Reformers affirmed, with equal insistence, that no such promise was ever made, nor were they ever in a position to send out a force.

Let us now turn to the other letter brought by the two cyclists, and see if we can discover anything in it which will support either contention. It was a joint production by Colonel Frank Rhodes and Lionel

---

[1] Select Committee, Willoughby, 5580–5581.
[2] Select Committee, Jameson, 4516.
[3] Select Committee, Willoughby, 5587.

THE RAID

Phillips; or, rather, the former wrote the letter – in pencil on a telegraph form – and the latter added a postscript. Jameson read it, and showed it to Willoughby and three or four others, and afterwards tore it up and threw the fragments on the veld. It is consequently one of the few papers that eluded the grasp of Major White, the recording angel of the expedition. But by one of the queer turns of fate some pieces of the letter were picked up, four months later, by a Boer, just where they had been left, and great ingenuity was displayed in putting them together and trying to reconstruct the original.

The bits of weather-stained paper, when arranged, revealed these words:

'Dear Dr.

'The rumour of massa . . . . Johannesburg that started yo . . . . relief was not true. We a . . . . right . . . . . . feeling intense. We have armed . . . . a lot of men. Shall be very glad . . . . to see you . . . . not in possess . . . . town. . . . . men to . . . . fellow.

'Yours ever,
'F. R.

'We will all drink a glass along . . . . . . you.
'L. P.

'31*st*, 11.30. Kruger has asked for . . . . go over and treat; armistice for . . . . to. My view is that they are in a funk at . . . . Pretoria, and they were wrong to agree from here.
'F. R.'[1]

---

[1] Cape Committee Report, Appendix, p. lxxii. The word 'wrong' in the last line is in italics, as if it had been inserted as a guess.

Various attempts have been made to supply the missing words, and the chief interest centres on those at the end of Colonel Rhodes's first note. Willoughby, when under examination by the Select Committee, gave the following version from memory:

> 'I will bring at least (or about) 300 men to meet you at Krugersdorp. You are a gallant fellow.'[1]

He was corroborated by Jameson, who, however, could not recall the actual number,[2] and by Raleigh Grey and Robert White.[3]

Colonel Rhodes filled the gaps in the letter quite differently, and as he wrote it his recollection of its terms must be accepted in the absence of definite proof to the contrary. His reconstruction was:

> 'I will send some men to show you your camp. You are a fine fellow.'

and he denied that it was ever in his mind to send out a force of men. Had that been his intention he would have sent them at the same time as the letter, which was only despatched on the morning of the day on which the column was expected to arrive.[4] Phillips confirmed this and said that it was impossible that even 200 should have been sent, as there were only 130 mounted men at their disposal.[5] Farrar and Sam Jameson made a statement to the same effect.[6] Both parties were so emphatic that an explanation would seem hopeless, if it were not for a clue supplied by sundry statements made by Rowland, which no one appears to have studied.

[1] Select Committee, 5573. [2] Select Committee, 5702.
[3] Select Committee, 5575. [4] Select Committee, 5404.
[5] Select Committee, 6963. [6] *The Transvaal From Within*, Appendix, p. 352.

THE RAID

This man, in addition to giving Jameson such news as he could as to the position in Johannesburg, and the strength of the Boers in Krugersdorp – not more than 350, according to him – must have discussed with Jameson the possibility of a force being sent out to meet the column. His evidence, although inconsistent, and difficult to explain, is worthy of attention. At the preliminary proceedings against Jameson and his officers at Bow Street in May 1896 he said :

> 'I asked Dr. Jameson if he wanted any assistance from Johannesburg. Dr. Jameson either said or concurred in the suggestion that if 2,000 men were sent out from Johannesburg – more for show than anything else – they would be of assistance.'

At Jameson's final trial in June of the same year Rowland went further :

> 'One of the despatches spoke of a force being sent out from Johannesburg – about 2,000 men. I cannot recollect from whom this despatch was.'

Lastly, when the Select Committee was sitting, Rowland wrote to the Chairman as follows :

> 'I notice that Sir John Willoughby states that in Colonel Frank Rhodes's despatch there is a statement that he would bring about 300 men to meet the Doctor at Krugersdorp. I read all the despatches we carried, and I can state that no letter from Colonel Rhodes contained any such statement.'[1]

From these conflicting utterances we may gather that

[1] Select Committee, letter read by Chairman, 5630.

Rowland's memory is untrustworthy, but it is nevertheless quite likely that under the influence of excitement, and with the self-importance inspired by the occasion, he indulged in some foolish talk about reinforcements, and that from his verbal communications Jameson and Willoughby got impressions on the subject which they afterwards attributed to something in Colonel Rhodes's letter. Rowland probably let his tongue wag, and talked in the same strain to some of the men. If so we have an explanation of the paragraph in Willoughby's report which reads :

' This news [i.e. the news as to support from Johannesburg and as to the small garrison of Boers at Krugersdorp] was communicated to the troops, who received it with loud cheers.'

Celliers, the second cyclist, gave yet another report of the interview with Jameson, the details of which are supplied in Fitzpatrick's book,[1] and may here be quoted :

' I reached the column between 9 and 10 o'clock. I saw Dr. Jameson personally. He received us very well, and was very glad with the news I brought him. He read the despatch, and asked me for full details. I told him the strength of the Boers and the dangers he was in. I told him that they had no guns, and all that I saw and heard that they had during my travels. I explained to him everything in detail. The Doctor seemed to be very brave. He told me that he had two scrimmages, and that no damage had been done. I said to him whether it would not be well for him to halt until we got through and sent him some help. The Doctor said he did not think there was anything

[1] *The Transvaal From Within*, pp. 143-144.

to fear, and at the same time he did not want to go to Johannesburg as a pirate, and it would be well for them to send some men to meet him. . . .'

The two messengers were handed the following reply for Colonel Rhodes, taken down by Colonel Harry White at the dictation of Jameson, who signed his initials:

> 'As you may imagine, we are well pleased by your letter. We have had some fighting and hope to reach Johannesburg to-night, but of course it will depend on the amount of fighting we have. Of course we shall be pleased to have 200 men meet us at Krugersdorp, as it will greatly encourage the men, who are in great heart although a bit tired. Love to Sam, Phillips and rest.'[1]

If anything, the above report and the letter support Jameson's contention that he was led to expect some assistance, but Fitzpatrick goes to considerable trouble to prove that no promises of the kind asserted were made in Colonel Rhodes's note, and quotes expert evidence that the gaps in the torn document could not have contained the words supplied by Willoughby. After all, the most convincing argument on the point is that no armed men were actually sent, and, further, that it is inconceivable that a man of Colonel Rhodes's character would have made such a promise with the knowledge that he could not carry it out. And there we must leave the matter.

---

[1] This note was concealed, like the others, in one of the bicycles. On their return journey both messengers were intercepted by Boers and abandoned their machines. One of them was subsequently found and brought into Johannesburg in a damaged condition. It was sent for repairs to a mechanic, who discovered Jameson's reply hidden in the tube – another example of the strange fate that pursued his private correspondence!

CHAPTER XVII

The Surrender

WHETHER because of Wolff's advice, or in the expectation of joining hands with the mythical reinforcements, Jameson and Willoughby decided to advance on Krugersdorp. Their decision was fortified by reports from their scouts that, in addition to the party of Boers hanging on to their rear, other bodies of some strength were keeping pace with the column on both flanks, while a further number were retreating before them and falling back on the town. Willoughby appears to have cherished some hope that he would be allowed to pass through Krugersdorp unmolested, as he sent a letter to the Commandant of that place to the effect that if his 'friendly force' met with opposition he would be obliged to shell the town. His instinctive reluctance to advance on Krugersdorp – overruled by Jameson – was no doubt sound. The movement suited the Boers, who were luring him towards their most favourable position by falling back on it while closing in on both flanks and from the rear.

Between van Oudtshoorn's and the next of Wolff's food-depots the progress of the column was delayed owing to part of the road being fenced on both sides with wire, which had to be cut to permit of free movement on the flanks, and while this was being attended to scouting parties were sent out in several directions. Shortly before the main body reached the depot, which was at Hind's store, about seven miles west of Krugersdorp, the advanced guard, under Lieut.-Colonel Harry White, surprised a couple of hundred Boers – a detachment of

THE SURRENDER

those who were retiring in front of the column – watering their horses at a small stream. They at once made off without showing fight, and White, although he had maxim guns and could have inflicted severe losses, refrained from opening fire upon them, the intention, according to Willoughby, being to reach Johannesburg, if possible, without bloodshed. The field guns were, however, sent forward and a few shots sent after the retreating Boers – an inconsistency which he does not explain.

At Hind's store they found that hardly any provisions either for men or horses were available (the Boers having probably been there before them), and after a short rest the march was resumed. Any illusion that the column was to be allowed a walk-over was quickly dispelled, for a few miles farther on the troops, having followed the track up a steep incline of 400 feet, and gained the summit of a ridge, found themselves looking over a valley, on the opposite slopes of which they became aware that the Boers held a strong line of defences. With their natural aptitude for taking cover they had made use of prospecting trenches, rough stone walls and the tailing-heaps and iron battery-house of the Queen's mine. A number could also be descried on the sky-line – of course well beyond rifle range. At the bottom of the valley the road led by a drift or ford across a broad water-course, making the Boer position still more difficult of approach.

At this moment the rear-guard was attacked by the force which had been dogging the footsteps of the column all day, and Willoughby thereupon gave orders for artillery fire with shrapnel to be opened on the positions in front of him, at 1,900 yards range. The Boers pursued their usual tactics of holding their fire, nor did they show themselves, until a shell bursting over the battery-house

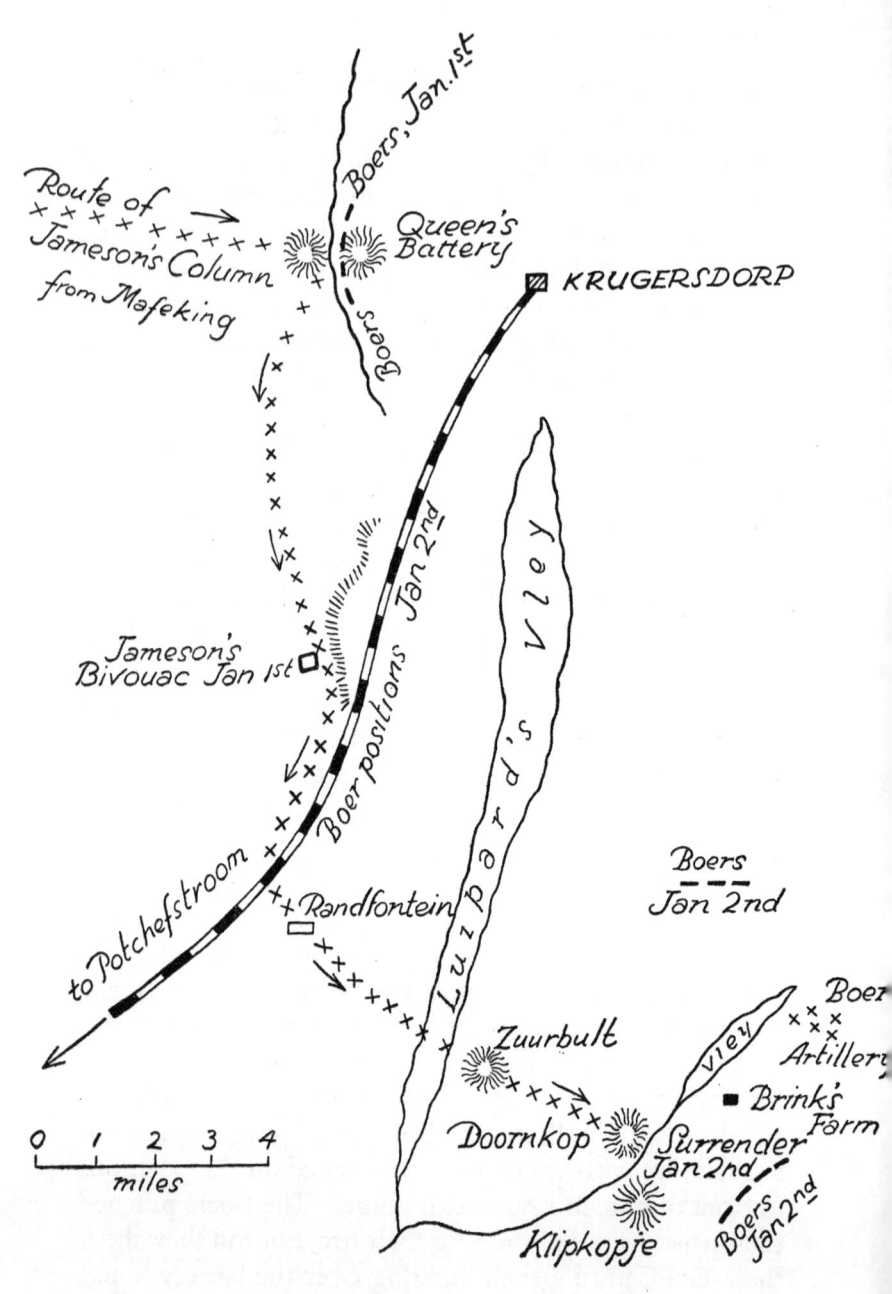

caused a few to vacate that position. The B.B. Police under Grey moved to attack the left of the Boer line, while Colonel Harry White, with the advanced guard and maxims, supported by a troop on each flank, went forward in skirmishing order towards the front trenches, which were supposed to have been evacuated. When nearing the water-course the frontal attack was checked by a heavy cross fire from all parts of the enemy's line, and White eventually had to fall back with some loss.

It was now late in the afternoon, and Willoughby realised that it was hopeless to continue the attempt to dislodge the Boers on the heights in front of him. He therefore began a flank march to the right (south) in the direction of Randfontein, a group of mines on the Potchefstroom railway, about twenty-five miles from Johannesburg, in the hope of striking a track which ran across a long swampy stream known as Luipard's Vley. From there, he was informed, a good road led direct into Johannesburg. To cover this movement Grey and the B.B.P., with their $12\frac{1}{2}$-pounder, kept up a continuous fire from the left on the Boers' positions and prevented them from advancing.

The main body had not proceeded very far in the new direction when, on ascending some rising ground, they heard maxim-fire on their left, and, according to some accounts, caught sight in the failing light of a large body of men moving towards the Queen's mine buildings. Willoughby – goodness knows why – immediately jumped to the conclusion that these were the reinforcements which he had convinced himself were being sent out by Colonel Rhodes from Johannesburg. ' To leave our supposed friends in the lurch ', he writes, ' was out of the question. I determined at once to move to their support '. Keeping here for a short space they shelled the enemy's *kopjes*, but they could not, in the long run, prevent the two Boer forces from joining hands. After this so heavy a fire was concentrated on Jameson's men that any further advance seemed out of the question.

In the small hours of the morning, before the bivouac had broken up, Jameson had sent a verbal message by one of his men – a bugler named Vallé – to Johannesburg. As repeated by this man it did not sound like a confession of defeat – hardly even an appeal for assistance. 'I am getting on all right, but you must send out to meet me.'

Why did he not swallow his pride and say candidly, 'Unless you send a force to my help I am done for'? It is impossible to think that he failed to grasp the extreme gravity of his position. His vision of a triumphant entry into Johannesburg as the champion of oppressed humanity could hardly have survived the failure to break through the Boer defences at Krugersdorp. The events of the past few hours should have convinced him that his chance of getting through at all was rapidly diminishing. All that he could hope for was to get his officers and men out of the hideous mess into which his overweening confidence had dragged them. However much one may admire his dogged refusal to own himself beaten, one cannot understand his failure, even at the eleventh hour, to send an urgent appeal for help.

No direct reply came to Jameson's message, but at 8.30 a.m. a member of the Reform Committee, Lace by name, arrived on the scene, accompanied by a despatch-rider from the British Agent, Sir Jacobus de Wet, and an escort. From the former Jameson learnt that there was no intention – never had been any intention – on the part of the Reformers to send troops to his assistance. From

THE SURRENDER

de Wet's despatches he learnt that the High Commissioner had proclaimed him an outlaw![1]

At this moment the column had just succeeded in clearing a ridge stated to be Doornkop, beyond which (according to information supplied to Willoughby by a guide picked up on the spot, who proved to be utterly untrustworthy) there was an open road through easy country to Johannesburg. But after carrying the ridge, under heavy fire which cost the column several further casualties – including Captain Coventry, severely wounded – it was found that in rear of it was another steep and stony *kopje*, 400 feet in height, held by hundreds of Boers, all securely under cover. This was actually Doornkop, which commanded the road along which the invaders were advancing, and the drift across a small *spruit* which lay just ahead of them.

The main body and guns were halted at a stone cattle kraal and an outhouse – part of the farm buildings of Vlakfontein, owned by one Brink, whose homestead was a few hundred yards to the north. Here for half an hour they made a final stand, keeping up a stubborn defence with field-guns and maxims, until the ammunition of the former began to fail, while the latter grew hot for want of water and jammed. The Boers, sheltered by boulders on the slopes of Doornkop, as well as from their entrenched positions beyond the *spruit* and from the cover

---

[1] The essential part of the High Commissioner's Proclamation was as follows :
'Whereas it has come to my knowledge that certain British subjects, said to be under the leadership of Dr. Jameson, have violated the territory of the South African Republic, and have cut telegraph wires, and done various illegal acts, and whereas the South African Republic is a friendly State in amity with Her Majesty's Government, and whereas it is my desire to respect the independence of the said State, Now therefore I do hereby command the said Dr. Jameson and all persons accompanying him to immediately retire from the territory of the South African Republic on pain of the penalties attached to their illegal proceedings. And I do hereby call upon all British subjects in the South African Republic to abstain from giving the said Dr. Jameson any countenance or assistance in his armed violation of the territory of a friendly State.'

of a stone wall in front, maintained a steady fire, and besides picking off an occasional trooper or horse, prevented any possibility of a further advance, for the ground in front of Willoughby's last position was open and exposed.

The country immediately surrounding them was reconnoitred, and it was found that there was no way round. Retirement was equally impracticable, and, in fact, they were in a trap. At this critical moment a body of the State Artillery – trained gunners from Pretoria – came into action from behind Brink's farm and opened fire at less than a mile range. The situation then became hopeless, as even Jameson realised. Abandoned by the friends on whom he had calculated – a proclaimed outlaw – his little force reduced by casualties to barely four hundred – the survivors worn out by hunger and want of rest – his plight was indeed a pitiable one, and there is no need to dwell on it.

It is immaterial who made the signal of surrender. Jameson himself was probably too overwhelmed to issue any orders. In that desperate moment his authority passed into other hands, and he no longer counted. Somewhere – by someone – a white flag was hoisted at 9.15, and the ' cease fire ' was sounded.[1] The weary rank and file flung themselves down where they stood, and Jameson, Willoughby and the officers gathered into a group and waited. A few Boers scrambled out from

---

[1] One of the surviving troop-officers – there are only four or five left – informed the writer that the white flag was not raised by any member of the force, but by Major Crosse, an ex-officer of the 5th Dragoons, who was at Mafeking for reasons of health when the column started, and accompanied it as a spectator, unarmed, for the fun of the thing. He was, however, made a prisoner with the others, and was only released on the representations of Sir Hercules Robinson (Blue Book C 7933, No. 217). From the accounts of several other eye-witnesses it appears that, no white material being available, the signal of surrender was made by means of a cotton apron, borrowed from a woman at the farmhouse, and tied to the end of a waggon whip!

"HERE . . . THEY MADE A FINAL STAND" (*p.* 187).

THE SURRENDER

behind their cover at one side of the *spruit* and advanced – cautiously at first, but more confidently as they saw that there was no further resistance. Willoughby wrote a short note, went forward and handed it to one of them to give to his commander, whose name, he learnt, was Potgieter:

'We surrender, provided that you guarantee us safe conduct out of the country for every member of the force.'

A reply was sent back that the Boer officers would assemble at once to consider terms, and in half an hour a second letter came of which a facsimile is here given, and of which the following is a translation:

'John C. Willoughby.

'I acknowledge your letter. The answer is that if you will undertake to pay the expense which you have caused the South African Republic, and if you will surrender with your arms, then I shall spare the lives of you and yours.

'Please send me a reply to this within thirty minutes.

'P. A. Cronjé,
'Commandant, Potchefstroom.'[1]

Willoughby's reply has not been preserved, but according to his own account he accepted the terms in writing, and asked the Boer General to bear in mind that his men had been without food for twenty-four hours.

The Boers now cantered up from all quarters, and while arms were being piled some of them gave hunks of bread and *biltong* to the famished English soldiers. Four of the principal commandants – Trichardt, who commanded the State Artillery, the above-mentioned Cronjé and Potgieter, and Malan of Rustenburg, interviewed Jameson.[2] Malan, who appeared to be the senior, began to bluster; accused Cronjé of acting without authority, and finally turned to Jameson and informed him that he declined to give any guarantee that his life or the lives of his chief officers would be spared. It was a question which must be decided by the *Krijgsraad* (war council). Jameson, who was past caring what befell him, made no

---

[1] It was afterwards pretended by the Boer Commandants Malan and Potgieter that Cronjé's undertaking was only meant to hold good until the prisoners were handed over to Joubert, the Commandant-General, at Pretoria. Cronjé himself made an affidavit in which he repeated the terms of his letter substantially as here given. He alleged, however, that the letter also contained a demand for the surrender of Jameson's flag, and that Jameson declared to him on oath that he had no flag. The letter was preserved, and from the facsimile it will be seen that there is no mention of a flag (Blue Book C 8063, No. 90, enclosure).

[2] The interpretation was carried on by Captain J. H. Kennedy, Quartermaster to Jameson's force.

reply and walked away. The arms had been given up and he was powerless, but having lost all else, he retained his self-control.

After some heated talk among the Boer leaders preparations were made for marching their prisoners off. They were taken away under strong escort – some of the officers and the wounded in Cape carts, and the remainder on their own horses – to Krugersdorp, where they were treated with rough consideration and given a good meal. The more serious casualties were left in a store fitted up as a temporary hospital, the principal officers were driven off to Pretoria in a mule waggon, while the rank and file, a worn out and dejected body of 400, were marched off a little later in charge of a large commando of burghers.[1] By nightfall all were safely under lock and key in the Boer capital. From that moment until they were handed over to the British Government on the Natal border three weeks later, no one of them was allowed to hold any communication with the outer world.

Note—Details of the casualties, so far as they were ascertained, are given in Appendix II.

[1] Captain Garraway was left with ten men and a guard of Boers at the scene of the surrender to attend the wounded and bury the dead. His journal contains the following entry:

'Nothing could exceed the kindness of the people, both Dutch and English, who came up afterwards. Milk, brandy, meat and bread were sent for the wounded, and ambulance carts came out from Krugersdorp. I was worked pretty hard all day, and only got to the burying late in the afternoon. To my surprise there were only six to bury—two B.B.P. and four B.S.A. men. One of ours was a youngster, not very long out from home. . . . All the B.S.A. were youngsters. The men from Roodepoort mine, which was close by, came over and helped me to bury the dead, which I did in one long trench. . . . It was dark when I got back to the farm-house where our men were, and I found an escort had arrived to take us to Krugersdorp. The men were put on a waggon and I on a horse, and we started off quietly. I had got most of the severely wounded in during the afternoon. . . . After a long cold ride we arrived at Krugersdorp at 1 a.m., and I was left at the temporary hospital while the men were taken down to the courthouse. . . . Every comfort and kindness was shown to the wounded. When I got there there were three doctors at work and a lot of volunteer nurses. . . .'

CHAPTER XVIII

Warnings

WE must leave Jameson for a while in order to relate what was happening at the other revolutionary fronts immediately before his incursion.

When Sir Hercules Robinson telegraphed on the 29th December to Chamberlain that 'the movement at Johannesburg had collapsed', he had every reason to be profoundly relieved, for within the preceding three days the feeling there had been suddenly raised to danger-point by the publication of the Leonard manifesto.[1] The interpretation placed on that document by the man in the street was that an outbreak against the Government was inevitable and imminent. The text of it does not, it is true, reveal any definite threat to resort to violence. It sets out at great – almost tedious – length the grievances of the Uitlanders – already familiar – and summarises their demands in a sort of schedule. The only words that can be translated into a hint of forcible action are contained in the last sentence:

'That [i.e. the schedule of demands] is what we want. There now remains the question which is to be put before you at the meeting of 6th January, viz., How shall we get it? To this question I shall expect

---

[1] Sir Hercules appears to have got from Graham Bower a somewhat muddled idea of what caused the collapse. In his official report, three weeks later, he explained it to Chamberlain in these words: 'The capitalists financing the movement had made the hoisting of the British flag a *sine qua non*. This the National Union rejected, and issued a manifesto declaring for a Republic. The division led to the complete collapse of the movement, and it was thought that the leaders of the National Union would probably make the best terms they could with President Kruger' (Blue Book C 8063, No. 13).

from you an answer in plain terms, according to your deliberate judgment.'

Still, it was generally understood that the manifesto was an ultimatum, and that the leaders of the National Union meant stern business. During Christmas week the news of their preparations began to filter abroad. It was whispered that they had arms and ammunition. None had actually been seen, but soon it was freely stated that numbers of rifles – magnified by report into many thousands – had, somehow or other, been smuggled into the town. It was said that machine-guns also had been obtained; that large stores of grain and flour were being accumulated, and other provisions made for a siege. For days past meetings had been held along the Reef, at which the miners and artizans had been addressed by one or other of the Reform leaders, and urged to join the Union, which was about to make a bold stand for their rights as citizens.

On Boxing Day the race-meeting – one of the most popular sporting events of the year in South Africa – opened at Johannesburg, but interest in it was shadowed by the prevailing anxiety caused by the manifesto and the warlike rumours. News of the crisis spread to the other colonies. The newspapers were full of ominous predictions. The *Cape Times* sent up its Assistant Editor as a special correspondent to watch the course of events, and his articles – afterwards reproduced in Edmund Garrett's book – give a vivid picture of the tension of popular feeling.[1]

In certain quarters there was something approaching a panic. Many of the Uitlanders decided to send their families away into safety until the storm blew over. On

[1] *The Story of an African Crisis*, Chapters IX.–XII.

Thursday and Friday crowds of women and children massed at the railway-stations and strove feverishly in the midsummer heat for seats in the trains going south. Advertisements appeared in the Press headed 'ENROL!' and several prominent Uitlanders began to organise corps of volunteers for service if needed. Mr. W. D. Davis ('Karri' Davis), an Australian, and an ardent member of the Union, busied himself in getting together a body of his own fellow-colonists – nominally for Red Cross work; another well-known officer – Colonel Bettington – had already collected the names of over a hundred men to form a mounted squadron, and now set to work to drill them and give them some training in musketry. The excitement spread along the Reef, and miners, inspired by the speeches at the recent meetings, flocked into the town, full of bellicose talk and eager for arms.

The one thing that did not become public – was never suspected indeed, except by those in the 'inner circle' – was Jameson's part, and the Reformers, secure in the conviction that their direct messengers to him, and their earnest representations to Rhodes, had effectively quelled his impatience, and would keep him quiet on the border till he was wanted – if that ever came about – were careful not to allow this side of the programme to get known. They had good reason for their reticence. It is obvious from passages in Fitzpatrick's account that they had never been quite easy in their minds as to their bargain with Jameson – made hurriedly, and when they were under the spell of his personal presence. They probably had a shrewd notion that the idea of enlisting outside assistance – especially assistance from Rhodesia and the Chartered Company – would be resented by the Johannesburgers, who would have looked askance at interference in a cause peculiarly their own.

On Saturday the 28th the agitation reached its peak. Women and children – and some men – began forming queues for the mail train many hours before it was due to start. A thousand people crowded on to it at Braamfontein, outside the town, where the trains were made up, and when it reached Park Station a further four or five thousand were found to be waiting in the vain hope of obtaining seats. A number of Cornish miners earned scorn by taking to their heels and seizing the accommodation which was being sought for by patient strings of women.

All this was known of course at Government House, Capetown. Some of it was cabled home to the Press in England, but it found the British public engaged in Christmas and New Year festivities and indisposed to exercise themselves over the affairs of a distant country, where troubles of one sort or another were always springing up. It was known also, and perhaps regarded more seriously, in Berlin, where the German Foreign Office was kept advised of every development by an assiduous consul at Pretoria. It was known at Pretoria, where Kruger had just returned from his country tour to celebrate *Nachtmaal* with his burghers, after his significant 'tortoise' speech. It was, in fact, fully intended by the Reformers that the President should be made aware that a crisis was at hand, and the object of the manifesto had been as much to convince him that they were in earnest as to brace the resolution of their own supporters. Had the Uitlanders been all of one mind the wily old man might have deemed it judicious to compromise and offer terms, for there was a strong party in his own Executive willing to grant some measure of reform. But he was quick to perceive that there were elements in the population of Johannesburg which

OR

shrank from extreme measures. Immediately on his return deputations waited on him from the American community, from the Mercantile Association and from the representatives of some of the big firms – the J. B. Robinson group for one – all seeking to find a way to avert an outbreak which they knew would be calamitous to trade and industry. As soon as he saw they were conciliatory his own resolve stiffened. 'The franchise', he said to one deputation, 'is for those who prove themselves loyal citizens, not for those who stir up agitation'. To others he made it clear that the manifesto must be withdrawn before he would consent to discuss concessions. In taking up this line with people who only wanted to prevent a catastrophe he committed an error of judgment, for it taught them that they could never expect any submission to their fair demands except at the point of the bayonet. Many of those who had before hesitated now made common cause with the Reformers.

Such was the position on Saturday evening, the 28th December, when Leonard and Hamilton telegraphed from Capetown that their colleagues must 'mark time', with the object of considering an entirely new programme; when Rhodes authorised Graham Bower to inform the Governor that the movement had 'fizzled out like a damp squib'; and when Jameson took a telegraph form and wrote – 'I shall start without fail to-morrow night'.

At 11 o'clock on Sunday morning J. A. Stevens, the Chartered Company's chief clerk, strolled over to the Capetown post-office. He was handed two telegrams, one of which had arrived the previous evening, but had remained undelivered because the Company's office had been closed for the week-end, while the other had only just come over the wires. They were Jameson's two last messages, and as soon as Stevens had decoded them he lost his Sabbath calm. He took a cab and drove off at once to show them to Harris, who lived a couple of miles off, at Three Anchor Bay, and Harris, after one glance at their contents, jumped into the same cab and went straight out to Rhodes's house at Rondebosch, on the opposite side of Capetown, a seven-mile drive. On his return an hour or two later he gave Stevens a telegram to send at once to Jameson in Rhodes's name, and ordered him to try and keep open the line to Mafeking – usually closed on Sunday – in case there might be further messages. But Stevens found that communication with Mafeking was broken, and though he made repeated efforts during the afternoon to get his telegram through, and stayed in the post-office until late in the evening, he did not succeed, and in fact it never went off. The draft was kept and produced by him before the Cape Committee. It was curiously worded and seems for the most part irrelevant to the occasion, but as a good deal of attention was bestowed on it by both the Cape and London Parliamentary Committees it may as well be repeated :

'Heartily reciprocate your wishes with regard to Protectorate, but the Colonial Office machinery moves slowly, as you know. We are, however, doing our utmost to get immediate transference of what we are justly entitled to. Things in Johannesburg I yet hope to see amicably settled, and a little patience and common sense is only necessary. On no account whatever must you move. I most strongly object to such a course.'[1]

The question now arises, did Harris send any further messages that day? Did he, for example, send a cablegram to Miss Flora Shaw? He was in regular correspondence with her, and had so far kept her posted every

[1] Cape Committee, Stevens, 308–377.

few days as to the progress of events in Johannesburg, while she in turn was in close touch with Mr. Fairfield of the Colonial Office, and had had discussions with him as to the crisis in Johannesburg.[1] The cables sent by Harris to her were afterwards produced by the Eastern Telegraph Company in obedience to orders from the Select Committee, and it appeared that the last message received by her before the Raid was dated the 27th December, and was as follows:

'Everything is postponed until after 6th January. We are ready, but divisions at Johannesburg.'[2]

Then there was a break until Monday the 30th, when Harris sent another marked 'Strictly confidential':

'Jameson moved to assist English in Johannesburg because he received strong letter begging Dr. Jameson to come signed by leading inhabitants....'[3]

The way in which this opens suggests that it was a sequel to a previous message announcing the fact that Jameson had moved – or was on the point of moving – and it would have been the natural thing for Harris to have sent such a message to Miss Shaw the moment he knew of Jameson's intention, but, as nothing of this kind has come to light, there is no warrant for assuming that he did so.

The importance of this will be seen when we try to solve the next puzzle – a remarkable communication despatched by Mr. Chamberlain the same afternoon,

---

[1] Select Committee, Miss Shaw, 9656, 9708, 9713, etc.
[2] Select Committee, Appendix 16, No. 941.
[3] Select Committee, Appendix 16, No. 1503.

before the receipt of Sir H. Robinson's cheerfully reassuring announcement that the movement had collapsed, *and just one hour before Jameson's force actually started.*

'(*Strictly Confidential.*)
'It has been suggested, although I do not think it probable, that an endeavour might be made to force matters at Johannesburg to a head by someone in the service of the Company advancing from Bechuanaland Protectorate with police.
'Were this to be done I should have to take action under Articles 22 and 8 of the Charter. Therefore, if necessary, but not otherwise, remind Rhodes of these Articles, and intimate to him that, in your opinion, he would not have my support, and point out the consequences which would follow.'[1]

At first sight there seem to be only two possible explanations of this message: either he had received some information from South Africa, or there was a coincidence so uncanny as to tempt us to agree with Garrett that it was a case for the Psychical Research Society. That the information which reached him was of a definite character was shown by a second and more explicit message despatched on Monday, before he could have received any official news of Jameson's advance, but *after* he had heard from Robinson that the whole affair had blown over:

'Your telegram received. Are you sure that Jameson has not moved in consequence of collapse?'[2]

The explanation afterwards given by Mr. Chamberlain was that his first warning had been prompted by a

[1] Blue Book C 7933, No. 2.   [2] Blue Book C 7933, No. 4.

suggestion from the Under-Secretary, Mr. Fairfield, who was 'put on the scent' by something which he saw in a newspaper article – something which hinted that Jameson might take the bit between his teeth.[1] This would be more convincing if it were not for the second cablegram – a strange one to be sent on the strength of a mere newspaper article; still, the period between Harris's first knowledge of Jameson's intended movement and the despatch of Mr. Chamberlain's cablegram was, making allowance for the difference between English and Cape time, barely seven hours. This seems to exclude the possibility of Miss Shaw having been employed as a link in the chain of communication. If, then, we dismiss the idea that Mr. Fairfield had other unofficial sources of information, Mr. Chamberlain's explanation must suffice. It is none the less extraordinary that a dénouement which was such a complete surprise to Rhodes, to Harris and to the leaders of the revolution in Johannesburg – all of them in daily and direct touch with Jameson – should have been foreseen with such accuracy by officials in the Colonial Office, 7,000 miles from the actual scene.

The announcement in Jameson's telegram was unquestionably a terrible shock to Rhodes, who, only the day before, had assured Leonard and Hamilton that he would keep him on the border six months or more if necessary.[2] The news reached him at Groote Schuur just before lunch time. He had some friends there, including the two Reform leaders, who were returning next day to the Rand, but he excused himself to them and discussed with Harris what was best to be done. Neither of them knew, of course, that the wire to Mafeking

---

[1] Select Committee, Mr. J. Chamberlain, 9562.
[2] Select Committee, Leonard, 7936.

had been cut, or, at any rate, it did not enter into their calculations. In the end Harris went back post-haste to Capetown with the telegram which has been quoted above.

For the remainder of the afternoon Rhodes was buoyed up by the hope that this firm veto would reach Jameson in time to stop him. If his nerves had been shaken he gave no outward sign, but chatted with apparent unconcern to the various friends who called. He kept open house at Groote Schuur, and there was the usual bevy of visitors who flocked to the fine old gabled Dutch mansion, and strolled about the spacious grounds in the shade of the pine-trees, or sat on the *stoep* and exchanged gossip over their tea. Among them was Mr. W. P. Schreiner, Rhodes's colleague in the Cabinet, in which he held office as Attorney-General. He came rather late, and was one of the last to leave. At 7 o'clock, when he rose to go, Rhodes walked along the *stoep* with him and for a minute or two the two men were alone together. Only then did Schreiner mention the topic of the hour – the situation at the Rand and the manifesto. 'Have you seen Charley Leonard?' he asked, and when Rhodes said 'Yes', he added, 'For goodness' sake be careful of that entanglement. Don't see too much of him, because people will be saying you are mixed up in the affair'. 'Oh, it will be all right', replied Rhodes, and Schreiner took his leave without having noticed anything unusual in Rhodes's demeanour, or suspecting that he was preoccupied with anxiety.[1]

At last, just after dinner, Harris came back with the news which Rhodes must, inwardly, have been dreading, that he had failed to communicate with Jameson, who was now beyond recall. In a flash he saw disclosed the

[1] Select Committee, Schreiner, 3233–3239.

precipice upon whose edge he stood. Even then his nerve did not desert him. He dismissed Harris, and for some time thought the matter out alone. It is almost cruel to pry into his mind at this moment. He had to face the bitter truth that at one blow his cherished ideal of a united South Africa had been wrecked by the mad impulse of another, and that other his greatest personal friend. No hushing up was possible. In a few hours the part which he himself had played would be trumpeted to the whole world. Before that happened there was one who must, in honour, be told – and by him – the Governor, whose chief counsellor he was, and whom he had kept in the dark.

Picking up the first piece of paper he saw – a telegraph form – he scribbled a hasty note to Graham Bower asking him to come at once to see him, and sent it by his coachman. Within half an hour Bower arrived and was shown to a bedroom, where Rhodes, who was alone, held out the telegram.

'Jameson has marched into the Transvaal', he said, and before the other could read the paper, or grasp the full import of what Rhodes meant, he went on, 'I have sent to stop him, and it may be all right yet. Do not be alarmed, it may come right yet'.

But in his heart he knew he was clutching a frail support. Just before midnight, when Bower was taking leave of him, the mask of stoicism which he had worn all day slipped down and revealed his utter dismay.

'I know I shall have to go', he burst out. 'I will resign to-morrow!'[1]

---

[1] Select Committee, Bower, 2572.

CHAPTER XIX

The Reform Committee

Harris and Rhodes were the earliest to hear of Jameson's intentions, but it was Pretoria which first got the news that he had actually started. Before 9 o'clock on Monday morning the State Secretary received a telegram from the *Landdrost* (District Magistrate) of Zeerust, the principal town in the Marico valley, through which the invaders passed after leaving Malmani. It briefly stated that a number of British troops had entered the Republic from Mafeking, and cut the telegraph wires, and were on the march towards Johannesburg.[1] A little later it was reported definitely that the invaders were close to the town of Rustenburg, which, as a matter of fact, lay well to the north of their route. The force was said to be composed of ' 800 Mashonaland troops ' well armed, with six maxims and ' four other cannons ', flying the English flag.[2] As nobody at Rustenburg could then have seen the force so as to be able to count the men and the guns there is something significant in the mention of 800, for it was the number of men expected by Johannesburg.[3] Is it possible that the people at Rustenburg had information beforehand of the supposed strength of Jameson's force, and when they heard that he was approaching assumed that he had that number with him?

Kruger at once sent for the British Agent – Sir Jacobus de Wet, a Cape colonial of Dutch descent – and read the telegrams to him. He urged him to call

[1] Blue Book C 7933, No. 6.   [2] Blue Book C 7933, No. 8.
[3] *The Transvaal From Within*, p. 110.

upon the High Commissioner to take immediate steps to stop the intruders from proceeding any further, and expressed his surprise that such serious movements should be allowed by Her Majesty's Government.[1]

One may imagine that the old President was startled. He was quite prepared for trouble, but expected it to come from Johannesburg, and although he cannot have failed to observe that the presence of a British force on the border was a potential menace, he could hardly have looked for the attack to be opened from that side. Not being cognisant of the eleventh-hour efforts made by the Reformers to keep Jameson in check, he would naturally now regard his movement as part of a pre-concerted plan, and as he had heard the prevalent stories of the supplies of arms – whose numbers were exaggerated by rumour – in possession of Johannesburg, he was justified in thinking that the next step would be the despatch of a force from there to co-operate with the 'Mashonaland troops'. Neither he nor General Joubert, who was with him, lost their heads. They were far from being novices in lawless military adventures. Indeed Kruger, who was now in his seventieth year, had, in early life, been to all intents a professional filibuster. A large part of his youth had been spent in expeditions against inoffensive native tribes in Bechuanaland, and in 1856 he had joined with Pretorius in leading a raid into the Orange Free State with the aim of upsetting the Government, a shameful feature of the affair having been an attempt to induce the Basutos to harass the Free State forces in rear while he and Pretorius with their supporters attacked them in front.

Kruger was well aware that the present crisis had been provoked by his obstinate refusal to allay grievances, and

[1] Blue Book C 7933, No. 8.

he had been prepared, in the last resort, to dole out some measure of relief if he found himself hard pressed. The moment had arrived, and his first impulse was to make belated overtures to the National Union, whose manifesto, followed so speedily by this new demonstration, showed that they were thoroughly in earnest. The tortoise had, in fact, put out its head.

Late on the evening of Monday, the 30th, he issued a proclamation which, while avoiding mention of Jameson's invasion, referred to the rumours of unrest at Johannesburg; warned 'evilly disposed persons' against any attempt at violence; called upon the law-abiding inhabitants of all nationalities to support him in his efforts to protect life and property, and announced that the Government was 'still prepared to listen to all complaints which may be properly submitted to them, and to consider them maturely, and submit them to the Legislature of the country without delay'.[1]

According to Sir Jacobus de Wet, this public gesture was accompanied by a secret step of a more sinister nature. In view of the incursion of an armed force of presumably British subjects reported to be carrying the British flag, he asked for the intervention of Germany and France through the Consuls of those Powers at Pretoria, who cabled the appeal to their respective Governments.[2]

The emergency found Kruger ready with a definite policy, and one which he had probably had in mind for some time, for he cannot have shut his eyes to the storm-clouds in Johannesburg. This is more than can be said for the Reformers, who were thrown into the utmost consternation on being suddenly confronted with a

---
[1] Blue Book C 8063, p. 123. Select Committee, Phillips, 7444.
[2] Blue Book C 7933, No. 9.

crisis which was partly the result of their own manœuvring. Nothing is more remarkable than the fact that they were taken so much by surprise. They had been aware for days that Jameson was being held back with difficulty; they knew he was a man who never faltered in his purpose; they had been warned by Heany and by Holden – his own officers – that he would most certainly carry out his plan in spite of all injunctions to the contrary, and yet they seem to have calmly assumed that the fuse which they themselves had lighted would die out without causing an explosion. They remind one of the boy who plays with the trigger of a gun, and when it goes off remarks, " I didn't know it was loaded ! "

The first thing that shook their composure was the receipt by Mr. Abe Bailey on Sunday afternoon of a telegram which came from somebody styling himself ' Godolphin ', and read :

> ' The veterinary surgeon has left for Johannesburg with some good horseflesh and backs himself for seven hundred.'

Having now become accustomed to the telegraphic pranks of the various persons involved in the plot we need feel no surprise at learning that this grotesque announcement emanated from Rutherfoord Harris, though why he should on this occasion have communicated with Mr. Bailey, instead of with Colonel Rhodes, to whom all his other telegrams had been addressed, and why he felt it necessary to adopt a new and fantastic code name, and to wrap up a vital piece of information in such obscure language, has never been disclosed. Whatever his purpose was, his method completely mystified the Reformers. Fitzpatrick tells us that neither Bailey himself, nor any of those to whom he showed it, understood the meaning of the message or could identify the sender, but there was a general impression that it related to Jameson, and it caused great uneasiness.[1]

A couple of hours later all doubt was removed when Mr. A. L. Lawley, another of the ' inner ring ' and a man whom nothing as a rule could ruffle, dashed into the Goldfields office, where some of the Committee were assembled, and excitedly produced a telegram which he had just received from the railway construction camp at Mafeking – veiled like the first one in queer terms, but alarmingly plain to understand :

> ' The contractor has started on the earthworks with 700 boys ; hopes to reach terminus on Wednesday.'[2]

Before those present could recover from their first incredulous shock confirmation was received from a Government official at Pretoria, with an intimation that the news had been known there for some hours, and that the burghers gathered in the town for *Nachtmaal* were already forming commandos.

Considering that the Reform leaders were taken by surprise, it must be recorded to their credit that they rose to the occasion with a fine spirit. Their procrastination fell from them like a discarded garment, and was replaced by a fierce activity. Messengers were at once sent out to summon all the prominent members of the National Union. Within an hour or two a meeting took place at Colonel Rhodes's office in the Goldfields building,

---

[1] *The Transvaal From Within*, p. 109.

[2] *The Transvaal From Within*, p. 109. Note the repetition of the figure 700. This points to some deliberate overstatement of the number at Pitsani, for the strength of the squadron of B.B.P. that left with Grey (122) must surely have been public property at Mafeking. It is strange, however, that Harris in his ' Godolphin ' telegram should also have mentioned 700.

and those present formed themselves into an executive body, which was styled the 'Reform Committee', and at once took charge of all arrangements for meeting the emergency. In the absence of Charles Leonard, who was still at Capetown, Phillips, the President of the Chamber of Mines, was appointed chairman, and a number of prominent Uitlanders immediately rallied round him, until eventually the Committee's numbers reached over sixty.

It will be recalled that the original plans of the leaders hinged on the seizure by surprise of the Pretoria arsenal, but now that the insurrection had gone off at half-cock all hope of carrying this out had to be abandoned, for Jameson's premature movement had put the Government thoroughly on their guard. The positions of the Government and the revolutionaries had, in fact, become reversed, and it was feared that a sudden attack might be made on Johannesburg, which was ill prepared to resist it. · Of the rifles so far delivered in accordance with Jameson's undertaking some 500 had been unpacked and were lying in the office; a further 1,200 were still in their cases at the mines to which they had been secretly consigned.[1] Orders were given for these to be brought in, and during the night members of the Committee worked hard in getting them unpacked, and removing the grease from them, in readiness for issue on the following morning.

On Tuesday the Government, with the avowed object of avoiding collisions, decided to withdraw from duty the 'Zarps',[2] or municipal police, who were moved to some barracks on Hospital Hill, a good strategic position overlooking the town. It then became urgently necessary

[1] Select Committee, Phillips, 6907.
[2] A slang name formed from the initials of their official title – *Zuid Afrikaansche Republiek Politie*.

THE REFORM COMMITTEE

to have a force to keep order, for immediately the news of Jameson's move became known some of the mines stopped work; the white employees flocked into town clamouring for arms; while the natives were left uncontrolled and became a source of danger. An Irish ex-dragoon, Andrew Trimble, formerly the competent chief of the Transvaal detective department, from which he had been dismissed owing to his nationality, was charged with the task of organising a force to ensure good order, and given plenary powers. Within twelve hours he had enrolled 500 men, including many old soldiers. The canteens were closed. Trimble set up a court of summary jurisdiction, and inflicted penalties – in one bad case of looting, lashes – on persons who defied his regulations for preserving order. Fitzpatrick records that never in the history of Johannesburg was the town so efficiently controlled.

Besides these measures for guarding against disorder within the town, hasty preparations were put in hand for defence against attack from outside. Earthworks were started at several commanding points and the few machine-guns in the hands of the Committee placed in position. Volunteers were enrolled in large numbers, and though only a small proportion could be armed, the approaches to the town were patrolled by Bettington's men and others, and a guard was mounted at the Goldfields office which was at once recognised as the headquarters of the defence organisation, and was surrounded by a huge crowd waiting for the rifles which it was said were to be distributed. A number of women and children were sent in from various parts of the Reef for safety, and the accommodation and feeding of these, and the rationing of the volunteer detachments, necessitated the formation of a sub-committee with power to commandeer stores and quarters. In these and many other directions the Reform Committee assumed the functions of a provisional government, and for several days was virtually accepted as such by the real one. On the whole it fulfilled its self-appointed task with success. There was no attempt to dispute its authority, and consequently there was no disorder and no privation.

In their attitude towards Jameson's incursion there was not the same unanimity or decisiveness among the members of the Committee. They were loth to repudiate him altogether, for the public, prepared by the manifesto, took it for granted, like Kruger, that the invasion was part of a programme for which the authors of that document were responsible. Moreover, there was a strong hope that his approach would frighten the Government into a submissive frame of mind. On the other hand, many of them were nervous of any open display of sympathy with him for fear of provoking an attack, against which their resources were so hopelessly inadequate. The majority of the new committee were in no way pledged to Jameson, but the original leaders could not in honour disclaim the responsibility of having made certain military arrangements with him and invited his assistance. They profoundly hoped that their ill-advised letter would never see the light of day, but it was there, and if produced would be regarded by those who did not know the whole story as a definite appeal for Jameson's help. There was a strong party too which sought to find excuses for his sudden decision to advance. After the first shock of surprise it was thought by them that some garbled report must have reached him and caused him to act precipitately, but in good faith – some rumour of disturbance, arrests or even massacres, of which plenty had been flying round in the preceding few days. There had been a persistent story that, on the issue of the manifesto, Phillips had been arrested by the Government on a charge of treason. Reports had been circulated locally as to fighting having taken place between Boers and Uitlanders at two of the mines,[1] and other equally wild statements had been current. Some of these might have reached Jameson; while, on the other hand, he might not have had the messages sent by Heany and Holden. It was inconceivable that with full knowledge of all the conditions he should deliberately have flouted their injunctions to wait.

It never occurred to anyone that he might be in need of assistance from Johannesburg. With 700 or 800 well-trained men, it was believed that he could easily force his way through, and in this confidence the Committee were strengthened by the opinion of Colonel Rhodes and other military men on the spot, including Colonel Heyman and Captain Charles White – the third of the White brothers – who was also there in connection with the plot. All of these were convinced that no force of Boers that could be mustered would be able to stop him.[2] Had the real truth as to the strength of his force been known there might perhaps have been less confidence.

In the afternoon the new Committee compromised by issuing a public notice, in which, while suggesting uncertainty as to Jameson's advance – a disingenuous evasion – they renounced any intention of defying the Government. It was posted on the door of the Goldfields offices and appeared in the *Star* on the morning of the 31st December. These were its terms:

'Notice is hereby given that this Committee adheres to the National Union Manifesto, and reiterates its desire

[1] *The Transvaal From Within*, p. 111.
[2] Select Committee, Phillips, 6909–6914.

to maintain the independence of the Republic. The fact that rumours are in course of circulation to the effect that a force has crossed the Bechuanaland border renders it necessary to take active steps for the defence of Johannesburg and the preservation of order. The Committee earnestly desires that the inhabitants should refrain from taking any action which can be considered as an overt act of hostility against the Government.'

By way of putting an accent on their earnest desire to avoid giving offence to the Government the Committee went further. Jameson – so their information went – was marching under the Union Jack.[1] That would never do for them. They must dissociate themselves at once from any taint of jingoism.

And so, almost simultaneously with the issue of the notice, the Republican ' Vierkleur ' – a striped banner of red, white, green and blue – was formally hoisted on the staff over the Goldfields building ! The gaping crowds in the street below rubbed their eyes and wondered what it all meant.

[1] According to Commandant Cronjé, Jameson declared to him on oath that he had no flag (Blue Book C 8063, p. 103 ; see also Select Committee, Colonel Rhodes, 5232).

CHAPTER XX

Troubles of the Reform Committee

IT is no easy matter to analyse the motives which impelled the Reform leaders during the next few crowded hours. They were suffering from a conflict of emotions, and their embarrassment was aggravated by the constantly changing attitude of the populace, who were swayed this way and that by rumours, and, in the absence of inside knowledge of what had led to the crisis, were completely bewildered by the turn of events. The Committee's most perplexing dilemma was in regard to Jameson. If they showed open approval of his action, or took any steps to give him assistance, they would be inviting an attack from the Boers. If, on the other hand, they formally cast him off they might not only be doing a gross injustice to one who was earnestly – if mistakenly – trying to help them, but might incur the rage of the mob, who, after their first startled uneasiness, were rapidly coming to regard him as a Paladin hastening to their deliverance.

Apart from the clash of impulses on this point, the Committee, having come into the open as an organised body, had thereby shouldered grave responsibilities. They had to secure the defence of Johannesburg against a Boer attack; to prevent disorder among the excited inhabitants; and to utilise the situation to procure redress of the common grievances in terms of the manifesto. On these three matters there was practical unanimity. The first danger seemed, on the 31st December, a very real one. Commandos, numbering several thousands, were reported to be assembling, with authority from General Joubert to march upon the town and shoot at sight all concerned in the plot. There was at Pretoria a trained force – the *Staats Artillerie* – 250 strong, with six Krupp heavy field pieces, besides Armstrong guns and a few maxims. In addition a large body of burghers was gathered there who could be quickly mobilised, and Krugersdorp, Klerksdorp, Lydenburg and Heidelburg would also be able to furnish their quota within a very short time. It was estimated that in five or six days an army of 5,000 could be put into the field ready to advance on Johannesburg. So critical did the position appear that they implored the High Commissioner by telegram ' to intervene to protect the lives of citizens who for years had agitated constitutionally for their rights '.[1]

As regards the internal management of the town there can be no denying that, in the absence of a strong controlling hand, the conditions would speedily have become chaotic, and rioting, looting and bloodshed would have been the inevitable sequel. The possibility of such outbreaks was generally realised. Shops were barricaded and jewellers packed their more valuable wares and placed them in the custody of a safe deposit company. On the other hand, there was a run on the banks, some customers illogically withdrawing their money and others converting Transvaal notes into gold. Numbers of business men hastened to send their families out of the danger zone. During Monday and Tuesday the exodus, which had started the previous week, continued, and every outgoing train was packed to suffocation. The rush to get away was only checked when the alarming news came that an overcrowded train which left Johannesburg on Monday evening for

[1] Blue Book C 7933, No. 177, enclosure.

TROUBLES OF REFORM COMMITTEE 215

Durban had run off the rails in rounding a sharp curve at Glencoe, near the Natal border, and that over thirty refugees had been killed and a large number injured.

The Committee had all their work cut out to keep the growing excitement within bounds. Speeches were delivered by several of the leaders from the Goldfields building. J. W. Leonard, brother of Charles, and like him a man of great eloquence, addressed the crowds and assured them that ample provision had been made to defend Johannesburg against any force that could possibly be brought against it. The Committee would be responsible for their safety, and would no longer allow their liberties to be trampled on by tyrants. They would carry on as a provisional government, but there was no intention to go against the feelings of the people or to impose a rule which they might not approve. This speech, and others in the same vein, inspired a certain amount of confidence. Somebody started singing ' Rule Britannia ', which, in spite of the Republican flag floating over the speakers' heads, was taken up lustily, and followed by ' God save the Queen '.[1]

For all their bold front, the Committee were greatly relieved when the Government made a conciliatory gesture by despatching two delegates to parley with them – Mr. Eugene Marais, editor of *Land en Volk*, the principal Dutch newspaper, a fair-minded man who had consistently striven to expose and remove abuses, and Mr. Malan, a respectable nonentity who was related to General Joubert. These emissaries arrived in Johannesburg on 31st December, prepared, in their own words,

---

[1] Telegram from the *Standard and Diggers' News*, 31st Dec., 1895; reproduced in *South Africa*, 8th Jan., 1896. See also Garrett, *The Story of an African Crisis*, pp. 168, 170–1.

'to hold out the olive-branch'. They assured the Committee that the Executive was genuinely willing to consider and redress their wrongs as set forth in the manifesto, and invited them to send a deputation at once to Pretoria to meet a Government commission. As their overtures were apparently made in good faith, and as they certainly presented an avenue to peace, they were immediately accepted. Before daybreak on the morning of the New Year a deputation of four, including Phillips the Chairman, started for Pretoria, where they were received by a Commission consisting of Chief Justice Kotzé, another judge (Ameshoff) and a member of the Executive (Koch).

Phillips, as spokesman, frankly admitted responsibility for the arrangement whereby Jameson was to hold himself ready with his force on the border to march on Johannesburg in case of extremity, but declared that his actual movement had been made without their knowledge or consent.[1] Accused of being rebels, the deputation said that they were only standing out for honest treatment, and as for Jameson, while they could not desert him, they would guarantee that if allowed to reach Johannesburg unmolested he and his force should leave the country at once. For the due fulfilment of this undertaking they offered themselves as hostages.

The Commission professed to doubt whether Phillips and his friends could speak for any considerable body of Uitlanders, and to this the delegates replied that the composition of the Reform Committee proved that it represented the whole of the industrial and professional interests of the Rand. They eventually telegraphed to Johannesburg for a complete list of members, and gave it to the Commission, thus gratuitously presenting the

[1] Statement of Reform prisoners at trial, 24th April, 1896.

Government with a valuable piece of evidence, which it was not slow to use when the time came.

The Boer Commissioners, in fact, found out all they wanted, and, in return, handed Phillips and his colleagues a statement which pledged the Government to practically nothing. It told them that Sir Hercules Robinson had offered to come up to use his good offices for a peaceful settlement; that his offer had been accepted, and that pending his arrival no hostile step would be taken against Johannesburg, provided the people there refrained from any hostile action against the Government – in other words, it sought to gain time by an 'armistice'.

The deputation were also informed of the High Commissioner's Proclamation ordering Jameson to withdraw with his troops, and solemnly calling upon all British subjects in the Transvaal to abstain from rendering him any assistance. This had just been received by Sir Jacobus de Wet, who had passed it on both to the Reform Committee and to the Government. It was couched in such peremptory language that the deputation felt, not only that it was impossible for Jameson to disregard it, but that it absolutely debarred them from taking any measures which could be construed as support for him. They ascertained that the Government was making arrangements through de Wet to send out the proclamation to Jameson in the field, and they took it for granted that, in this respect at all events, their own responsibility was at an end.

They returned to report to their Committee with some relief, if not with positive elation. They found the streets outside their headquarters packed by a surging multitude, greedy for news and shouting for the arms which were not there. The spirit of New Year's exhilaration was perhaps uppermost, but there was a sinister undercurrent of suspicion that the truth was being kept from them. Phillips pluckily consented to address the throng from the balcony, and his speech, teeming as it was with indiscretions, went a long way to reassure them. He gave a glowing version of the encounter with the Government Commission, and told them that the High Commissioner was on his way to mediate. As to the proclamation he was silent, but he assured the excited crowd that there was no intention of forsaking Jameson, who had gallantly marched across country with his brave troops to support them, and might be expected in Johannesburg within a few hours. This announcement was greeted with rapturous enthusiasm, and cheered again and again.[1]

All this was on the evening of Wednesday, the 1st of January – just about the time when Jameson, driven back from the Boer entrenchments outside Krugersdorp, was preparing, under heavy fire, for his last bivouac on the rising ground west of Luipard's Vley.

Meanwhile Kruger and Joubert, having received the report of Judge Kotzé's commission, and having assured themselves that no immediate aggressive movement need be feared from Johannesburg, released the *Staats Artillerie*, which had so far been kept back to defend Pretoria, and ordered them to join the burgher commandos encircling the raiders.

At the request of de Wet the Committee supplied an escort for the despatch rider who was to hasten out to Jameson with the proclamation, the Boers having provided the man with a safe conduct through their own lines. This was a heaven-sent opportunity for the Committee to send the Doctor a letter explaining the development

---

[1] *The Times* special correspondent, quoted in *South Africa*, 1st Feb., 1896. See also Garrett, *The Story of an African Crisis*, p. 182.

of the situation and exhorting him, in the strongest language at their command, to obey the proclamation and desist from a further advance. They were not aware of the plight into which he had fallen; they had so far had no word from him, and for all they knew he might be advancing without encountering resistance, but even on that assumption it was of the highest importance that they should seize the occasion to warn him that the Boers were making ready to oppose him with all their resources, and that by proceeding he would not only endanger his own troops, but would seriously jeopardize the cause for which he started. This was the more necessary because their last message to him – sent only the day before – had been one of approval and encouragement, that fatuous joint note from Colonel Rhodes and Phillips, patting him on the back; telling him what a fine fellow he was; how glad they would be to see him and have a drink with him; saying that the Government were 'in a funk', and that Johannesburg had armed a lot of men. The whole tone of that note – as far as can be gathered from its salved fragments – was to urge him to come straight on, and now their whole object was to try to prevent him from coming, or, if he came, to get rid of him as quickly as possible.

It is conceivable that if Jameson had learnt fully what had taken place, with defeat staring him in the face and with the terrible sentence of outlawry threatening him, he might, late as it was, have sought and found an opportunity of opening negotiations with the Boer Commandants opposing him, and thus have saved himself and his following from the extremity of humiliation which was awaiting them. We cannot, however, waste time in considering what might have happened. What did happen was that the Committee accepted the offer of

Mr. Lace to accompany de Wet's despatch rider, and gave him some verbal message, which could not have been very explicit – judging from the brief way in which Fitzpatrick refers to it – and of which, according to Willoughby, the main purport was that no troops were being sent out to meet the column.[1] What ensued has already been told.

Shortly before Lace started the bugler, Vallé, to whom Jameson had confided the only message that got through, arrived at the Goldfields office and reported that 'the Doctor was getting on all right, but wanted them to send out to meet him'. Although this was very vague, Colonel Rhodes, who first interviewed him, guessed the truth, and, on his own responsibility, ordered Bettington to saddle up at once and go out with as many men as he could muster – he had not more than 120 or so, all told – to his support. It was a chivalrous impulse, and just what one would have expected from a man of Rhodes's instincts, but when some of the others heard what he had done they were seized with alarm lest his action should be held to be a breach of the armistice, and a defiance of the proclamation. No doubt this view was the 'correct' one, and their discretion should be applauded. Bettington, to his intense chagrin, was recalled before he had gone more than two or three miles. In any case, the force that he had with him was too small to have affected the course of events.

The story of Johannesburg must now be interrupted in order to describe the repercussions of the Raid in the other African Colonies, in Great Britain and on the Continent; but before this chapter is closed something may be said about the 'letter of invitation,' which had

---

[1] *The Transvaal From Within*, pp. 135, 333.

a career as strange and romantic – or sordid – as any document ever penned by mortal man.

It will be remembered that the letter – which should never have been written to begin with, and which seems to have demoralised everyone who afterwards handled it – was given to Jameson at Johannesburg in November. It was left undated, but was signed by Charles Leonard, Phillips, Colonel Rhodes, Hammond and Farrar. The first named afterwards declared that he was most reluctant to sign it, but eventually gave way under pressure from the others.[1] On the other hand, Fitzpatrick says that he actually drafted it,[2] and the diction is certainly similar to that of his manifestos. On his return to Capetown, Jameson showed it to Rhodes, but Harris knew nothing about it until his arrival from England on 17th December, when he heard of it for the first time. A day or two later he telegraphed to Jameson, in Rhodes's name, for a copy,[3] and when it arrived he found that the date had been filled in as 20th December, which was the day on which it was posted from Pitsani.[4]

The next development came on Monday the 30th, the day after Jameson started. Rhodes's recollections of what happened on that unhappy day were very confused. He did not go into Capetown at all, but is said to have spent his time riding alone on the slopes of Table Mountain. But he did remember giving orders that the letter should be cabled to London, to give the people at home some explanation of Jameson's action, and to show that he had been in communication with the Johannesburg leaders before the Raid.[5] Harris accordingly

---

[1] Select Committee, Leonard, No. 7945. [2] *The Transvaal From Within*, p. 100.
[3] Cape Report, Appendix, p. liii. [4] Select Committee, Harris, 6318.
[5] Select Committee, Rhodes, 140, 148.

cabled the text, *en clair*, to Miss Flora Shaw on that day (30th), prefacing it with certain directions of his own :

'Following letter was received by Dr. Jameson before he decided to go, but you must not use letter for Press until we cable authority ; it is signed by leading inhabitants of Johannesburg.'[1]

He signed the cablegram form ' *F. R. Harris, for C. J. Rhodes, Premier,*' and he did another strange and apparently foolish thing ; he altered the date on the letter from 20th December to 28th December.[2] If this was with the object of suggesting that it only reached Jameson at the last moment, and that he had acted on it at once, he overreached himself, for it was impossible for a letter written in Johannesburg on the 28th to have reached Pitsani on the following day – the day of the Raid.

On the 31st, Harris sent a second cablegram to Miss Shaw :

'You can publish letter.'[3]

and on the 1st January it appeared in *The Times*, with this introduction :

' The following letter, signed by leading inhabitants of Johannesburg, was sent on Saturday [i.e. the 28th December] to Dr. Jameson, Mafeking.'

There is one point to be noticed about the text as

[1] Select Committee, Appendix 16, No. 1557.
[2] Select Committee, Harris, 6318.
[3] Select Committee, Appendix 16, No. 1687.

printed in *The Times*. The last paragraph of the letter as handed to Jameson opened with these words :

'It is under these circumstances that we feel constrained to *call upon you to come to our aid should a disturbance arise here*. The circumstances are so extreme that we cannot but believe that you and the men under you will not fail to come to the rescue of people who will be so situated. . . .'

In the version published in *The Times* there is a full stop after the word 'aid', and the next words, 'should a disturbance arise here', are made to start the succeeding sentence. The result is a material alteration in the sense, but it is charitable to believe that the mistake occurred in the course of telegraphic transmission.

The effect of the publication of this letter was, as will be shown later, that the public was completely taken in. There was a strong outburst of sympathy with Jameson and a corresponding contempt for the Reform leaders, who were placed under the odious stigma of having entreated Jameson to come to their aid, and within five days abandoned him to his fate.

The remaining history of this evil letter is no less painful. A certified copy, dated 29th December, was placed by Major R. White in the despatch-box which was taken in by him with the column, and fell into the hands of the Boers after Doornkop. The certificate was signed by White himself as a Magistrate of the Chartered Company, and after being taken prisoner he made a further affidavit at Pretoria verifying his own signature.[1] The only plausible explanation of this is that it was an

---

[1] Evidence of A. R. Fleischak at the trial of Dr. Jameson and his officers in London, July 23rd, 1896.

attempt to keep up the fiction that Jameson entered in consequence of the invitation, but the unfortunate result was that it became a damning piece of evidence against the four remaining signatories – Leonard having escaped arrest – who, on the strength of the letter, were treated at the trial of the Reformers as the arch-delinquents.[1]

[1] The full text of the letter is printed in Appendix II.

CHAPTER XXI

Reverberations

SIR GRAHAM BOWER, the Imperial Secretary, left Rhodes on Sunday about midnight, and returned to Newlands, a suburb of Capetown about a mile beyond Groote Schuur, where the Governor had a summer residence. Apart from his official anxiety at the sudden turn of events, he must have felt considerable disquietude as to his own position, for, sooner or later, he would have to disclose to his Chief that he had been privy to at least part of the Jameson plan. It may be taken for granted that he did not get much repose during the remaining hours of the night, for at 5 a.m. on Monday morning he was writing a note to Sir Hercules asking him to come to town early : ' There is ', he said, ' bad news from Jameson. He seems to have disobeyed Rhodes and taken the bit between his teeth.'[1]

Sir Hercules was not in the best of health, but on receipt of this information – vague and meagre as it was – he hastened to his office in Capetown, where he heard Bower's account of his conversation with Rhodes of the night before, and, to add to his discomfiture, found awaiting him the strangely prophetic cablegram from Chamberlain hinting at a possible attempt at invasion of the Transvaal on the part of the Company's police. Within the next few hours came the agitated series of telegrams from Sir Jacobus de Wet reporting the receipt of the news at Pretoria, and asking for instructions. In spite of his age and indisposition Robinson at

[1] Blue Book C 8063, Appendix, No. 1.

this stage seems to have acted with vigour and discretion. His first step was to telegraph to Newton, the Commissioner at Mafeking, directing him, if it really was true that Jameson had started, to send a messenger after him on a fast horse ordering his immediate return and warning him and his officers of the grave penalties to which they were laying themselves open by their reckless conduct. These instructions could not, however, be despatched till about midday, when the telegraph line was once more in working order. Newton's action on receipt of them will be referred to by and by.[1]

Robinson must have thought it strange that Rhodes neither came to see him nor made any sign. He sent Bower to look for him; to show him the various reports, and to urge him to co-operate in recalling Jameson, but although he went several times to the Prime Minister's office, as well as to the Chartered Company's, Rhodes was not to be found. Bower then sent a somewhat acid letter to his private house, hinting plainly the Governor's annoyance at not having seen him and giving his views as to Jameson's conduct, and followed this up by another, conveying what he described as a 'paraphrase' – it was really a garbled version – of Chamberlain's cablegram.[2] The perusal of this caused great irritation to Rhodes, and goaded him into despatching a most indiscreet message to Miss Shaw, which was one of those afterwards laid before the Select Committee :

---

[1] Blue Book C 8063, Part II., No. 13.

[2] The text of the cable ran : ' It has been suggested that an endeavour might be made to force matters at Johannesburg to a head by *someone* in the service of the Company advancing from the Bechuanaland Protectorate with police. . . . ' In the version transmitted by Bower the word ' someone ' was replaced by ' *Rhodes and Jameson or somebody else* '. There were also other alterations. See Blue Book C 8063, Appendix, No. 10.

'To Telamones, London.
'Capetown, 30th December, 1895.

'Inform Chamberlain that I shall get through all right if he supports me, but he must not send cable like he sent to High Commissioner in South Africa. To-day the crux is I will win and South Africa will belong to England.

'C. J. RHODES.'[1]

Miss Shaw came to the conclusion that this message really emanated from Harris, using Rhodes's name for greater effect (she may have been right, as the telegraph form was again signed by '*F. R. Harris, for C. J. Rhodes, Premier*' as sender) and wisely refrained from taking any action on it.[2] But even if it actually was from Rhodes – and the use of the word 'crux,' a favourite expression with him, suggests that it was – it can be explained by his agitated and unbalanced frame of mind at the time.

Other people were trying to get hold of Rhodes that day. One of them was Schreiner, the Attorney-General, who was amazed and shocked when, from official sources, he learnt what had occurred. As soon as the line was opened there arrived from Boyes, the Mafeking magistrate, a report of the departure of the Bechuanaland Police for the Transvaal. At first Schreiner refused to credit it, and administered a severe snub to Boyes for paying attention to alarmist rumours.[3] Only when the statements were corroborated by an additional telegram from Inspector Fuller did he realise that there was no mistake. He went off at once to find Rhodes; but Rhodes was still riding alone on the slopes of Table Mountain, trying to find a way out of the hideous tangle in which

[1] Select Committee, Appendix 16, No. 1556.
[2] Select Committee, Miss Shaw, Nos. 9733–9736 and 9676–9688.
[3] Select Committee, Schreiner, 3255–3257.

he was enmeshed. He did not return until late in the afternoon, and then sent a brief note of excuse to Bower's stiff official communication:

> 'MY DEAR BOWER,—Jameson has gone in without my authority. I hope our messages may have stopped him. I am sorry to have missed you.
> 'Yours, &c.,
> 'C. J. RHODES.'[1]

This is another example of Rhodes's confusion. Only one message had been prepared, and that never went off.

He next sent a note to Schreiner asking him to come and see him. The Attorney-General, then in his fortieth year, was an Afrikander of German descent and a man of unusual intellectual gifts, though his judgment was apt to be swayed by his ardent and impulsive temperament. His natural honesty and singleness of purpose made him incapable of discerning any but the most exalted motives in those to whom he gave his allegiance, and he had of late become intoxicated by Rhodes's ideals of a united South Africa with a sinking of racial antagonisms, and dominated by the personality of Rhodes himself. He was completely unprepared for the discovery that one whom he had made his idol could have feet of clay.

The account which Schreiner furnished to the Cape Committee of his interview with his colleague that evening has become historical, and, making allowance for the introduction of emotional colour, it probably gave a fair picture of a most dramatic meeting.

'I suppose I reached Groote Schuur about half-past eight', he said, 'and I was talking to Mr. Rhodes till

---

[1] Blue Book C 8063, Appendix, No. 11.

nearly twelve. I went into his study with the telegrams in my hand. The moment I saw him I saw a man I had never seen before. His appearance was utterly dejected and different. Before I could say a word he said, "Yes, yes, it is true! It is all true! Old Jameson has upset my apple-cart" – reiterating in the way he does when he is moved. I was staggered. I said, "What do you mean; what *can* you mean?" He said, "Yes, it is quite true; he has ridden in. Go and write out your resignation. Go; I know you will". And so I said, "It is not a question of my resignation". I asked him, "Why did you not say anything to me yesterday when I was here?" Rhodes replied at once, "I thought I had stopped him. I sent messages to stop him, and did not want to say anything about it if I stopped him". I elicited a great many facts in relation to this matter, and I told him it was his duty to convene a Cabinet meeting at once.'[1]

Later in his evidence Schreiner stated that, although he did not extract the whole story of Rhodes's connection with the plot – as was natural, for Rhodes was not in a condition to make a consecutive statement – he heard enough to make up his mind, then and there, that his resignation – carrying with it, of course, the resignations of the rest of the Cabinet – was imperative.

Schreiner added one significant thing. Something, he thought, had been 'brought to Rhodes's consciousness' since he had talked to him on the previous evening – something had occurred to make a mental change in him. It might, he thought, have been the communication from Chamberlain to Robinson. Looking, however, at all the circumstances, it appears more likely that Rhodes, having had the whole of Monday to fight the

[1] Cape Committee Report, p. 216. Select Committee, Schreiner, 3269–3277, 3290–3301, 3988–3990.

matter out with his own conscience, and to weigh the consequences, had decided that, whatever personal sacrifice it entailed, loyalty to his friend was his only course. And he may have clung to the hope that if Jameson got through – and at that time there was nothing to indicate that he would not get through – he would be whitewashed and forgiven, and all might yet be well. Both these thoughts peeped out when Schreiner put the question, "Why do you not stop him?" to which his answer was "Poor old Jameson! Twenty years we have been friends, and now he goes in and ruins me. I cannot hinder him. I cannot go and destroy him!"[1]

During the entire interview Rhodes seemed absolutely broken down in spirit, and there can be no doubt that the agony he went through in those few days shook him both mentally and physically. Sir Lewis Michell, who saw him four days after Schreiner, was struck by his 'shattered appearance',[2] and when, three months later, he arrived in Rhodesia and threw himself into the critical business of the Matabele rebellion with unimpaired vigour, the physical change was obvious to all who knew him, the present writer among them. But when the first shock was over he braced himself with admirable courage to look the world in the face and to maintain an outward demeanour of confidence. On the 12th January he was at Kimberley, where he was enthusiastically welcomed by a crowd of many thousands, who flocked to the railway-station to greet him. In a short speech of thanks he said, 'There is an idea abroad that my public career has come to an end. On the contrary, I think it is only just beginning, and I have a firm belief that I shall live to do useful work for this country'.[3]

[1] Select Committee. Schreiner, 3301.
[2] Report of speech in *South Africa*, 8th Feb., 1896.
[3] *Life of Rhodes*, p. 276.

His naturally sanguine temperament did, in fact, enable him to rise superior to the strain of the Raid and completely to recover his sanity of judgment, and some of his greatest achievements were carried through in the remaining seven years of his life, but nothing could efface the marks left on his countenance. His brown hair rapidly whitened; his fresh complexion became prematurely lined and coarsened. Though still in the early forties, he acquired the facial characteristics of a man twenty years older.

On the day following the interview with Schreiner there was a short meeting of the Cabinet at which Rhodes stated his intention of resigning. Immediately afterwards he called on the Governor, and informed him that Jameson had acted without his authority, and that his attempts to stop him had been frustrated by the cutting of the telegraph wire. He then formally tendered his resignation. For the moment Robinson hesitated to accept this offer, but his confidence in his Prime Minister had been rudely disturbed, and while he had been holding aloof, battling with his own problems, others had not been slow to offer their counsel. Chief among them was Mr. Jan Hendrik Hofmeyr, the leader of the Dutch Afrikander party and of recent years Rhodes's close ally in the policy of drawing together the two white races in South Africa. On learning of the Raid, and on receiving information of Rhodes's complicity in the revolutionary movement in the Transvaal, he found it impossible to doubt that both were part of an organised programme to force British domination upon the whole of the South African States. He threw friendship to the winds, and urged Robinson, as High Commissioner, to issue a proclamation publicly repudiating Jameson, as the only course likely to avert civil war. This advice was accepted, and in the circumstances it is hard to find fault with it, but Rhodes had not been consulted, and only heard of the intention when the proclamation had been drafted, and was on the point of publication. He was greatly upset, and, calling upon Robinson, protested that it would make Jameson an outlaw, and urged him to withhold it, or at any rate to delay issue till the next day, clinging, no doubt, to the hope that by next day Jameson would be in Johannesburg, and the situation would have developed beyond Robinson's power to restrain the rush of events. But the High Commissioner had made up his mind that Hofmeyr, though an unofficial adviser, was right, and the proclamation was published in a special Gazette the same evening.[1] Its reception by Jameson and its effect on the Reform Committee have already been described.

A digression may here be made to relate the action of the Resident Commissioner at Mafeking on receipt of Robinson's instructions to do his utmost to recall Jameson. The telegram conveying them was the first message to get through after the line was restored, and reached Mafeking about 1 o'clock on Monday. In less than an hour Newton sent off Sergeant White with letters to Jameson, Willoughby and three of the Bechuanaland Police officers – as many as could be written in the time. The sergeant was given the best horse in camp and told to use every endeavour to overtake the column, which had already had nearly twenty hours start. Shortly after crossing the border he fell in with a party of armed Boers who took him to the Landdrost of Malmani. There he was detained about four hours while his papers were examined. Ultimately he was allowed to proceed in charge of Field-Cornet Louw, a burgher official, who,

---

[1] Blue Book C 8063, Part II., No. 13.

however, after accompanying him through the night, found he could not stay the course, and gave him back the package containing the despatches. White then went on alone, and at 11 a.m. on Tuesday morning, 10 miles beyond the Eland River, or about eighty from Mafeking, he came up with the column, as described in a former chapter. On his return journey, with a verbal message from Willoughby, he met further parties of Boers following the invaders, but was not interfered with, and eventually reached Mafeking, having accomplished the double journey of 160 miles in fifty-two hours on one horse.[1]

Jameson's telegram announcing his intention to advance was received on Sunday evening by Napier and Spreckley, the two senior officers of the Rhodesia Horse, who were holding themselves ready at Bulawayo to move with their corps in support as soon as they received the signal. By the following morning the news had been broadcast and created wild excitement. 'The Doctor's' popularity in Rhodesia was unbounded, and his old pioneers were ready to follow him to a man. They were not concerned with the rights or wrongs of the case; in fact, they knew nothing of the reasons for the incursion beyond what they learnt at a mass meeting held on the market square on Monday morning, when Jameson's telegram was read. All that they grasped was that their old leader in previous hazardous expeditions was engaged in a crusade of some kind to help their fellow-countrymen on the Rand, and was said to need them. Napier asked for a thousand volunteers, and it was resolved with enthusiasm that the Rhodesia Horse should at once be made up to that number, and should

---

[1] Blue Book C 8063, Part II., No. 12, enclosure. Evidence of Sergeant White at Jameson's trial, 22nd July, 1896.

proceed to the Transvaal via Mafeking. The great distance to be travelled and the difficulties of transport in the rainy season were forgotten or ignored, as was also the fact that it would be impossible to provide horses and other equipment for so large a number. Names were freely handed in and there was eager competition to join the force.[1]

As soon as Kruger heard, through Press telegrams, of this new threat he reported it by a direct cablegram to Chamberlain, and asked for the co-operation of Her Majesty's Government in repelling it. The fact that Bulawayo was taking a hand seemed to him conclusive evidence that the whole conspiracy was being engineered by the Chartered Company, and Chamberlain was disposed to take the same view. He summoned the Directors to meet him, and ordered them to issue peremptory instructions to stop the intended use of their troops and ordnance.[2] He also enjoined Robinson to send up an Imperial officer to meet the force and turn it back, and to call upon Rhodes to restrain his Bulawayo hotheads. But Rhodes had anticipated these orders. One of the few decided actions he took in those days of indecision was to telegraph to Spreckley on 1st January sternly prohibiting any movement of the volunteer forces.[3]

Harris, on the other hand, seems to have had some idea of keeping the movement in Bulawayo alive by encouraging the people there to think that Jameson was succeeding. On the same day, without Rhodes's knowledge, he repeated to Spreckley by telegraph a

---

[1] The excitement was confined to Bulawayo and the neighbourhood. In Mashonaland, owing to a temporary breakdown of the telegraphic service caused by the heavy rains, nothing was known of the Raid until it was all over.

[2] Blue Book C 7933, No. 31.   [3] Cape Report, p. 289.

rumour from Johannesburg that Jameson had had a fight and won, adding:

> 'I believe he is now safe with his friends in Johannesburg. You may be quite sure that no one who knows him will leave him, even with fifty proclamations against him.'[1]

In fact, throughout those anxious days Harris kept up a pretence that all was going well. To Miss Shaw he telegraphed on the 30th December:

> 'We are confident of success. Johannesburg united and strong on our side. Dissensions have been stopped except two or three Germans.'[2]

And as late as 2nd January, when Jameson had actually surrendered – though he can hardly have known it – he kept up the farce – this time in a message to Napier:

> 'Latest news dated two-thirty to-day, Johannesburg, is that heavy hostilities going on just outside the town. Jameson steadily pushing his way in. That is latest news this afternoon, and is authentic....'[3]

Immediately afterwards came the announcement of Jameson's surrender with his whole force, which effectively damped down any smouldering impulse to rush to his assistance and changed the impetuosity of the Rhodesians into a feeling of blank dismay. They saw too clearly that any demonstration on their part would increase the danger of reprisals on the prisoners, and they could only gnash their teeth in impotent rage.

[1] Select Committee, Rhodes, 422.
[2] Select Committee, Appendix 16, No. 1503.
[3] Cape Report, Appendix, p. ccxlvii.

The above efforts, it may be added with relief, were the last of Harris's acrobatics on the telegraph wire, and he now drops out of the story.

Let us turn to England, where the news of the Raid was not received until the last day of the year, and came upon the public as a thunderclap. Telegraphic communication between Johannesburg and Capetown being interrupted, very few definite details could at first be obtained and, in the absence of precise information, the moderate section of the Press refused to pronounce judgment on Jameson's conduct, although, when the 'letter of invitation' was published, more than one newspaper pointed out how little there was in it to show that the dangers it foreshadowed were imminent, or sufficient to warrant any precipitate steps for relief. The extreme Radical Press was less guarded, and, while taking it for granted that the Raid was inspired by the Chartered Company, and hinting plainly that share manipulations were at the bottom of it, could hardly find words bitter enough to hurl at Jameson himself. The public at large were frankly puzzled, but were generally inclined to regard the venture as a foolish display of quixotism. The publication of Jameson's unfortunate letter to the Commandant of Marico put an unfavourable complexion on his conduct. It was not, after all, it seemed, to succour helpless women and children, but to support a political agitation that he had gone in.

When the report of the surrender came there was a moment of profound gloom, mingled with disgust that British prestige should once more have suffered a blow at the hands of this primitive race of fighting farmers. But immediately afterwards a variety of circumstances began to set up a current of feeling in Jameson's favour. The repudiation of him by the Colonial Secretary, the

High Commissioner and the Chartered Company were more or less understood, but provoked some compassion – a tendency not unusual in our countrymen, always prone to take the part of a man when he is down. This was succeeded by an outburst of indignation when it appeared that the Uitlanders, at whose invitation he had started, for whose cause he had made such a gallant effort, had utterly failed to support him. Indeed one cabled item reported, on the strength of a statement by Sir Jacobus de Wet, that the majority of the Uitlanders disclaimed his action. What did it mean? First they implored his assistance and then they left him in the lurch! The only conclusion was that he had been betrayed, and opinion veered still more strongly in his favour.

The culminating touch was supplied from a most unexpected quarter – Berlin. The Transvaal State Secretary, Dr. Leyds, whose name was quite unknown to the British public, had been in Germany for some weeks – ostensibly undergoing treatment for an affection of the throat, but without doubt using every endeavour to ensure support for Kruger in the event of trouble with the British element of the community at the Rand. It afterwards came out that the German Foreign Office was being carefully, and very intelligently, supplied with information as to the progress of the Uitlander movement by their Consul, Herff, at Pretoria, and that when the crisis arrived he was directed to arrange, with the consent of the Portuguese authorities, for a party from a German cruiser which was at the moment in Delagoa Bay, to land, nominally for the protection of the lives and property of their countrymen at that port, but with further instructions to hold themselves ready to proceed to Pretoria if the necessity arose, to guard the consulate against the insurgents. A second cruiser was at the same time ordered to Delagoa Bay from Zanzibar.¹

On 3rd January, on receiving intelligence of the defeat of the Rhodesian force at Doornkop, the Kaiser despatched the following cablegram to President Kruger:

> 'I express my sincere congratulations that, supported by your people, and without appealing for the help of friendly Powers, you have succeeded by your own energetic action against armed bands which invaded your country as disturbers of the peace, and have thus been enabled to restore peace, and safeguard the independence of the country against attacks from outside.' – William, I.R.

This blazing indiscretion even the Radical Press in England found it hard to condone, for the terms of the message were tantamount to an assertion that the Transvaal was an independent Power, that Germany was her ally, and that if Kruger had asked for help against invasion he, William, would at once have buckled on his 'shining armour' and come. The Transvaal question emerged as an international issue of the first order, for the Kaiser's telegram flouted the Suzerainty of the British Crown.² All the latent anti-Prussian instincts of the public in England were roused, and not only in England, but throughout the Empire. Even Jan Hofmeyr was moved to say to the Press that this sort of bluster would find no sympathetic echo in Afrikander circles. 'Nobody,' he said, 'knows better than His Imperial Majesty that the first German shot fired against England would be followed by a combined French and Russian attack on *das Vaterland*, and by the acquisition

---

¹ Translation of documents presented to the Reichstag, and printed in Appendix 5 of the Report of the Select Committee.
² See Appendix III.

by England of all German Colonies, Damaraland included, which would not be an unmixed evil for the Cape.'[1]

The official reply to the Kaiser's interference was the prompt commissioning of a special service squadron of four cruisers and their complement of destroyers, which assembled at Spithead in readiness to proceed at a moment's notice to sea. The unofficial result was remarkable. The German Emperor proved Jameson's best friend. By a rapid, if illogical, process in the public mind the man who, a day or two before, had been regarded as a troublesome adventurer was raised to the supreme pinnacle of popularity. It was a position which, in modern times, can only be compared with that which General Boulanger attained and held for a short time in France ten years earlier. The leader of the Raid and his officers and men were extolled as martyrs in a righteous cause. Extraordinary demonstrations in their favour occurred at the theatres, the music halls, and even in the streets of London. Had Kruger committed any rash reprisals at that moment he would infallibly have caused an outburst resulting in war, imperilling the existence not merely of his Republic, but of the German colonies in Africa as well.

The Jameson furore led to curious manifestations in unexpected quarters – in some cases ridiculous. Mr. Alfred Austin, who, as Poet Laureate, should have preserved some sort of official dignity, gave to the world a doggerel which, for sheer sloppiness and unreal sentiment, has no equal in the English language. It was entitled *Jameson's Ride*, and this over-long chapter may be closed by quoting the last stanza, as a melancholy example of the depths to which men of education are

[1] Interview reported in *Cape Argus*, 13th Jan., 1896.

capable of sinking when essaying to interpret public emotions:

> I suppose we were wrong, were madmen,
>   Still I think at the Judgment Day,
> When God sifts the good from the bad men,
>   There'll be something more to say.
> We were wrong, but we aren't half sorry,
>   And, as one of the baffled band,
> I would have rather have had that foray
>   Than the crushings of all the Rand.

CHAPTER XXII

Humiliation

ON the 1st January, when the outcome of Jameson's venture was still uncertain, Chamberlain had suggested to Sir Hercules Robinson that he might 'intimate to Kruger his intention of proceeding to Pretoria as peacemaker, and with a view to a reasonable settlement of the Uitlanders' grievances'.[1] Hofmeyr was also in favour of this course, and the Reform Committee besought de Wet to ' demand ' that the High Commissioner should come up in person.[2] On 1st January, therefore, on hearing that Johannesburg had risen in arms, and that a provisional government had been declared, Robinson telegraphed to know whether such a step ' would be agreeable ' to Kruger,[3] and, after some hesitation, a reply came back accepting the offer – not, however, because of the assumption of authority by the Reform Committee, of which the Government professed ignorance,[4] but in order that he might 'assist to prevent further bloodshed', Jameson having defied the order to retire, and having fired on burghers of the Republic. Either Kruger, in accepting, or de Wet, in transmitting the acceptance – the telegram is not clear on the point – advised His Excellency ' for cogent reasons ' to come straight to Pretoria, and to receive no deputations, either there or at Johannesburg, until there had been a personal meeting between himself and the President.[5]

Some weeks earlier it had been understood that if the

---

[1] Blue Book C 7933, No. 24.   [2] Blue Book C 8063, Appendix, No. 58.
[3] Blue Book C 8063, Appendix, No. 45.   [4] Blue Book C 8063, No. 56.
[5] Blue Book C 8063, Appendix, No. 61.

position at the Rand became so critical as to require the High Commissioner's presence he should be accompanied by Rhodes. This was now manifestly out of the question, but he was reluctant to undertake his delicate mission single-handed, and in his extremity turned to Hofmeyr, who, he thought, might exercise a moderating influence on both sides. Hofmeyr saw objections, and when at Charles Leonard's earnest request Robinson repeated the invitation by telegraph from the train on his journey north, he replied in rather a pontifical manner:

'Owing to physical complaint shall go only when supreme necessity arises, which is not yet.'[1]

His refusal is perhaps a matter for regret, for though steeped in Afrikander traditions, Hofmeyr was under no illusions as to the rottenness of the Transvaal system of government, and had no particular regard for Kruger himself. A Dutchman, and an honest one to boot, he was about the only man in Africa who was Kruger's equal in tactical ability, and his presence would have been a safeguard against any attempt to throw dust in the eyes of the British representative. As it was, Robinson had to proceed alone, except for Graham Bower and one or two members of the Secretariat.

The proposal for the visit had been made when Jameson was still on the march, and its declared object was to co-operate in bringing about a peaceful settlement. But Robinson did not start until 2nd January, after the Doornkop surrender, so that Kruger had already scored heavily by capturing the most important piece on the board, and was fully alive to the advantage this gave him. There still remained in Kruger's mind, however,

[1] Blue Book 8063, Appendix, No. 135.

two disquieting thoughts – the fear of a further invasion of Rhodesians from the north, and the probability of an attack from Johannesburg, where, he was led to believe, the Reform Committee could put into the field 20,000 armed men. At an early stage he had received an offer of help from the Government of the sister republic of the Orange Free State, where mobilisation orders had immediately been issued to the burghers. At Bloemfontein, during his journey, Robinson received in his special train a deputation of Free-Staters, who expressed uneasiness at the reports of further invasions from Rhodesia. On this point he gave them satisfactory assurances, which he repeated by wire to Kruger, so that by the time he reached Pretoria the latter had only one big anxiety – the possibility of an appeal to arms by Johannesburg.

The only other incident of the journey that need be mentioned was that Robinson received by telegraph from Rhodes a renewed offer of resignation, on the ground that the position of affairs was so strained that he could not continue in office. This time the offer was accepted.[1]

Robinson's only knowledge of the Doornkop capitulation was that derived from two telegrams received by him from de Wet just before starting. The purport of these was that the surrender was *unconditional*.[2] Presumably this is what de Wet had been informed by the Transvaal authorities, and he does not seem to have taken the trouble to make any further enquiries. Sir Hercules also accepted the information, and remained under a false impression on the subject during the whole of his visit. Indeed, in reporting to Chamberlain on the 20th January

[1] Blue Book C 7933, No. 81.
[2] Blue Book C 8063, Appendix, Nos. 81, 83.

– some days after his return – he treated it as an established fact. 'Dr. Jameson's force', he wrote, 'surrendered unconditionally to Boer commando near Krugersdorp on 2nd January.'[1] He was therefore seriously handicapped in his negotiations with the President. And in other respects he was no match for him. The two men were both seventy years of age, Robinson being the senior by a few months, but whereas one had had to fight his own way in the world by his wits, and had attained his present position by a combination of patriotism and tenacity of purpose, the other had throughout his career moved along the precise grooves of the British Public Service, and, for all his experience, he was not much more than a superior type of well-trained administrator.

Kruger's character was rugged and patriarchal. Out of his narrow *Dopper* creed he had evolved a fanatical conviction – which he had succeeded in imparting to his people – that he was the special *protégé* of Divine Providence. He was not, as is commonly thought, a hypocrite – no man can be a hypocrite who sincerely believes in himself – nor was there any conscious guile in his political methods, but he had a natural gift for diplomacy, and his intellectual make-up was largely composed of that subtle quality expressed by the untranslatable Dutch word *slim*. His conservatism made him resent all new-comers and all new ideas. It was to secure freedom from the restless and progressive interference of the British that his parents and the other *Voortrekkers* had fled, sixty years earlier, from Cape Colony, and if he could have had his way he would have placed a barrier across South Africa which should shut out for ever all intruders on the national privacy

[1] Blue Book C 8063, Part II., No. 13.

PAUL KRUGER

(face p. 244)

which they had at first secured. The spectre that now haunted him was not the further shedding of blood, to which he so constantly referred – his own past had been too turbulent for that to disquiet him – but his certainty of designs against the hard-won independence of the Republic. It was not perhaps an unnatural obsession, though it made him all the more intransigent and difficult to deal with.

Sir Hercules Robinson approached the conference in a wholly different spirit – the spirit of an apologist and a defeatist. His dominant anxiety was at all costs to smooth matters over, and he betrayed it by deprecating any suggestion that he thought might irritate the Boers, and by thrusting into the background all incidents that might have an unpleasant flavour. When Chamberlain hinted at the desirability of sending troops to Mafeking he protested, almost we may gather with tears in his eyes, that it would hamper his negotiations, and implored that he should be allowed a free hand.[1] Although by no means certain that the risk of trouble from Rhodesian quarters was at an end, he again and again insisted that nothing of the sort could occur. In short, so intense was his fear of ruffling the susceptibilities of the Transvaal Government that it made him relegate to a minor place – almost to overlook – the Reformers' case, the oppressions which the Rand community had been suffering for years, and which had led to the whole catastrophe. Apart from this he was a sick man, physically unfit for the strain now imposed upon him, and his only advisers were de Wet, whose letters and telegrams reveal the state of panic he was in, and Sir Sidney Shippard, who, on retiring from Bechuanaland, had accepted some business appointment in

[1] Blue Book C 7933, Nos. 84 and 93.

Johannesburg – not wholly unconnected, it was said, with Rhodes's company – and now offered to put his experience at Robinson's disposal.

Robinson arrived in Pretoria late on Saturday night, and, after interviewing de Wet, but without seeing any member of the Reform Committee, sent a cabled summary to Chamberlain of the situation as it had been represented to him.

On the part of the Government, he said, there appeared a desire to show moderation, but the burghers displayed a tendency to get out of hand and to demand the execution of Jameson. He understood that Kruger would insist on the disarmament of Johannesburg as a condition precedent to negotiations. He went on to state that Kruger's military preparations were complete, whereas Johannesburg could not hold out owing to shortness of water and coal. On the side of the Reformers, he told Chamberlain that they too desired to be moderate, but demanded that Jameson's safety should be guaranteed. They also claimed that the concessions promised on the basis of the manifesto should be assured before they laid down their arms. If these conditions were refused they would elect their own leaders and fight the matter out in their own way. This being the position, he saw great difficulty in avoiding civil war.[1]

We know that Jameson's life was Kruger's trump card, but he was not going to be so foolish as to order or allow him to be shot, for he was fully aware that such an act would have instantly provoked a conflagration throughout South Africa, and would have brought Nemesis on himself and his corrupt Government. It was a clever contrivance therefore to let it be understood that, while he and the Executive were inclined for

---

[1] Blue Book C 7933, No. 80.

clemency, it might be impossible to control the burghers, who, on the least sign of hostility in Johannesburg, would take matters into their own hands, and shoot not only Jameson, but his officers as well.

The first meeting took place next day, the President being supported by the members of the Executive. Kruger at once took a high hand. The fate of Jameson and the other prisoners had not, he said, yet been decided. Grievances could not be discussed till Johannesburg laid down its arms unconditionally. As he had 8,000 burghers collected and ready to attack, and they could not be kept indefinitely on commando, he must have an answer about this within twenty-four hours.

Such was his ultimatum, and it seems to have thrown Robinson completely off his balance. He at once leapt to the conclusion that the lives of Jameson and his comrades in captivity depended on Johannesburg's submission. Without ascertaining what would be Kruger's next move if the disarmament were accomplished, without attempting to stipulate for any conditions, he telegraphed, through de Wet, to the Reform Committee, informing them of the Government's terms and urging their acceptance. It is instructive to contrast Robinson's timidity with the attitude adopted three and a half years later at Bloemfontein by his successor, Sir Alfred Milner, who refused to be brow-beaten by Kruger and warned him in plain language of the inevitable consequences of his outrageous treatment of the Uitlanders.

The twenty-four hours allowed by Kruger, which were due to expire at 4 p.m. on the 7th January, gave the Committee no time for counter-proposals or representations to the High Commissioner, but his telegram aroused the greatest resentment and suspicion among them. Some were for rejecting the terms and making a dash to rescue the prisoners – an insane suggestion, which was soon dropped, as was the idea of an appeal to arms, for the Boer commandos were now in great strength round the town, and Johannesburg, though in possession of a limited quantity of rifles and ammunition, was a huge unwieldy place, with a large non-combatant population and no facilities for defence. It was felt, however, that the ends for which they had been agitating should not be abandoned without a further struggle, and, to quote Fitzpatrick, 'that if a firm stand were taken, such was the justice of the cause of the Uitlanders, that the Government would not be able to refuse definite terms as to what reforms they would introduce, besides assuring the safety of Jameson'.[1]

Late that night, as no reply to his telegram had been received, Robinson, who was determined to leave no stone unturned in his efforts to procure the submission of Johannesburg, decided to send de Wet personally to interview the Committee. A meeting took place on Tuesday morning, at which the British Agent read the following amazing instructions which had been telegraphed to him by Robinson, and had reached him on the train :

> 'You should inform the Johannesburg people that I consider that if they lay down their arms they will be acting loyally and honourably, and that if they do not comply with my request they will forfeit all claim to sympathy from Her Majesty's Government, and from British subjects throughout the world, as the lives of Jameson and the prisoners are now practically in their hands.'[2]

Questioned as to the redress of their grievances, which

---
[1] *The Transvaal From Within*, p. 163.
[2] Blue Book C 8063, Appendix, No. 208.

had been the subject of the agreement made with Judge Kotzé's commission on New Year's Day, de Wet assured them that they would be safe in putting themselves unreservedly in the hands of the High Commissioner. He scouted the suggestion that the Government contemplated any such treachery as first to disarm them and then to make reprisals on the leaders. ' Not a hair of the head of any man in Johannesburg will be touched ' – ' Not one of you will lose his liberty for a single hour ' – were among the asseverations he is said to have made in reply to various doubting enquirers.[1]

In the end the Committee gave way. They felt that all considerations must be subordinated to the jeopardous situation of Jameson and his fellow-captives. There was thus no alternative but to comply with the High Commissioner's advice, and they passed a resolution agreeing to lay down their arms, coupling it with a statement that their decision was prompted ' by a paramount desire to do everything possible to ensure the safety of Jameson and his men, to advance the amicable discussion of terms of settlement with the Government and to support the High Commissioner in his efforts in this respect '.[2]

It was all very well for the Committee to pass this resolution, but it was quite another matter to bring about the actual surrender of the arms which had been distributed. Outside the Goldfields offices there had collected a seething mass of several thousand people who had got wind that de Wet had arrived with the Government's decision as to the prisoners. They were fiercely impatient to hear the result. Their cheers for Jameson and boos and groans for Kruger reached the Committee-room, and told those within plainly that they were in a highly explosive mood. At the earnest request of the

---

[1] *The Transvaal From Within*, p. 164.   [2] Blue Book C 7933, No. 98.

Committee de Wet consented to address the excited crowd from the veranda of the Rand Club, not far away, where he was accompanied by Sir Sidney Shippard, and a few of the Committee, including Hamilton, the *Star* editor, and J. W. Leonard. It required a good deal of courage to face the angry mob with proposals which were bound to be unpalatable, and de Wet deserved every credit for undertaking so unpleasant and even dangerous a duty. His speech, extracts from which, taken from the Press reports, are given below, was a strong appeal to the emotions, and although interrupted by protests and dissent it served his purpose of impressing upon them the dismal alternative of surrendering their arms or surrendering Jameson to a firing-party.

' I beg you ', he said, ' to use your judgment, and not to allow your English blood, your English courage, or English valour to violate your judgment. . . . I ask you to listen and abide by the appeal I am about to make to you . . . and for the sake of humanity to sacrifice your personal feelings. First of all I have to announce to you officially that Dr. Jameson and his brave little band, misguided though they may have been – but brave they were (*loud cheers*) – a terrible mistake has been undoubtedly committed by Dr. Jameson which has placed all of you in a most awkward and painful position (*some uproar*). It has also placed Her Majesty's Government in a most painful position. I rejoice, however, to be able to announce that Dr. Jameson and his men will be honourably handed over to Her Majesty's Government to be dealt with at their discretion. But before that can be done you men of Johannesburg must lay down your arms. (*Loud cries of* " Never ! " *and* " Who to ? "). . . . I am speaking with the High Commissioner's full consent. . . . His wish, his appeal to you is to set aside your national sentiments, the national feelings by which you are inspired, and which run high at the present moment. Put these aside, and lay down your arms. . . . Let me tell you as sensible men, as a man who has myself been in war, and has grown old in the service of the country, that it is absolutely impossible for you to hold your position against the forces opposed to you. With all your valour, with all your determination, with all your pluck, you will have to die; and what is the good of dying? Why should you sacrifice your lives? If you don't care for your own lives – and brave men do not care for their own lives – consider the lives of the women and children (*cheers*), of many innocent people who have nothing in the world to do with this movement; consider the condition of this town – that it may be in ashes if you persevere in your course. (*Signs of dissent*.) . . . Are you, as men, as fathers, as Christians, most of you, as men who have been brought up in a civilised country, to sacrifice the lives of women and children? (*Uproar, and a voice,* " *We are going to defend them.*") You may also sacrifice the life of your countryman, that brave man who came through here at the request of some men in Johannesburg, and who has fought so bravely. If you will listen to me you will save his life – he will be handed over, according to the usage of civilised nations, to Her Majesty's Government to be dealt with. If you do not listen to me you don't know what the consequences may be. If this place is shelled (*a voice,* " *Don't frighten us !* ") – if the cannon play on every house in the town, what is to become of the hundreds and thousands of unfortunate women and children? (*A voice,* "*What are the conditions if we lay down arms ?* ") As the representative of the Queen I beseech you as British subjects to consider the serious position in which you are placed. In this terrible crisis I have found the Government disposed to be lenient. (*A voice*, "*We shall have to take it now.*")'

A telling speech, no doubt, but somehow – it does not seem to ring quite true!

Shippard also spoke, and, though constantly interrupted, made his points.

'The High Commissioner', he said, 'has come up determined to do his very best to secure your rights by every constitutional means, and he told me himself that the very first condition that would enable him to do so would be the laying down of arms. If that is done I have every reason to believe that not only will the lives of Jameson and his men be safe, but also the welfare of those concerned in this movement – I mean the leaders. ... I, whose heart and soul are with you, beg you to go home to your ordinary avocations, deliver up your arms to your High Commissioner, and you will have no occasion to repent it.'

After this there was nothing for it but to swallow the bitter pill. Sullen, baffled, doped with words, and with no further thought of resistance, the crowd melted away. Kruger's terms had been jockeyed through.

During the following day the process of collecting the arms was carried on vigorously, the Government sending three commissioners to take delivery at the Reform Committee's office. By Wednesday afternoon nearly 1,900 rifles (all but 500 of the total issued), the maxim guns (three in number) and the stores of ammunition had been handed in and the enrolled men had been paid off and disbanded, with the exception of a few retained to keep order in the town till the Government resumed control. In spite of the Committee's assurances, and of the facilities given by them for searching in suspected quarters, the Boer commissioners could not believe that the rifles collected were more than a fraction of the whole in their possession. They had expected to find 20,000, and it was only with extreme difficulty that they were convinced that a large number were not still being hidden. They also thought there were field-guns. Robinson attributed these delusions to 'the previous boasting of the Uitlanders, who had stated publicly that they had 20,000 rifles and a large number of cannon',[1] but the only evidence he produced of this was contained in certain affidavits by Boer officials and others which were mutually contradictory, and in other respects patently untrustworthy. A person called Malan, for instance, testified that J. W. Leonard and Abe Bailey told him *before* and after the Raid that they had 30,000 rifles, and that Lionel Phillips, when travelling to Pretoria to meet the Government Commission, had made out that there were 45,000. He also said that he had seen between 3,000 and 4,000 armed men assembled in Johannesburg during the crisis. Another swore that he had seen a cannon ten feet long in Commissioner Street ![2]

On 9th January Kruger played his next card. Under the pretext that a final time-limit must be fixed for the completion of the disarmament he issued a proclamation stating that those who by 6 p.m. on the following day had surrendered their rifles and ammunition should be exempt from prosecution and pardoned for all that had occurred in Johannesburg, '*with the exception of all persons and bodies that may appear to be the principal criminals, leaders, instigators or perpetrators of the troubles*'.[3] On the

---

[1] Blue Book C 8063, No. 13, para. 31.
[2] Blue Book C 8063, Appendix, No. 317.
[3] Blue Book C 8063, Appendix, 290.

same evening, when the ink on this document was hardly dry, warrants were issued for the apprehension of those persons whose names were on the list of the Reform Committee so conveniently obtained from Phillips's deputation. About half of them were pounced on at once and detained in the lock-up at Johannesburg. The remainder were arrested during the night and early next morning. The whole of the Committee – 64 in number – were put on the train and taken to the gaol at Pretoria.

In this same gaol Jameson and his officers and men had been lying for over a week. It was now inconveniently over-crowded, and the Government were forced to consider how to deal with the Raiders, whom they had consented to hand over to the Imperial authorities. But they were loth to part with them too easily, and, like a cat playing with a mouse, Kruger began to haggle with the High Commissioner as to the conditions to be observed in regard to their surrender. He had found out that Robinson could be bullied, and in two hectoring letters he formulated his terms.

Jameson and the members of his force would have to be conveyed from Pretoria to England without any demonstration.

They would be taken as prisoners to Durban, and on a British man-of-war to England, and there they would have to be tried and punished.

The sub-officers (N.C.O.s) and men would be sent off first, and Jameson and the officers would follow.[1]

Almost in the same breath Kruger suggested that the time had come for Robinson to take his leave, tempering the hint by a polite intimation that ' the Council placed a high value on a personal meeting for farewell '.[2]

[1] Blue Book C 8063, No. 315. [2] Blue Book C 8063, No. 342.

When Robinson demurred at the ridiculous demand that the rank and file should be tried, Kruger replied that in that case the whole question of their surrender would have to be reconsidered.[1] In this quandary the High Commissioner cabled to Chamberlain for guidance. Within a few hours he had an answer, and it is a pity that he did not take it straight to Kruger, who might have realised, earlier than he eventually did, that Chamberlain was not a man to be trifled with, for his answer, given below, did not mince matters:

'11th January. Astonished that Council should hesitate to fulfil the engagement which we understood was made by President with you, and confirmed by Queen, on the faith of which you secured disarmament of Johannesburg. Any delay will produce worst impression here, and may lead to serious consequences. I have already promised that all leaders shall be brought to trial immediately, but it would be absurd to try the rank and file, who only obeyed orders which they could not refuse. If desired, we may, however, engage to bring to England all who are not domiciled in South Africa; but we cannot undertake to bring all the rank and file to trial, for that would make a farce of the whole proceedings and is contrary to the practice of all civilised Governments. As regards a pledge that they shall be punished, the President will see, on consideration, although a Government can order a prosecution it cannot in any free country compel a conviction. You may remind him that the murderers of Major Elliott, who were tried in the Transvaal in 1881, were acquitted by the jury of

[1] Blue Book C 7933, Nos. 125 and 129.

burghers. Compare also the treatment by us of Stellaland and other freebooters.'[1]

Robinson toned this down into a polite official despatch – omitting the stings at the end – and was relieved when Kruger, who really wanted to get rid of the responsibility of detaining the prisoners, allowed himself to be convinced.[2]

The Raiders had now been confined in Pretoria Gaol for a fortnight, and during that time were strictly debarred from receiving visitors or letters, or holding any communication with the outer world. Their food was coarse and their quarters verminous, but they seem to have been treated with rough consideration by their gaolers. Indeed, except for a short demonstration on their first arrival in Pretoria, there was at no time any display of rancour against the Doornkop prisoners, whose filibustering exploit had several parallels in the history of the Boers themselves, and may even have aroused some admiration. They reserved their bitterness for the Reform leaders, whose presence as plotters in their midst seemed to them far more odious than a raid from outside.

[1] Blue Book C 7933, No. 132. The murder of Major Elliott took place shortly after the Bronkhorst Spruit massacre, which was the opening incident of the Boer War of 1880-1. Elliott, the Paymaster of the 94th Regiment, and another officer – the only two left unwounded – were made prisoners, but were offered liberty on promising to leave the Transvaal for the Free State and to refrain from further participation in the war. They agreed and were escorted to the Vaal River at a point where there was no ford. The Boers in charge made them attempt to cross, but the current was so strong that the vehicle in which they were seated was washed back and upset on the Transvaal side. The escort thereupon fired a volley, killing Elliott on the spot. The other was wounded, but managed to swim across. On the conclusion of the war two of the escort were tried at Pretoria by a jury composed of eight Boers and one German, and, although the facts were perfectly clear, were acquitted.

The Stellaland freebooters were a party of Boers who, in 1883, invaded Bechuanaland from the Transvaal and founded a so-called republic. By an arrangement effected by Rhodes in the following year they were allowed, on accepting annexation by Britain, to retain their land-holdings.

[2] Blue Book C 8063, Nos. 354 and 364.

On the 20th January Jameson and thirteen of his officers were handed over to the Governor of Natal (Sir Walter Hely-Hutchinson) at Charlestown, on the border; from there they were conducted under escort to Durban, and placed on the troopship *Victoria*, which left for England on the following day. The remaining prisoners – 26 officers and 399 other ranks – were taken over a few days later and embarked on a mail steamer, specially chartered. Those whose homes were in South Africa were allowed to land at Cape ports, the remainder being conveyed to England. Captains Coventry and Barry, together with nineteen rank and file under treatment for wounds, were left in hospital at Krugersdorp and Pretoria, and, with the exception of Barry, who died of his wounds, were handed over later.[1]

Sir Hercules Robinson took his departure on the 14th, having spent ten days at the Transvaal capital – miserable and anxious days for him, no doubt, and unfortunate for those who had so strongly counted on his mediation. During the whole of his stay he had not visited the Doornkop prisoners or held personal communication with any member of the Reform Committee. The omission to do so was presumably in deference to Kruger's wish, but in view of his instructions from Chamberlain it can only be regarded as a lamentable misconception of his duty.[2]

In the despatch which he afterwards sent to the Colonial Secretary he claimed credit for issuing his proclamation, which had restrained Johannesburg from

---

[1] Blue Books C 7933, No. 209, and 8063, Part II., No. 17.
[2] Robinson's Military Secretary was allowed on two occasions to visit the Doornkop prisoners, to enquire into their health and to obtain information as to the casualties in the field, but before he could get authority to see them he had to undertake not to discuss any other points. Consequently Robinson remained ignorant of the terms of surrender until, on March 2nd, he learnt them from Chamberlain (House of Commons proceedings, 5th March).

giving assistance to Jameson; for procuring the unconditional submission and disarmament of the Reformers; and for bringing about the delivery of Jameson and his following to the British authorities. He also said that he had deemed the occasion inopportune for urging any redress of the Uitlanders' political grievances.[1]

Poor Sir Hercules! His age and his state of health must be remembered. The burden which he was suddenly called upon to bear was heavy enough to break the back of all but one man in thousands. He did not happen to be that one. His mission was a triumph for Kruger, who engineered it entirely to his own advantage. He left behind him a jubilant Dutch community and an embittered British one. He succeeded in bringing about a superficial peace, but he had only damped down the fires. In a short time they blazed up more fiercely than ever.

He arrived in Capetown on the 16th January. Rhodes, having heard of all that had taken place, had sailed for England the day before.

[1] Blue Book C 8063, Part II., No. 13.

CHAPTER XXIII

Kruger's Magnanimity

APART from minor proceedings against individuals, such as the prosecution of Mr. Gardner Williams, the General Manager of De Beers, and of Mr. H. H. Rutherfoord, the Chartered Company's forwarding agent at Capetown, on charges connected with the smuggling of firearms, there were four official investigations into events connected with the Raid – two criminal and two political. Some account of all of these will be attempted in the next two chapters.

First came the trial at Pretoria of the sixty-four members of the Reform Committee for treason, beginning with a preliminary examination before a judicial commissioner on 3rd February, and closing with their conviction by the High Court on 28th April, 1896.

The proceedings against Jameson and his senior officers in London started at Bow Street on 25th February and resulted, after a ' Trial at Bar ', in the conviction of six of them on 28th July.

At the end of May an investigation was opened by a Select Committee appointed by the Cape House of Assembly, which issued its report in the following July.

Finally there was the enquiry by the Select Committee of the House of Commons, which, though appointed in August 1896, did not conclude its work till July 1897.

The overlapping of the first three led to some confusion and embarrassment. The Cape Committee was prevented from hearing important witnesses who were attending Jameson's trial, and the simultaneous holding, at different places, of three separate enquiries was prejudicial to an impartial survey of the facts by any one of them. The House of Commons Committee was the only tribunal which was able to take evidence from Rhodes, Jameson, members of the Reform Committee and the principal officials concerned, and to weigh their statements side by side.

Outstanding points from the evidence given at all except the Pretoria trial have already been quoted, and it is not proposed to do any more than supply a general description of the circumstances under which they were held and to note some peculiar features in each case.

To start, then, with the Reformers, who were, without exception, men of education and high business standing – many of them wealthy, and all accustomed to the refinements of comfortable homes. A number were managers and directors of mining companies; others professional men – the principal lawyers and doctors in Johannesburg were among them; three were retired British officers; one was the editor of the leading newspaper on the Rand. There were also half a dozen Americans, including Captain Mein, who was manager of one of the biggest mines – the 'Robinson'. Finally there were Phillips, Rhodes, Hammond and Farrar, the heads of the mining industry, and Fitzpatrick, also a prominent mining man, and the Secretary of the Reform Committee. The only absentees were Charles Leonard, against whom a warrant had been issued, but who was still in Capetown, and Dr. Wolff, who had managed somehow or other to slip away.

They were arrested, as already stated, on the 9th and 10th of January, and escorted in two batches to Pretoria. The first arrived at night time, but the second was marched through the streets from the railway station by daylight, and had to run the gauntlet of a disorderly mob, hustling them, hurling foul insults at them, and even spitting on them as they passed. One of the prisoners, the above-mentioned Captain Mein, an elderly man, was knocked down and kicked by a bystander, and was with difficulty rescued by his companions from further violence. They were all eventually lodged in the common gaol, searched, and crowded into cells usually tenanted by natives and felons of the lowest character.

The four principal accused were from the outset placed on a different footing from the others, and were thrust into one cell, windowless, and not more than twelve feet square, and here for the first three nights they were locked up for twelve or thirteen hours at a stretch.[1] Their sufferings in the summer heat of Pretoria, where the temperature frequently rises above 100 degrees in the shade, were appalling, especially in the case of Hammond, who was in bad health. But the others were no better off. The cells, to each of which four or five were allotted, were even smaller – 6 feet by 10, swarming with vermin and devoid of any furniture, unless dirty straw palliasses, previously used by kaffirs, could be so regarded. In these horrible quarters they were confined for nearly a fortnight. Their head gaoler was an unfeeling bully, but by the aid of his more kindly assistant and the efforts of friends outside they were gradually able to get a few necessaries, such as bedding and decent food, smuggled in, and to obtain changes of clothing and linen. Nothing, however, could be done to improve the disgusting sanitary arrangements, or to get rid of the bugs and other vermin with which the whole building was infested.

For a few days Jameson and a number of his officers and men were there too, but were kept apart, chalked

[1] *Some South African Recollections*, by Florence Phillips, p. 111.

lines being marked out in the exercise yard to prevent any mingling of the two parties, and although opportunities could no doubt have been found for communication there was no desire to seek them. On the day after Jameson's departure the majority of the accused were released on heavy bail, but the four leaders, with Fitzpatrick, were kept in close confinement till after the preliminary examination opened. They were then allowed to remove to a cottage on the outskirts of the town, where, although strictly guarded, they were granted several privileges – a daily bicycle-ride under escort, the right to purchase their own food and to have their personal servants, and to receive, and even to entertain, as many visitors as they liked.

None of the Reformers knew at first what evidence was to be produced against them, and they were staggered later when they heard of the mass of compromising documents which the Transvaal authorities had discovered in White's despatch-box, among them the certified copy of the 'letter of invitation', the very existence of which was unsuspected by many of them.

On February 8th they were brought up for preliminary examination. Space will not permit a detailed description of the proceedings, but they were marked by an utter disregard of the ordinary rules of evidence, and by incidents which showed them that the Government were resolved to resort to every device – including the intimidation of witnesses – to make sure of their conviction.

The trial was fixed for 27th April, and before that date arrived significant preparations – official and otherwise – were made for the occasion. One was the importation, especially to try the case, of Mr. Gregorowski, the State Attorney of the Orange Free State. Of the five regular

KRUGER'S MAGNANIMITY   263

Transvaal judges two had been members of the Commission which had made terms with the Reformers, and the other three were held to be unsuitable for various reasons. The introduction of an outsider was justified by the Government on the ground that it would ensure impartiality. As his name indicates, Mr. Gregorowski was certainly no Boer; but he had a reputation for extreme severity and pronounced anti-British sentiments. Unpleasant stories gained currency pointing to his having made up his mind beforehand. On arrival in Pretoria, for instance, one of his first actions was to beg the loan of a black cap from one of the other judges, and this before he had heard or read a word of the evidence.[1]

Another ominous incident – so generally vouched for as to be beyond dispute – was the private purchase in Cape Colony by one of the Transvaal commandants of the identical beam upon which a number of Boer rebels had been hung, eighty years before, at Slagter's Nek by the British authorities, and its conveyance to Pretoria.[2]

The indictment against the Reformers was contained in four counts. Briefly they were charged, first, with agreeing with Jameson for a hostile invasion; secondly, with supporting him after he had started and inciting the people of Johannesburg to assist him; thirdly, with issuing arms and taking other hostile measures for the object of undermining the Government; and lastly with

[1] *The Transvaal From Within*, p. 182. *South African Recollections* (Mrs. Phillips), p. 142.

[2] The episode of Slagter's Nek is well known in South Africa. The sentence of death was unquestionably a harsh one, and its public execution was marked by a shocking accident. The rebels – five in number – were at first hung together, when the scaffold broke under their united weight. They were partially strangled, but recovered sufficiently to beg for mercy amid the cries and sobs of their friends. The scaffold, however, was repaired and they were then put to death one by one. The tragedy was never forgotten by the Boers, and many oaths were taken to avenge it.

assuming the functions of government, forming their own police, and investing ex-detective Trimble with judicial powers. Shortly before the trial a compromise was arrived at between the lawyer defending the accused and the State Attorney – the latter undertaking that if the four leaders would plead guilty to the first charge and the remaining sixty to the third and fourth he would not press for exemplary punishment. The disclosure of the documents found in the despatch-box had put the leaders in a very critical position, but, in spite of their experience that arrangements made with Transvaal officials were unsound planks to rest on, they generously accepted the proposal, in the hope and expectation that the minor offenders would be let off with a moderate fine. There were, moreover, certain advantages to all in avoiding a long trial with separate defences in individual cases. No honest defence could be made without impeaching the Government, and the dice were already so heavily loaded against the accused that it was deemed impolitic to adopt any course that might aggravate the official hostility to them. There was also the possibility of damaging facts being elicited against Jameson, whose ordeal was yet to come.

The trial opened on Friday, 27th April, in the Market Hall of Pretoria, which was packed to overflowing with burghers, Government officials and their womenfolk, and the friends and relatives of the accused men. They pleaded guilty, as arranged, and the State Attorney put in the various incriminating documents and formally asked for conviction. On behalf of the four leaders their Counsel, Mr. Wessels, a distinguished Cambridge scholar and a member of the Inner Temple, read, on the resumption of the trial on Monday, a long statement the pith of which was contained in the last clause :

'We admit responsibility for the action taken by us. We frankly avowed it at the time of the negotiations with the Government, when we were informed that the services of the High Commissioner had been accepted with a view to a peaceful settlement. We submit that we kept faith in every detail in the arrangement with the Government, that we did all that was humanly possible to protect the State and Dr. Jameson from the consequences of his action, that we have committed no breach of the law which was not known to the Government at the time, and that " the earnest consideration of your grievances " was promised. We can now only lay the bare facts before the Court, and submit to the judgment that may be passed upon us.'

Mr. Wessels then delivered an eloquent address in mitigation of sentence, and sat down in the belief that all was over except for the judge's summing up.

To everybody's surprise the State Attorney immediately claimed, and was allowed, the right to make a further speech, in which he completely forsook the moderate attitude he had promised to adopt. His language was of the most violent nature. He demanded that the death penalty prescribed by the old Roman-Dutch laws should be inflicted on the four principals, and that their property should be confiscated. He strode up and down the court, shouting and brandishing his arms in a state of uncontrollable excitement. The accused men had little knowledge of Dutch, but they comprehended all too well the words *Hangen bij den nek*, which he repeated over and over again, and which told them that once more they had been betrayed by Boer duplicity.

Judgment was deferred until the following day (Tuesday, 28th April), when it was seen that the courthouse was surrounded by a large body of police and mounted burghers; that an immense crowd filled the square in front, and that inside a separate dock had been provided for the four leaders, who were ceremoniously ushered into it. As the judge at great length reviewed the law and the evidence it became manifest to all present that the worst anticipations were to be realised. At the conclusion of his speech the usual formalities were gone through; Gregorowski put on his borrowed black cap, and sentenced Lionel Phillips, Frank Rhodes, George Farrar and John Hays Hammond to death.

The interpreter broke down as he repeated the terms of the sentence in English, and the effect in court was overpowering. All women had previously been ordered out of the building, but strong men lost their self-control and wept, while one spectator fell down in a fit. The most impassive persons were the four, who, whatever their thoughts may have been, allowed no sign of distress to escape them. Someone shouted out a word or two of encouragement to them; whereat Frank Rhodes turned, and, catching his eye, slowly and deliberately winked – not a piece of bravado this, but just a characteristic effort to put heart into a friend.

The other accused were sentenced to two years' imprisonment and a fine of £2,000 in each case. They were taken back to the filthy gaol, and as they were being marched away Dr. Leyds, the Hollander State Secretary who had returned shortly before from his trip to Berlin, stood on the steps of the Government buildings and watched them pass with a smile of malevolent gratification.

The news of the sentences created a wave of horror

and passionate resentment throughout South Africa, and whatever the original intentions of the President may have been he must have learnt from the widespread indignation that he could never dare to carry out the extreme penalty. He decided to make a virtue of necessity, but forfeited any claim to magnanimity by letting his mercy fall, like the gentle rain from heaven, in drops. On the day following the conviction it was announced that the death sentence would be commuted, though it was not for some weeks that any disclosure was made as to what punishment would be substituted. Great pressure was then brought to bear on the remaining prisoners to admit their guilt and humbly supplicate for mitigation, and, repugnant as such a course was, they were in the long run induced by threats and terrorism to comply with the demand in all but two cases. Before this, however, one of them, unnerved by the mental agony he had gone through, cut his throat.

On 19th May the Executive proclaimed, as an act of clemency, that the sentences of imprisonment would be reduced to varying terms ranging from twelve to three months, while eight were released at once on payment of their fines. The four principal offenders were to be imprisoned for fifteen years – fifteen years in that awful gaol! In the meantime organised efforts were being made throughout South Africa to procure the release of all. Meetings were held, and petitions framed in the principal towns of Cape Colony, Natal and Rhodesia, urging upon Kruger a spirit of generosity and amnesty. Finally, on the 9th of June a deputation of fifty Mayors and other representatives started for Pretoria to interview the President in person. Kruger then began to see that his 'magnanimity' would have to be accelerated. He hurriedly announced that the whole of the prisoners would be set free upon payment of their original fines and signing an undertaking to abstain from political agitation, and that in the case of Phillips, Rhodes, Farrar and Hammond the fines would be £25,000 each. The two who had declined to petition the Government – Messrs. Sampson[1] and W. D. Davis – were excluded from this remission, and as they persisted in their refusal they were compelled to endure the torture of existence in Pretoria gaol until the following year, when they were liberated – nominally as a gracious act of clemency to mark the occasion of Queen Victoria's Diamond Jubilee, but really because they had worn down the patience of the Executive, who found that their continued confinement was a source of irritation to the whole of South Africa, and had become heartily sick of keeping them.

[1] Afterwards Sir Aubrey Wools-Sampson, K.C.B.

CHAPTER XXIV

Regina versus Jameson

THE troopship *Victoria*, bearing Jameson and thirteen of his officers, arrived on Monday evening, the 24th February, at Gravesend, where they were arrested by Scotland Yard officials, and driven in omnibuses direct to Bow Street police court. A large gathering of curious people, including many well known in society, had been waiting there since three o'clock, and when the Raiders entered the court they were greeted by a frantic burst of cheering, which the presiding magistrate was quite unable to check. Formal evidence was taken and they were remanded on substantial bail, but they had some difficulty in getting away through the enthusiastic admirers who thronged the approaches to the building. They were brought up on seven subsequent occasions, and ultimately, on the 15th June, six – Jameson, Willoughby, Grey, Coventry (who had arrived by a later steamer) and the two Whites – were committed for trial, the remaining nine being discharged.[1] At the close of these preliminary proceedings Jameson's Counsel, Sir Edward Clarke, stated that he had been instructed by his client to say that he alone was responsible for all that had happened, and that the remaining defendants had acted under his direction in loyal obedience to his orders. He therefore hoped that further

[1] The nine discharged were Majors Stracey and Villiers, Captains Kincaid-Smith, Foley, Munro, Lindsell, Holden and Gosling and Lieutenant Grenfell. It may be mentioned that the *Harlech Castle*, carrying the remaining members of the force, arrived at Plymouth the day before Jameson, and, after being kept for some weeks at the expense of the Chartered Company, they were shipped back in detachments to South Africa, where they arrived in time to join a column organised by Colonel Plumer, for the relief of the Rhodesian settlers, who were being hard pressed by the rebel Matabele.

discharges would be sanctioned by the legal advisers to the Crown. But the appeal met with no response. Later, at the instance of the Attorney-General, an order was made for the final proceedings to take the form of a ' Trial at Bar ', a procedure rarely used and reserved for cases of the highest importance. It involved certain technical peculiarities, one being that the actual hearing would be conducted in the Court of Queen's Bench before a special jury and not less than three judges, each of whom was entitled to deliver a separate opinion.

The case of ' Regina *versus* Jameson and others ' opened on 20th July. The Court was composed of the Lord Chief Justice (Lord Russell of Killowen), Mr. Baron Pollock and Mr. Justice Hawkins. The defendants were charged with contravening the ' Foreign Enlistment Act ' by organising and conducting from the Queen's dominions a military expedition against a friendly State. A distinguished array of Counsel was engaged in the case, the Crown being represented by no less than six, headed by the Attorney-General (Sir Richard Webster), while Sir Edward Clarke, Mr. E. H. Carson (now Lord Carson), Mr. C. F. Gill and Sir Frank Lockwood were among the eight retained for the various defendants. The first day was taken up by a prolonged controversy as to whether the Foreign Enlistment Act was in operation in Mafeking and Pitsani, a tedious and highly technical discussion which had the effect of lowering the public interest in the trial, up to then regarded as a first-class sensation, coming opportunely at the end of the London Season. The hearing of the case occupied, in all, seven days ; a large amount of evidence was given by members of the Bechuanaland Police and Transvaal officials, and most of the correspondence with which we are already familiar was read.

The main line of defence – that there was no hostile intention in the Raid – did not impress the Lord Chief Justice, whose summing-up was strongly against the defendants. The jury, having agreed on the main facts, endeavoured to avoid a direct conviction by putting forward a rider to the effect that provocation had been created by the state of affairs in Johannesburg, but were overruled by Lord Russell, who directed them to find a verdict of guilty.

Jameson, who throughout the proceedings had never opened his mouth, and gave the impression of being a worn-out and thoroughly beaten man, was sentenced to fifteen months' imprisonment without hard labour, Willoughby to ten, Robert White to seven and the other three to five months each.

They were taken to Wormwood Scrubs, and were at first compelled to wear the regulation convicts' dress and to perform various menial duties such as cleaning out their own cells, according to the ordinary prison routine, but even so there was nothing in their punishment to be compared with the vindictive severity of that meted out to the Reformers. As no reflection had been made on their honour by the prosecution or the judges, the Home Secretary a few days later ordered them to be removed to Holloway Gaol and to be treated as first-class misdemeanants. Willoughby, Grey, Coventry and the Whites were compulsorily retired from the Army.[1]

The British public, better educated about the Raid than in the first flush of excitement six months before, were inclined to view the verdict and sentence without emotion. It was recognised that, although no sordid or dishonourable motive had been proved against them,

---

[1] Their commissions were in every case subsequently restored in recognition of outstanding services in other fields of action.

these men by their recklessness had plunged Great Britain into serious international difficulties, and might have involved the country in war. For example's sake they must be punished, and the punishment was not unduly severe. The Press generally took the same line and wagged its head in solemn platitudes. The Continental Press also approved, though both in France and Germany hopes were expressed that Rhodes would be brought to justice. One French paper – *La Liberté* – made the interesting comment that 'the colonial greatness of European peoples consists in successful *coups à la Jameson*'.

After a few weeks' imprisonment Jameson's health grew so bad that he had to undergo a serious operation. It was represented to the authorities that further confinement would gravely endanger his life, and he was released after serving about four months of his sentence.

Of the two Parliamentary enquiries that instituted by the Cape House of Assembly needs no more than a passing glance. It was presided over by the Attorney-General, Sir Thomas Upington, and was composed of seven members, of whom the best known were Rhodes's former colleague, Schreiner, and Mr. John X. Merriman, who at different times had been his colleague and his opponent. The Committee achieved a good deal of dull but useful work in collecting evidence, both documentary and oral, and its report, while acquitting Rhodes of responsibility for the actual Raid, expressed strong condemnation of his conduct in mixing himself up in the intrigues of which it was the outcome. No opportunity occurred of examining any of the principal characters. Rhodes was in Rhodesia, fighting the Matabele, and the others were prisoners, either in London or Pretoria.

The Imperial Government very properly abstained

from setting on foot any official enquiry while criminal trials were pending, but immediately after Jameson's conviction agreed to constitute a Select Committee of the House of Commons to investigate not only the Raid, but the whole of the administration of the Chartered Company, and on 11th August, fifteen members of the House – nine of them Unionists, five Radicals and one Irish Nationalist – were nominated to serve on it. The Unionists included the Attorney-General (Sir Richard Webster), the Chancellor of the Exchequer (Sir Michael Hicks-Beach) and Mr. Chamberlain. Mr. Henry Labouchere, an extreme Radical, who, both from his seat in Parliament and in the columns of his weekly paper *Truth*, had consistently displayed the greatest animus against Rhodes, the Chartered Company and all their works, successfully asserted his claim to membership. Apart from him, there was no one against whom the charge of partisanship could be brought, but, as the enquiry developed, it became obvious that certain members – notably Sir William Vernon Harcourt – were resolved to make use of it to implicate Chamberlain and the Colonial Office, and thereby to bring discredit on the Government. All the serious work of the Committee was deferred till the following year, when sittings took place two or three times a week from February to June.

Frequent extracts have already been given from the voluminous evidence, and no further reference need be made to it, but there were some dramatic moments which may briefly be mentioned. One of these occurred when Chamberlain interposed during the evidence of Rutherfoord Harris and took his seat in the witnesses' chair to deny that the latter had conveyed, directly or by hints, the real purpose of the concentration of police on the Transvaal border. Another incident which broke the serenity of the meetings was the refusal of Mr. Bourchier Hawksley, as solicitor to Rhodes, to produce certain cablegrams 'between London and Capetown, which had been used to support Rhodes's action in South Africa'. These had been seen confidentially by Chamberlain, but Hawksley, pleading professional privilege, declined point-blank to divulge them without Rhodes's consent,[1] and, in spite of dire threats of further action, successfully maintained his contumacy. The effect was to invest these communications with an air of mystery, and to give rise to suspicions that they contained evidence of complicity on the part of Chamberlain or his official subordinates. They have remained buried, and possibly no longer exist, but the suspicion regarding them has never entirely died down.

Rhodes's own evidence extended over six days, during which he was asked more than 2,000 questions. He proved a most embarrassing witness, partly because of a real or affected vagueness on matters of detail, and also because he frequently turned the tables on his interrogators by using their questions as a means of ventilating his own ideas of the political issues in South Africa, and of delivering homilies on the duty of the Government there and in the colonies generally. Neither Sir William Harcourt, a past master in the art of cloaking dangerous insinuations under a bland and innocent guise, nor Labouchere, by his more direct and frontal attacks, was able to entrap Rhodes into any admissions which could weaken the impression that he had acted in a genuine desire to alleviate the burdens under which the British inhabitants of the Transvaal were suffering, and to benefit

[1] This was on the 25th May, by which time Rhodes had returned to South Africa.

South Africa at large. The honesty of his purpose was absolutely transparent, though he never attempted to justify the mistake he had made in his methods.

One other satisfactory result was attained, and as many hard things have been said of Rutherfoord Harris in the course of this story it is pleasant to be able to record that he was the chief means of giving the quietus to a scandalous rumour. It had been freely hinted that certain of the principals – Harris himself, Alfred Beit and Lionel Phillips among others – had engineered the revolutionary scheme in the Transvaal for the sordid object of ' bearing ' large blocks of Chartered and other South African shares, and were members of a secret syndicate formed with that design. Mr. Labouchere was the main propagator of this rumour, and had not only affirmed its truth in a speech in the House of Commons, but, after his appointment as a member of the Select Committee, had repeated it in a more offensive form in a signed letter to a French journal – the *Gaulois*. During his examination of Harris he unwarily put a question which enabled his victim to drag this insinuation into the enquiry, and to claim the protection of the Committee against the slanderer. This caused one of the few breezes that enlivened the proceeding, and Harris had the satisfaction of persuading the Committee to pass a severe censure on Labouchere, who eventually had to eat his words and make an abject apology.[1]

In the end the Select Committee added very little to the general knowledge of the facts, and, in endeavouring to steer clear of the political malice which had become so obvious during their proceedings, and to please everybody so as to secure unanimity, they did not succeed in getting much colour into their report. They evidently

[1] Select Committee, evidence, p. 459.

felt that Jameson had been sufficiently punished, for they did not explicitly reprimand him, but they dealt out mild censure in varying proportions to Rhodes, the Chartered Company and to certain Imperial officers in South Africa (honourably excluding Sir Hercules Robinson, who had just received a peerage). They also entirely acquitted the Colonial Office of any guilty knowledge.

Labouchere, who submitted a report of his own, the extreme shrewdness of which in some respects was marred by the patent vindictiveness of his attitude towards the Chartered Company, found himself in a minority of one.

CHAPTER XXV

The After-Cost

THE first sufferers from the Raid were the Chartered Company and the Rhodesian settlers. The former, regarded two months before as a colonising instrument of supreme value, was now a dangerous beast whose claws must be cut without delay. Within a fortnight of the Raid the whole of its rifles and ordnance were taken possession of by the Imperial authorities, and soon afterwards it was deprived of the control of its military establishments. The citizens of Rhodesia were also suspect, and provision was made for their closer surveillance. The Government decided that an Imperial watch-dog must reside permanently in the territory – a Resident Commissioner, as he was called – to see that no further misbehaviour occurred.

These precautions were in both cases based on illogical assumptions. If the Company were to blame for giving too free a hand to their principal agents on the spot, what about the High Commissioner and even the heads of the Colonial Office, who, up to the end of 1895, were allied in a common purpose of allowing the utmost latitude to Rhodes and his lieutenants? Unfortunately, however, the Raid was closely followed by the native rebellion, which induced a large section of the public and Parliament to a conviction that the Company was incapable of keeping its house in order, and that the white population had been guilty of acts of oppression. This view was reflected in the terms of reference to the Select Committee, which was appointed not merely to enquire ' into the origin and circumstances of the incursion into the South

African Republic', but also 'into the administration of the British South Africa Company, and to report what alterations are desirable in the government of the territories under their control'.

The Committee shirked the latter part of the enquiry, and in the long run it was abandoned. With regard to the former they came to the somewhat ambiguous conclusion that it was the duty of the Board to maintain a due supervision not only in respect of the commercial interests of their company, but also 'in regard to the Imperial relations of the dominion under their control.'[1] On a literal interpretation of these words it would again have been a reasonable retort that the trouble which had occurred was largely due to inefficient supervision by the high officials of the Colonial Office, who were very much in the same position as the gentlemen who formed the Company's Board.

As regards the Rhodesian settlers not one in a thousand had the slightest conception of what was on foot, or took anything more than a passing interest in the Uitlanders and their grievances. Their mistake – if mistake it was – lay in the enthusiastic impulse to rally to Jameson's assistance when they learnt he was riding to the relief of their fellow-countrymen. On the strength of this – there was no other crime that could be laid at their door – they were saddled with the odium of being an irresponsible and dangerous community, and years elapsed before they could entirely shake off this reputation.

In South Africa generally the Raid led to a revival of the racial animosities between the English and Dutch. In spite of such blunders as the rebuff given by the British Government to the Orange Free State, when they sought,

---

[1] Select Committee Report, p. xii.

THE AFTER-COST

in 1858, a union with the Cape Colony, and the annexation and subsequent retrocession of the Transvaal, this feeling had been more or less dormant since the days of the Great Trek, but the events of 1895 gave it a new impetus which is still felt, and which has defied the efforts of such wide-minded men as Botha and Smuts to check it. Had the Uitlanders and the Boers of the Transvaal been allowed to settle their difficulties without outside interference Kruger would have found very little sympathy among the Dutch section of the population in Cape Colony and Natal. Among the champions of the Uitlander cause in Johannesburg were many men of Dutch descent from the two colonies, who were just as much the victims of oppression as the British. The moment it was suspected, however, that a treacherous attempt was to be made to rob the Transvaal Boers of their independence, a fellow-feeling was stirred up among their kith and kin in the south.

Enough has already been said about the stir caused in England by the Raid and the acute tension created by the German Emperor's ill-advised interference. It was the first overt sign which he gave of his jealous hatred of Great Britain, and the beginning of the friction between the two nations which lasted till the Great War.

Far reaching as were the political waves of the Raid, the fortunes of the individuals concerned, with a few notable exceptions, were not permanently or adversely affected. A remarkable number of those mixed up in the plot in South Africa became prominent in politics, or war service, or both, in later years. They cannot all be mentioned here, and no mention is necessary in the case of Sir Lionel Phillips, Sir Abe Bailey, Sir Percy Fitzpatrick and others who are still living, whose eminent public work is well known, and has been recognised by their Sovereign; or of others like Sir George Farrar and Sir Aubrey Wools-Sampson, who played a gallant part for the Empire and have passed from the stage.

Of the four Reform leaders who were sentenced to death, Colonel Frank Rhodes was perhaps the most to be pitied, as having sacrificed his personal interests – purely through loyalty to his younger brother – for a quarrel in which he had no real part. After his trial and sentence he was ordered to resign his commission in the Army – a cruel blow to a man with an honourable record in one of the finest cavalry regiments in the Service; a man who had gained the Distinguished Service Order for his work in the arduous march to the relief of Gordon at Khartoum, and further laurels as one of Sir Gerald Portal's expedition to Uganda. But this punishment and the ordeal of standing in a felon's dock and undergoing sentence of death were probably not so hard for him to bear as the stigma, under which he and his fellow conspirators were compelled by an ill-informed public to rest for some time, of having deserted Jameson. He determined to shake off the experience like a bad dream, and made heroic efforts to live it down. He found some relief by taking part in the repression of the Matabele rebellion, for active service was the breath of his life. A further opportunity came in the Sudanese campaign of 1898, when he accompanied Kitchener's army as special correspondent for *The Times*. He was present at the battle of Atbara, and a few weeks later was wounded in the operations round Omdurman. He had behaved with conspicuous gallantry and was rewarded by reinstatement in the army in his old rank. The Boer War found him once more at the front. He was a prisoner in Ladysmith during the siege, and when that was over became Intelligence Officer to Colonel Mahon in the final dash for the relief of Mafeking. A high tribute was paid to his work in that capacity and he was awarded the C.B. He had retrieved his honour – to those who knew him it was never sullied – but at the cost of his health, for he was no longer a young man. The death of his brother Cecil in 1902 was a blow from which he never properly recovered, and he only survived him by three years.

Mr. John Hays Hammond, another of 'the four', is still a man of innumerable interests. He has spent the later years of his life in his native country, and has devoted himself to scientific and public work. He has also been an outstanding figure in politics, and had the distinction of representing the President of the United States at the coronation of His Majesty King George.

Such were a few of the men who fought the battle of the Uitlanders in the Transvaal. They were not naturally rebels, and their only object was clean government. Had Kruger, instead of mistrusting, spurning and maltreating them, realised that they were providing the life-blood of his country and sought their co-operation, he might have averted the calamity of the war which brought ruin to himself and a heavy burden of misery and suffering to his burghers.

After the failure of the revolution the President was left to outward appearance standing more strongly than ever. It was a golden opportunity for him to embark on a policy of moderate reform. Had he seized it he could, without loss of dignity, have entrenched himself and his Government in an impregnable position, and he would have gone down to history as a wise and patriotic ruler. There was no need for him to be over-generous about the franchise, for although this ultimately became the battle-cry of the Uitlanders, they desired it not so much as an end in itself as a means of removing abuses. By purifying the administration; putting a stop to the iniquitous system of concessions; prohibiting the sale of drink to natives; and permitting the use of the English language in schools he would have disarmed their hostility and might still have kept the balance of voting power in the hands of his own people. But shrewd as he was in some directions, his statecraft was not profound enough to make him grasp this. He was swollen with self-satisfaction at having once more got the better of the *verdomde rooinek*; he failed to see that his success was due, not so much to his own strength as to the mistakes of his antagonists, and his one idea was to exact the uttermost price of victory. Not content with extorting over £200,000 in fines from the Reformers, he put in a claim for £600,000 for material loss against the Chartered Company, to which he added £1,000,000 for 'moral and intellectual damage'. So far from alleviating the position of the Uitlanders, he increased their burdens. The scandal of concessions and monopolies went on unchecked. The heavy duties on foodstuffs remained, and no reduction was effected in the exorbitant railway tariffs. Kruger even attempted to tamper with the independence of the Courts of Justice. In every way he showed that, having got the upper hand of the Uitlanders, he was determined to keep them in the condition of helots. A sinister feature of his policy was the appropriation of the revenue he derived from them towards a colossal expenditure on war-material and fortifications, far in excess, as Fitzpatrick points out, of what could possibly be used by the whole Boer population, and therefore believed to be designed for the use of others outside the Transvaal. The ease with which he had crushed resistance had turned his head, misled him into thinking he could dominate the whole of South Africa, and rendered him incapable of discerning that retribution was waiting for him.

Finally a few words may be said of the effects of the miscarriage of their plans on Jameson and Rhodes.

The sentence of imprisonment was probably the least part of Jameson's punishment. He had to endure the bitter mortification of feeling that by his own hand he had robbed his closest friend, if not irretrievably, at any rate for years to come, of his cherished ambition – the ambition of welding the white races of South Africa into a harmonious whole; the common cause for which he too had been pledged to fight. He had cut himself off from the colony which he had helped to create and had nursed through its infancy; and that at the most critical moment in its existence, for within four months of the Raid the Matabele broke out into open and bloody rebellion. He may even have reproached himself with the idea that the native rising was a direct consequence of his own act in removing the police, as many were eager to assert.[1] Perhaps the most galling thought was that he could not be there to help.

Poignant as these reflections must have been, he kept them to himself, and bore the pain of them without outwardly flinching. He accepted full responsibility and never tried to shuffle the least part of the blame on to others. He was bitter, but his bitterness was not against people, but against his luck – the true gambler's philosophy. 'I know perfectly well', he said, 'that as I did not succeed the natural thing has happened, but I also know that if I had succeeded I should have been forgiven'.[2]

---

[1] Undoubtedly the defeat of the Rhodesian troops and their capture by the Boers injured their prestige in the eyes of the Matabele, who had thought them invincible; but the causes of the outbreak were many and complex, and the removal of two or three hundred police had very little to do with it.

[2] Select Committee, Jameson, 4605.

But no outward acceptance of his fate could mask the fact that for a time he lost heart, and thought the future had nothing in store for him. He did not make a quick recovery from his illness and operation. He was waiting for a sign from Rhodes. Had that not come he would probably have died. For a year the two men had not met nor held any communication, but in January 1897 Rhodes came to England to give evidence before the Select Committee, and when he heard of Jameson's condition he at once went to see him in his nursing-home.

What passed between the two cannot be known, but if there had been doubts before on either side this meeting dissipated them. It revealed to both that their mutual regard was unshaken and intact. If Jameson had thought that his career was ended something must have been said by Rhodes to put new heart into him, for from that moment he began to mend. New motives inspired him. To make atonement to Rhodes – that was his first care, and then perhaps to live down his blunder and take a share once more in Rhodes's work.

The psychological difference between them was very strongly brought out by their first behaviour in their common adversity. They were of the same age, and both were handicapped by bodily ailments (in Rhodes's case constitutional, in Jameson's mainly due to the exposure and hardships of the past few years), but while the mercurial temperament of Jameson had kept him for the time being cowed and spiritless, Rhodes was saved partly by his imagination and partly by his greater stability of character. After his first, short, passionate outburst he had pulled himself together. He had been the greatest sufferer, but he displayed in public the greatest courage. He set forth to prove that he was by no means a beaten man, and he had this advantage – that he was free, and if

CECIL RHODES
From a woodcut by
WILLIAM NICHOLSON

(face p. 284)

his presence was embarrassing in Capetown he was badly needed elsewhere. South African politics might take care of themselves for a while; there were other big things to attend to. Rhodesia was in dire straits and sorely needed a leader. He flung himself heart and soul into the task of suppressing the rebellion, and when he had finished there he had his railway extension, his transcontinental telegraph scheme which was to link Capetown with Cairo, and, at the back of his mind, no doubt, he had begun to evolve the great educational bequest to cement the English-speaking races of the world. All these were distractions, and enabled him partially to recover from the shock of his failure elsewhere. While Jameson effaced himself and licked his wounds, Rhodes found his mind too fully occupied to brood. The next four or five years were, in fact, the most crowded, and in some ways the most creative, of his life. Nevertheless, the abrupt shattering of his hopes in the Transvaal had told heavily on his nerves and his constitution, and the anxiety and hardships which he suffered in the Rhodesian rebellion, followed by the general tumult of the Boer War, did not mend matters. During the siege of Kimberley his irritability and impatience of military routine showed that his health was failing; and he was conscious of it. While Jameson's buoyancy of mind was beginning to help him to rise superior to misfortune, and inspiring him with ideas of further achievements, Rhodes was haunted by the realisation that his own time would be too short for all there was to do.

Splendid as is the thought that the bond between these two was strong enough to survive the strain imposed upon it, there is something equally impressive – as showing the hold which Jameson was able to exert on less established friends – in the complete disappearance of ill-will on the part of those others to whom he had been the cause of so much trouble – the Reform leaders. Frank Rhodes, Phillips, Hammond, however much they may have suffered through his actions, were unable to resist the man himself, and as soon as he was out of prison were visiting him in his sick-room and encouraging him to feel that the past was wiped out. Jameson never lost a friend through the Raid, and, in the long run, made innumerable friends in spite of it – even among the Boers. General Smuts, President Steyn of the Free State, and General Louis Botha, when brought into personal contact with him, learnt to appreciate his quality, and the last named became his close ally.

This is not a biography of Jameson, and there is no need to dwell on the details of his subsequent life. Posterity will judge him by his whole career; they will put the Raid between brackets, as a temporary aberration, and will attach more weight to his recovery.

And what a recovery it was! When we think of the passions, the malice, the party feuds and racial differences which his mistake provoked, is it not wonderful that he, the foremost delinquent, should within eight years have become the Prime Minister of a Colony which was the stronghold of Afrikanderism, and a Privy Councillor, and ultimately should have been adopted as the president and guiding spirit of the great corporation whose very existence he had imperilled less than twenty years before?

A daring adventurer; an opportunist, maybe; but a leader and moulder of men, and therefore a great soul.

APPENDIX I

The Letter of Invitation

(This was handed to Dr. Jameson by the leaders of the Reform movement at Johannesburg, in November 1895. It was then undated. The certified copy which fell into the hands of the Boers after the surrender of Dr. Jameson bore the date 20th December, 1895. The version in *The Times* was dated the 28th December.)

' Johannesburg.

'Dr. Jameson.

' DEAR SIR, – The position of matters in this State has become so critical that at no distant period there will be a conflict between the Government and the uitlander population. It is scarcely necessary for us to recapitulate what is now a matter of history. Suffice it that the position of thousands of Englishmen and others is rapidly becoming intolerable. Not satisfied with making the uitlanders pay virtually the whole of the revenue of the country while denying them representation, the policy has been steadily to encroach upon the liberty of the subjects and to undermine the security of property to such an extent as to leave a very deep-seated cause of discontent and danger. A foreign corporation of Hollanders is to a considerable extent controlling our destinies, and, in conjunction with the Boer leaders, is endeavouring to cast them in a mould which is wholly foreign to the genius of the people. Every public act betrays the most positive hostility, not only to everything English, but to the neighbouring States as well. In short, the internal policy of the Government is such as to have roused into antagonism not only practically the whole body of uitlanders, but a large number of the Boers, while its external policy has exasperated the neighbouring States, causing the possibility of great danger to the peace and independence of the Republic. Public feeling is in a condition of smouldering discontent. All the petitions of the people have been refused with a greater or less degree of contempt, and in the debate on the Franchise petition, signed by nearly 40,000 people, one member challenged the uitlanders to fight for the rights they asked for, and not a single member spoke against him. Not to go into details, we may say that the Government called into existence all the elements necessary for armed conflict. The one desire of the people here is for fair play and the maintenance of the independence and the preservation of their public liberties, without which life is not worth having. The Government denies these things, and violates the national sense of Englishmen at every turn. What we have to consider is what will be the condition of things here in the event of conflict, with thousands of unarmed men, women and children of our race. They will be at the mercy of well-armed Boers, while property of enormous value would be in the greatest peril. We cannot contemplate the future without the gravest apprehension, and feel that we are justified in taking steps to prevent the shedding of blood, to ensure the protection of our rights. It is under these circumstances that we feel constrained to call upon you to come to our aid should a disturbance arise here. The circumstances are so extreme that we cannot avoid this step, and we cannot but believe that you and the men under you will not fail to come to the rescue of the people who would be so situated. We guarantee any expense that may be incurred by you in helping us, and ask you to believe that nothing but the sternest necessity has prompted this appeal.

'We are, yours faithfully,
'(Signed) CHAS. LEONARD.
'FRANCIS RHODES.
'LIONEL PHILLIPS.
'JOHN HAYS HAMMOND;
'GEORGE FARRAR.'

APPENDIX II

Composition of Dr. Jameson's Force and Details of Casualties

Note. – The sources from which the following particulars have been obtained are : (*a*) The data supplied to the High Commissioner by Mr. F. J. Newton, Resident Commissioner of the Bechuanaland Protectorate, printed in Blue Book No. C 8063, pp. 34-6, with supplementary figures by Captains Ellis and Walford of the B.B. Police; (*b*) The marching-out state appended to Sir John Willoughby's report to the War Office, written in Pretoria Gaol. This document is printed as an Appendix to *The Transvaal From Within*, by Sir Percy Fitzpatrick. The report was not officially made public, but its genuineness is confirmed by quotations from it made in the course of Willoughby's examination before the Select Committee, which correspond word for word with the text as printed by Fitzpatrick (see questions 5580, 5587, etc.). (*c*) Cablegram from Sir Hercules Robinson to Mr. Chamberlain of 10th January, 1896 (Blue Book C 7933, No. 121).

The figures differ slightly in the various statements, but the utmost care has been taken in this appendix to ensure accuracy. The names of officers have in some cases been corrected, and Christian names supplied by the author, from personal knowledge.

The details of casualties are obtained mainly from Sir H. Robinson's cablegram of 11th January, 1896, to Mr. Chamberlain (Blue Book C 7933, No. 135).

COMPOSITION OF DR. JAMESON'S FORCE

(Those marked D. are now deceased.)

In general charge : Dr. Leander Starr Jameson, C.B. D.
In military command : Lieut.-Col. Sir John Christopher Willoughby, Bart. (Major, Royal Horse Guards). D.
Staff Officers:
Major Hon. Robert White (Captain, Royal Welch Fusiliers), Senior Staff Officer.
Major Charles Hyde Villiers (Captain, Royal Horse Guards).

Captain Kenneth J. Kincaid-Smith (Lieut., Royal Artillery), Artillery Staff Officer.
Captain Charles Frederick Lindsell (late Royal Scots Fusiliers), i/c Scouts. D.
Captain James Hutchinson Kennedy (B.S.A. Co.'s Civil Service), Quartermaster. D.
Captain E. Holden (Derbyshire Yeomanry), Assistant Quartermaster.
Surgeon-Captain W. Farmer (B.S.A. Co.'s Civil Service). D.
Surgeon-Captain Seaton Hamilton (late 1st Life Guards).
Lieut. Harold M. Grenfell (1st Life Guards), Remount Officer.
Lieut. James Charles Jesser-Coope (Rhodesia Horse Volunteers), Transport Officer.
Veterinary Surgeon-Lieut. A. H. C. Masters (Mashonaland Mtd. Police).

Attached to Staff:
Major John Bourchier Stracey (Scots Guards).
Major Maurice Heany (late Mashonaland Pioneer Corps). D.
Captain Cyril Foley (3rd Royal Scots).
Lieut. H. R. Holden (late Grenadier Guards).

Mashonaland Mounted Police

In command: Lieut.-Col. Hon. Henry Fredk. White (Major, Grenadier Guards). D.

Second in command: Major William Bodle (Chief Inspector, M.M.P.). D.

A Troop:
 Captain Martin Straker (Inspector, M.M.P.). D.
 Lieut. Rowan Cashel (Sub-Inspector, M.M.P.). D.
 Lieut. Harry J. Scott (Sub-Inspector, M.M.P.).

B Troop:
 Captain Lawson Leigh Ballantyne Dykes (Inspector, M.M.P.).
 Lieut. A. T. Tomlinson (Sub-Inspector, M.M.P.).
 Lieut. H. Chawner (Sub-Inspector, M.M.P.).

C Troop:
 Captain William John Barry (Inspector, M.M.P.). D.
 Lieut. A. Cazalet (Sub-Inspector, M.M.P.). D.
 Lieut. G. H. P. Williams (Sub-Inspector, M.M.P.). D.

D Troop:
 Captain Gordon Vallancy Drury (B.B.P., attached M.M.P.). D.

APPENDICES

Lieut. W. E. Murray (Sub-Inspector, M.M.P.). D.
Lieut. Harry Constable (Sub-Inspector, M.M.P.).
Artillery:
Captain Frank L. Bowden (Inspector, M.M.P.). D.
Lieut. W. S. Spain (Sub-Inspector, M.M.P.).
N.C.O.'s *and men,* 356.

BECHUANALAND BORDER POLICE

In command: Lieut.-Col. Raleigh Grey (Major, 6th Dragoons).
Second in command: Major Hon. Charles J. Coventry (3rd Worcesters). D.
G Troop:
Captain Audley Vaughan Gosling. D.
Lieut. A. H. J. Hore.
Lieut. Edward Allen Wood. D.
K Troop:
Captain C. L. D. Munro (Seaforth Highlanders).
Lieut. W. G. McQueen. D.
Medical Officer:
Surgeon-Captain Edward Charles Frederick Garraway.
Veterinary Officer:
Veterinary-Lieut. W. Lakie.
N.C.O.'s *and men,* 113.

SUMMARY

Staff	officers	17	other ranks	—
M.M.P.	,,	16	,,	356
B.B.P.	,,	9	,,	113
	Total	42		469
	Grand total (white troops)			511

In addition to the officers named above, Major Crosse, late 5th Dragoons, accompanied the column as a spectator.

There were 8 maxim guns, 2 7-pounder guns and 1 12½-pounder gun, 640 horses and 158 mules with the force, and about 150 native drivers, leaders, etc.

UR

A Few Notes as to Some of the Officers

Dr. Jameson became Prime Minister of Cape Colony and afterwards President of the Chartered Company. He was created a baronet and a Privy Councillor.

Major R. White is now Brigadier-General White, C.B., C.M.G., D.S.O.

Captain Kincaid-Smith is now Colonel Kincaid-Smith, C.B., C.M.G., D.S.O.

Major Bodle (now deceased) became Brigadier-General Bodle, C.M.G.

Major Stracey is now Colonel J. B. Stracey-Clitherow, C.B.E.

Colonel Grey is now Sir Raleigh Grey, K.B.E., C.V.O., C.M.G.

Major Coventry (now deceased) became Colonel Coventry, C.B.

Lieut. Wood (now deceased) became Brigadier-General Wood, C.M.G., D.S.O. (3 bars).

Captain Garraway became Resident Commissioner of Basutoland and is now Lieut.-Colonel Sir Edward Garraway, K.C.M.G.

Of the officers on the list the following have died since the Raid: Jameson, Willoughby, Lindsell, Kennedy, Farmer, Heany, H. F. White, Bodle, Straker, Cashel, Barry, Cazalet, Williams, Drury, Murray, Bowden, Coventry, Gosling, Wood and McQueen.

Casualties during the Raid

	Officers	Other ranks	Total
Killed in action	—	16	16
Wounded severely	1 (*died of wounds*)	14	15
Wounded, not seriously	3	38	41

Dr. Jameson and 13 officers were despatched by troopship *Victoria* to England on 20th January 14
26 other officers and 399 rank and file were despatched to Cape ports and England by s.s. *Harlech Castle* on 26th January . 425
The wounded left in hospital at Pretoria and Krugersdorp at that date numbered 21
The number known to have been killed was . . . 16

Total accounted for 476

APPENDICES

If this figure is deducted from the total strength of the force which started from Pitsani and Mafeking (511) there remain 35 unaccounted for.

After the surrender about 25 men were reported missing, but it is known that the majority of them escaped.

Uniform

The M.M.P. wore grey felt ' smasher ' hats with left side pinned up and a blue puggaree with white spots (commonly known as ' guinea-fowl ' or ' bird's-eye ' pattern). Their tunic and breeches were of dark grey Bedford cord (copied from the Cape Mounted Riflemen), and they had dark blue puttees.

The B.B.P. hat was a brown ' smasher,' with *right* side pinned up, and white puggarees. Their tunic and breeches were of khaki twill, and their puttees were dark blue.

Dr. Jameson wore civilian clothes during the march. He had a double ' Terai ' hat, with the crown dented in like a cup. On the morning of the surrender at Doornkop he also wore a light fawn-coloured dust-coat with full skirts. He rode a sixteen-hand black entire.

Further Notes

An account of the manner in which Dr. Jameson, and those of his officers who were to be the subject of criminal proceedings, were dealt with has been given in the body of the book. I am permitted by Sir Edward Garraway to supplement this by the following extracts from his journal, describing the adventures of the remainder of the column:

' . . . At last on Friday morning, the 10th, our brother officers were all marched down to us, except Jameson, Grey, the two Whites, Willoughby and Stracey. They were all looking well and had got clothes given them when in Jail. They had been well fed and looked after there, but were locked up at sunset. . . . On Saturday 11th, about 9 a.m., a guard of the Pretoria Volunteer Corps came down and we were marched up to the railway station in two separate lots and put into special trains, which left Pretoria about noon. We were very well treated and a Dr. Laxton, surgeon to the *Staats Artillerie,* was sent with us as well as a strong escort. We officers were put into first-class carriages and well supplied with fruit and liquor. We were cheered as we left the station, and at every station as we passed. . . . We got into Standerton about 9 p.m. Here some kind people had a cold collation for us officers in the railway refreshment room, and lots of bully beef and bread for the men. A number of ladies were outside the room and asked if they might shake hands with the officers as we passed out. . . . At 6 a.m. on Sunday we arrived at Volksrust, a small town on the border. Here to our disgust we were taken out of the train and marched into a large goods shed, and told the Natal authorities not being yet ready for us we would be kept there until they were. A large escort of burghers under Landdrost Schiffer of Utrecht looked after us, and not having had a share of the fighting were full of blood and rather aggressive at first. It was rather sickening as we were only about 1,000 yards from the Natal border and we could see Charlestown about ¼ of a mile away. Here too we were quite close to Majuba Hill, which we had ample opportunities of studying in the distance for the next twelve days. The sick were taken up and comfortably lodged at an hotel in the village. We were well fed here twice a day. Bread and butter and good meat were brought down to us and coolies came with pineapples, bananas and other fruit which we bought. . . . But it was very monotonous waiting and wondering what they were going to do with us, while the nights on the hard floor of the shed were colder than at Pretoria. . . . On Wednesday General Cox of the Natal district appeared on the scene with his staff – all in mufti, of course. They were not over civil at first and made us feel more like felons than prisoners of war. The Natal law adviser of sorts was with them and we were all paraded and signed a sort of parole saying that we would not attempt to escape, etc. Our domiciles were also fixed, and such of us as were homeborn told that we would be sent home to be tried. . . . The General and staff stayed at Charlestown, coming over by train every day. All the inhabitants too came down to look at the wild beasts again. The Landdrost, a dear old man, and the Commandant were more than kind to us, indeed we experienced far greater kindness from the Dutch than from our own people. . . . No parson came near us on Sunday, though I saw one among the people who came to look at us. . . . On Tuesday . . . a train came in about 7 a.m. and the Imperial officers were all marched up to the station. We were allowed to see them off and in the train we found Jameson, Willoughby, the two Whites, Stracey and Grey . . . and were allowed a few minutes conversation. They all looked well and hearty too. They are to be shipped on the trooper *Victoria* at Durban and sent home. We are all to follow in the *Harlech Castle*, which has been specially chartered for us. When they left we

APPENDICES 295

marched back, feeling very low, to our shed with the prospect of two days more imprisonment there. . . .

'Thursday morning the 25th we were all up at daylight and did not take long getting into train and soon to the border. Here we saw the welcome red coats of the detachment of the West Riding Regt., which was to take us over and relieve our Boer guards, whom we cheered as we steamed away. A few minutes more we were at Charlestown, and here coffee was served out to us and our food for the journey was put into the train. The Governor of Natal and Lady Hely-Hutchinson, General Cox and staff were here too. They did us officers well. Cold fowl, ham and beef, beer and fruit in abundance, and the men were equally well looked after. We had a very pleasant journey, though it got very hot later in the day. Every station we passed through we were cheered enthusiastically though we never stopped quite at a station, but a little way at either side to avoid demonstration. . . .

'26th. About daylight we got to Durban . . . detrained at the jetty, and marched on board a tug and a lighter and taken out to the *Harlech Castle*, which was lying out in the bay. . . . We have an escort; Major Evans, 7th Hussars and 8 men, Lieut. Dennistown, R.A., and 8 men and 8 men W. Riding Regt.

'On board ship after a few days the effect of our imprisonment at Volksrust began to show itself. Three undoubted cases of typhoid broke out. A B.S.A. officer, Spain, is one of them. It is due to the utter absence of sanitary precautions at Volksrust, and there was typhoid in the village at the time. . . . Gambling goes on freely on board, for the men are full of money, having been given a bonus of £10 each by some sympathiser in Capetown (? Rhodes) as well as their December pay, before the ship left Natal. . . . My kit consists of a blue serge suit, " off the peg," two vests and one pair socks. These all were presented to me before leaving Durban. I also have the clothes I went to war in, and a cavalry cloak, so am well prepared for the cold. . . .

'Feb. 6th. Trooper Spurrier, B.S.A., died of typhoid. Three other very suspicious cases. . . .

'Feb. 17th. Las Palmas. Orders received from Major Evans here that we are to proceed to Madeira, and there pick up some official from the Treasury, who is to hold an enquiry on board this ship as we sail home. . . .

'Feb. 18th. Arrived at Madeira. Took the Treasury man, called Lewis, and a man called Froest, from Scotland Yard. . . .

APPENDIX III

The 'Suzerainty'

AT the time of the disturbances in the Transvaal, and especially when the German Emperor intruded with his famous telegram, it was contended in some quarters that the 'Suzerainty of Her Majesty the Queen' – a term first used in the Pretoria Convention of August 1881 – had been expressly abrogated by the later convention of February 1884 known as the 'London Convention'. The most cursory examination of the two instruments shows, however, that this view is incorrect.

The Convention of 1881 consisted of a 'Preamble' and thirty-three 'Articles,' and the reservation of Her Majesty's Suzerainty was contained in the Preamble, of which the following is the text:

'Her Majesty's Commissioners for the settlement of the Transvaal territory, duly appointed as such by a Commission passed under the Royal Sign Manual and Signet, bearing date the 5th day of April, 1881, do hereby undertake and guarantee on behalf of Her Majesty that, from and after the 8th day of August, 1881, complete self-government, *subject to the suzerainty of Her Majesty, her heirs and successors,* will be accorded to the inhabitants of the Transvaal territory, upon the following terms and conditions, and subject to the following reservations and limitations:'

Then follow Articles I to XXXIII.

The Convention of 1884, which was in force at the time of the events described in this volume, states, in an opening clause, that representations have been made by the Government of the Transvaal State that the old Convention 'contains certain provisions which are inconvenient, and imposes burdens and obligations from which the said State is desirous to be relieved'; that Her Majesty has been pleased to take the said representations into consideration, and directs that 'the following articles of a new Convention ... shall, when ratified by the Volksraad ... be *substituted for the* articles embodied in the Convention of 3rd August, 1881....' Then follow twenty new articles.

The effect of this is to leave the 'Preamble' of the old convention, and consequently the Suzerainty, untouched, and to cancel only the articles, which are replaced by new, and in some respects less irksome ones.

In the 1881 convention the foreign relations of the 'Transvaal State' were dealt with in Article II, which provides that Her Majesty reserves to herself, her heirs and successors, *inter alia*,

> 'the control of the external relations of the said State, including the conclusion of treaties and the conduct of diplomatic intercourse with Foreign Powers, such intercourse to be carried on through Her Majesty's diplomatic and consular officers abroad.'

The corresponding article in the 1884 Convention was No. IV, the terms of which were as follows :

> 'The South African Republic will conclude no treaty or engagement with any State or nation other than the Orange Free State, nor with any tribe to the eastward or westward of the Republic, until the same has been approved by Her Majesty the Queen.'

It may be noted that Paul Kruger was one of the signatories to both Conventions.

INDEX

Abercorn, Duke of, Director of Chartered Co., 68
Arms, purchased by Dr. Harris, 68, 69
secret introduction into Transvaal, 82, 85, 99, 100
numbers received at Johannesburg, 208
Austin, Alfred, Poet Laureate, poem on Raid, 239, 240

Bailey, (Sir) Abe, at Kimberley in 1889, 5
connection with Reform movement, 120, 130
receives telegram from 'Godolphin', 206
Banwell, W., Editor of *South Africa*, introduction viii.
Barnato, 'Barney', at Kimberley in 1889, 5
Barotseland, rumoured expedition to, 46
Barry, Captain W. J., fatally wounded, 185
Bathoen, Bechuanaland chief, 52
visit to England, 63, 67 (footnote)
Bechuanaland (Crown Colony), political status of, 51, 52
Bechuanaland (Protectorate), within sphere of Chartered Co., 51
chiefs and tribes of, 52
chiefs required to surrender strip for railway, 65
transfer of, to Chartered Co., 66
Bechuanaland Border Police, 52, 102
assembled at Mafeking, 103
character of force, 163
Beit, Alfred, at Kimberley in 1889, 5, 6
and Eckstein group, 31
correspondence with Phillips, 32, 33
Director of Chartered Co., 68
sails for S. Africa, 70
discusses revolutionary plot, 71, 73
financial support of Reform movement, 99, 120
reassuring messages to Reformers, 121
Bettington, Col., enrols mounted squadron, 194
rides out to meet Jameson, 220

Bivouac of Jameson's column, on Jan. 1st, 1896, 184
Bodle, Major W., 2nd in command, M.M.P., 163
leads charge against Boers, 185
Botha, J. D. L., Commandant of Marico, writes to Jameson, 166
Bouwer, D., carries despatch to Jameson from British Agent, 171
Bower, Sir Graham, Imperial Secretary, made aware of Rhodes's plans, 114
interview with Rhodes on day of Raid, 202
Boyes, G. J., Civil Commissioner of Mafeking, 161
reports Raid to Cape Government, 162
Bulawayo, sympathy with Jameson, 233
Burgher forces mobilised, 214

Cape Parliamentary Committee, 259, 272
Capetown, position in regard to mining industry, 3
Casualties in Jameson's force, 292 (appendix)
Cawston, Geo., Director of Chartered Co., 68
Cazalet, Lieut. A., wounded, 185
Celliers, cyclist, brings despatches to Jameson, 172
account of meeting, 178
Chamberlain, Mr. Joseph, Colonial Secretary, 54, 55
interviewed by Harris, 55
account of interview, 57, 58
attitude regarding transfer of Protectorate, 63, 65
his policy criticised, 66
mystery of cablegrams anticipating Raid, 199
action on learning of Raid, 234
firm stand with Kruger, 255, 256
evidence before Select Committee, 273
Charter of British South Africa Co., 13
Chartered Co.'s Board, sanctions increase of Rhodesian forces, 37
ignorance of Rhodes's schemes, 37, 38, 68

INDEX

Chartered Co's. Board (*contd.*)
  summoned to meet Chamberlain, 234
  reprimanded by Select Committee, 276
  deprived of military power, 277
Coghlan, (Sir) Charles, at Kimberley in 1889, 5
Colonial Office, how far privy to Rhodes's plans, 57–61
Colquhoun, A. R., Administrator of Mashonaland, 17
  relations with Jameson, 17
  resignation of, 19
Colvin, Ian, introduction ix
  biography of Jameson, 2
Coventry, Hon. Charles, officer of B.B.P., 159
  wounded, 187
  tried and sentenced in England, 269–271
Cronjé, Boer Commandant, accepts Jameson's surrender, 189, 190

Davis, W. D. ('Karri'), and flag question, 127
  enrols volunteers for Red Cross work, 194
  detained in gaol, 268
De Beers Co., and the smuggling of arms, 99
De Wet, Sir Jacobus, British Agent at Pretoria, 171
  orders Jameson to turn back, 171
  summoned by Kruger, 203
  urges Reform Committee to submit to Kruger, 248, 249
  addresses crowd in Johannesburg, 250
Disarmament of Johannesburg, 252, 253
Doornkop, fighting round, 187
Drifts, closed by Kruger, 75

Eckstein, Herman, 4
  group, 31
Elliott, Major, murder of, 255, 256 (footnote)
Eloff, Saul, Transvaal officer, made prisoner, 170
England, popular feeling regarding Raid, 236
Esselen, Ewald, interviewed by Jameson, 73

Fairfield, present at Harris's interview with Chamberlain, 56
  knowledge of 'Jameson plan', 59
  letter to Chamberlain, 60

Farquhar, Sir Horace, Director of Chartered Co., 68
Farrar, (Sir) George, 100
  qualifications as Reform leader, 110
  trial and sentence, 260–266
  later career, 280
Faure, J. H., telegram to Rhodes, 135
Fife, Duke of, Director of Chartered Co., 68
Fitzpatrick, (Sir) Percy, historian of Reform movement, introduction vii, viii, 80
  as Reform leader, 110
'Flag controversy', 127–133
Forbes, Major P. W., Commander of Matabele expedition, 22
Franchise, Uitlanders' efforts to obtain, 29, 71
  rejection of petition in Volksraad, 74
Fuller, Inspector J. W., B.B.P., 159, 160

Garraway, Sir Edward, introduction viii
  journal of the Raid, 152 (footnote), 165 (footnote), 293
German Emperor, telegraphs to Kruger, 238, 239
Germany, Kruger's advances to, 30, 39, 40
Gibbs, Captain J. A. C., adjutant of Rhodesia Horse, 107
  receives instructions from Willoughby and Jameson, 107
Gifford, Lord, Director of Chartered Co., 68
Glencoe, railway accident at, 214, 215
Goldfields of South Africa Co., 31, 32
Gregorowski, Judge, imported to try Reformers, 262, 263, 266
Grey, (Sir) Raleigh, commanding B.B.P., 79
  antecedents of, 79
  informed of Jameson's intentions, 103, 159
  departure from Mafeking, 160
  wounded, 185
  tried in London and sentenced, 269–271
Griqualand West, absorbed in Cape Colony, 4

Hamilton, F. H., Editor of *Star*, deputed to interview Rhodes on 'flag' question, 132, 141

INDEX

Hammond, J. H., Goldfields engineer, 25, 26, 32
visits Rhodesia, 25
conversations with Rhodes and Jameson, 26
telegram to Rhodes, 138
trial and sentence of, 264–266
later career of, 281
Harris, Dr. F. Rutherfoord, at Kimberley in 1889, 5
character of, 9, 10
accompanies Jameson to Matabeleland, 11
Secretary of Chartered Company, 14
leaves Mashonaland, 20
mission to England, 55
interviews with Chamberlain, 55–61, 63
cable correspondence with Rhodes, 62, 67
buys rifles, 68, 69
arrangements with Miss F. Shaw, 69, 70
sails for South Africa, 70
telegrams to Jameson and Reformers, 124–133
responsibility for 'flag controversy', 129–131
informs Jameson that Johannesburg movement has collapsed, 141
learns Jameson's intention to advance, 197
cablegrams to Miss Shaw, 198
the 'Godolphin' telegram, 206
encounter with Labouchere at Parliamentary enquiry, 275
Hawksley, Bourchier, refuses to produce cablegrams at Parliamentary enquiry, 274
Heany, Maurice, sent to Johannesburg, 118
charged with message to Jameson, 134, 146
interviews Jameson at Pitsani, 147, 149
Heyman, (Sir) H. Melville, appointed to command Matabeleland volunteers, 45
at Johannesburg, 117, 118
Hofmeyr, J. H., offers unofficial advice to Governor, 231, 232
deprecates action of German Emperor, 238
refuses to visit Pretoria, 242
Holden, Captain, charged with message to Jameson, 134
reaches Pitsani, 146

Hull, H. C., at Kimberley in 1889, 5

Ikaning, Bechuanaland chief, 52
cedes territorial jurisdiction to Rhodes, 64

Jameson, Leander Starr, temperamental peculiarities of 2, 7
medical practice at Kimberley, 7
visits Matabeleland, 9, 11
and Lobengula, 12
returns to Kimberley, 13
second visit to Matabeleland, 14
final visit to reassure Lobengula, 15
friendship with Willoughby, 15, 16
accompanies Pioneers to Mashonaland, 16
relations with Colquhoun, 17
explores Pungwe route, 17
secures Gazaland concession, 18
frustrates Boer trek, 19
appointed Administrator of Mashonaland, 19
deals with Matabele raiders, 21
leads expedition to Matabeleland, 22
reception on visit to England, 23
lecture at Imperial Institute, 23
conversations with Hammond, 25, 26
first thoughts of action in Transvaal, 27, 34
visits Pretoria and Johannesburg, 35
discussions with Colonial Office, 36
second visit to Johannesburg, 44
forms volunteer corps in Rhodesia, 44, 45
negotiations with Khama, 54
appointed Resident Commissioner of Southern Protectorate, 64
fixity of purpose, 71
third visit to Johannesburg, 73
discloses plans to Reformers, 75
final visit to arrange details, 80
his account of plot compared with Reformers' statements, 81–92
responsibility to Rhodes, 91
self-confidence of, 92
efforts to prevent postponement of rising, 117, 125, 136
erroneous estimate of forces available, 95
reveals plans to Grey and Newton, 103, 104
impatience at hesitation of Reformers, 118–125, 133

INDEX

Jameson, Leander Starr (*contd.*)
  apprehension of Boer suspicions, 125
  and Heany, 147
  decides on invasion, 149
  telegrams to Napier, Spreckley, and others, 149–151
  announces intention by telegraph to Rhodes, 151
  reads 'letter of invitation' to troops, 153
  starts from Pitsani, 155
  his letter to Commandant of Marico, 166, 167
  his letter to British Agent, 171
  his letter to Col. Rhodes, 179
  surrenders at Vlakfontein, 188, 189
  in gaol at Pretoria, 191, 254
  conditions of his delivery to British authorities, 254
  embarkation at Durban, 257
  tried and sentenced, 269–271
  illness leads to release, 272
  first meeting with Rhodes after Raid, 284
  recovery from effects of Raid, 285
  subsequent career, 286
Jameson, Sam, in business at Johannesburg, 44
Jeppe, Carl, supports Uitlander petition for franchise, 74
Johannesburg, in 1889, 4
  plans of Reformers, 81–92
  races in Christmas week, 111
  exodus of women and children from, 194
  disarmament of, 252
Joubert, P. (Commandant-General), alleged letter to Jameson, 167

Khama, principal chief in Bechuanaland Protectorate, 52
  visited by Jameson, 54
  visit to England, 54, 63, 65
Kimberley, conditions of, in 1889, 5, 6
Kotzé, Judge, member of Commission to parley with Reformers, 216
Kruger, President, attitude to Uitlanders, 27, 30
  favours Hollanders, 30
  pro-German policy of, 30, 39–41
  obdurate on franchise question, 74, 196
  closes drifts, 75
  his 'tortoise' speech, 97, 195
  interviewed by deputations of Uitlanders, 196

Kruger, President (*contd.*)
  his reception of news of Raid, 203, 204
  issues proclamation, 205
  asks for intervention of France and Germany, 205
  disturbed by threats from Rhodesia, 243
  sketch of his character, 244
  meeting with Robinson, 247
  demands submission of Johannesburg, 247
  dictates terms for delivery of Raiders, 254
  reduces sentences on Reformers, 267
  short-sighted policy after Raid, 281, 282
Krugersdorp, Boer positions at, 173, 177, 181
  repulse of Jameson's force from, 183

Labouchere, Henry, member of Parliamentary Committee on Raid, 273
  his imputations against Harris, Phillips and others, 275
  submits minority report, 276
Lace, sent by Reform Committee with message to Jameson, 186
Lawley, A. L., advised of Raid by wire from Mafeking, 207
Leonard, Charles, Chairman of National Union, 72
  approached by Beit, 73
  and by Jameson, 73
  visits Rhodes at Capetown, 75, 76
  head of Reform Executive, 110
  attitude on 'flag controversy', 127, 132
Leonard, J. W., member of Reform party, 151
  speeches during crisis, 215
'Letter of invitation', text of, 287
  conflicting accounts as to purpose of, 89, 90
  read to troops at Pitsani, 153
  use made of, by Harris and others, 221–224
Leyds, Dr., State Attorney of Transvaal, 30
  gratification at conviction of Reformers, 266
Linchwe, Bechuanaland chief, 52
Lobengula, King of Matabele, sends mission to Queen Victoria, 8
  falls under Jameson's influence, 12

INDEX

Lobengula, King of Matabele (*contd.*)
  orders execution of councillor, 13, 14
Loch, Sir Henry, retirement of, 42

Mafeking, B.B. Police assembled at, 103
  start of troops from, 159, 160
Maguire, Rochfort, in 1889, 6
  Rhodes's agent at Bulawayo, 8
  Rhodes's alternate on Chartered Board, 68
Malan, farmer on road to Johannesburg, 102, 168
Malan, Boer delegate to Reform Committee, 215
Malmani, junction of Pitsani and Mafeking columns at, 165
Marais, Eugene, Boer emissary to Reform Committee, 215
Mashonaland Mounted Police, arrival at Pitsani, 94
  character of force, 163
  details of personnel, 290, 291
Mashonaland, pioneer expedition to, 14, 16, 17
  early conditions of, 19, 20
Matabele Concession, obtained by Rhodes, 8
  opponents of, 8, 11, 13
Matabele, raid of, into Mashonaland, 21
Matabele war, 22, 23
Mathers, E. P., Editor of *South Africa*, introduction viii
Metcalfe, Sir Charles, association with Rhodes in 1889, 6
  at Mafeking at time of Raid, 162
Meyer, Lukas, favours grant of franchise, 74
Moffat, J. S., British Resident at Bulawayo, 12
Montsioa, Bechuanaland chief, 52
  cedes territorial jurisdiction to Rhodes, 64

Nachtmaal, at Pretoria, 112
Napier, William, officer of Rhodesia Horse, 106
  receives orders as to mobilisation, 106, 149
  calls for volunteers in Bulawayo, 233
National Union, 31
  leaders of, approached by Beit, 72
  issues manifesto on Uitlander grievances, 113, 192

Newton, (Sir) F. J., learns purpose of Jameson's force, 103
  decides not to participate in movement, 104
  sends despatches recalling Jameson, 232

Officers of Jameson's force, reassured as to commissions, 156–158
  personal notes as to, 289–292
Orange Free State, mobilisation of burghers of, 243

Phillips, (Sir) Lionel, at Johannesburg in 1889, 4
  and Uitlander grievances, 29, 32
  President of Chamber of Mines, 31
  correspondence with Beit, 29, 32, 33
  character of, 72
  approached by Beit, 73
  and by Jameson, 73
  visits Rhodes at Capetown with Leonard, 75, 76
  warns Transvaal Government in speech, 78
  one of revolutionary executive, 110
  attitude on flag question, 127
  Chairman of Reform Committee, 208
  heads deputation to parley with Government, 216
  speech to crowd on return, 218
  trial and sentence, 264–266
  later career, 279
Pioneer expedition to Mashonaland, 14–17
Pitsani Botluko, camp at, 65, 93, 153
  arrival of Rhodesian police at, 94
  departure of Jameson's force from, 153–155
Pretoria, arsenal at, 81

Queen's Mine, Boer position at, 181

Races at Johannesburg, 111
Raid, incidents of, 163–191
Reform Committee, formation of, 208
  activities of, 208–212
  attitude towards Jameson, 210
  decide on disarmament, 249
  members arrested, 260
  trial of members, 263–266
  sentences, 266
  later careers of members, 279–281
Reformers, efforts to postpone rising, 116–135

304 INDEX

Reinforcements from Johannesburg, controversy as to, 173-179
Reuters, telegram as to acute position in Johannesburg, 145
Rhodes, C. J., at Kimberley in 1889, 5, 6
acquires Matabele Concession, 8
in England in 1894, 13, 36
negotiations with Colonial Office on Bechuanaland, 36
railway and other schemes, 36
and Kruger's intrigues with Germany, 39, 41
and retirement of Sir H. Loch, 42
his responsibility for appointment of Sir H. Robinson, 42, 43
and Bechuanaland, 52
negotiations with Bechuanaland chiefs, 64
annoyance at terms of Bechuanaland settlement, 67
relations with Chartered colleagues, 67, 68
interview with Leonard and Phillips 76, 77
his objects in supporting Uitlander movement, 77, 128
his intentions as to Jameson's force, 77
his financial support for Reformers, 99
to proceed to Johannesburg on outbreak of rising, 113
and 'flag controversy', 128-130
regards movement as 'fizzled out', 142
telegrams sent in his name, 143, 144
his action on learning Jameson's decision to move, 200-202
meeting with Schreiner, 201
interview with Bower, 202
indiscreet cablegram to Miss Shaw, 226, 227
sends for Schreiner, 228
his mental and physical strain, 230
his resignation as Prime Minister, 231, 243
gives evidence before Parliamentary Committee, 274
reprimanded in Committee's report, 276
friendship with Jameson unimpaired, 284
after-effects of Raid on, 285
Rhodes, Ernest, represents his brother on Goldfields Board, 32

Rhodes, Frank, acts as Administrator of Rhodesia, 49
character of, 49
military member of Council, 50
negotiations with Bechuana chiefs, 64
present at interview with Leonard and Phillips, 76
sent to organise military details at Johannesburg, 78
unsuitability as leader of revolution, 110
telegram as to High Commissioner's visit to Johannesburg, 121, 122
reconstruction of his letter to Jameson, 175, 176
orders Bettington to assist Jameson, 220
trial and sentence, 262-266
later career, 280
Rhodesia Horse Volunteers, formation of corps, 44-46
use to be made of, 95, 105
strength of, 107
eagerness to assist Jameson, 233, 234
Rhodesian settlers, effects of Raid on, 277, 278
Rifles for Johannesburg, *see* 'Arms'
Robinson, Sir Hercules, appointed Governor of Cape Colony, 42, 43
to act as mediator on outbreak of rising, 113
difficulties involved, 115
informs Chamberlain of collapse of movement, 142
action on hearing of Raid, 225, 226
proposals for mediation, 241
accepts Rhodes's resignation, 243
ignorance of terms of Jameson's surrender, 243
attitude of mind in regard to negotiations, 245
meeting with Kruger at Pretoria, 247
urges Reform Committee to disarm, 248
unfortunate results of his visit to Pretoria, 257, 258
Rowland, cyclist despatch-rider, brings letters to Jameson, 172
his contradictory accounts of contents, 176, 177
Rudd, C. D., Rhodes's partner, 6
and Matabele Concession, 8
Rustenburg, reports as to Jameson's advance, 203

INDEX 305

Sampson, (Sir) A. Wools, connection with Reform movement, 120, 130
  and flag question, 127
  detained in gaol, 268
  later career, 280
Schreiner, W. P., calls on Rhodes without suspicion, 201
  painful later interview with Rhodes, 228–230
Sebele, Bechuanaland chief, 52
  visit to England, 54, 63, 67 (footnote)
Secret service in Transvaal, 96
Selborne, Lord, present at meeting between Harris and Chamberlain, 56, 58
Select Committee of House of Commons, 259
  composition of, 273
  dramatic moments during enquiry, 273–275
  findings of, 275–278
Shaw, Miss Flora, relations with *Times*, 69
  engagement by Harris, 70
  cablegrams to Rhodes, 70, 119
Shippard, Sir Sidney, Administrator of British Bechuanaland, 64
  supports Robinson at Johannesburg, 245, 252
Slagter's Nek, execution of Boers at, 263 (footnote)
South Africa, racial animosities revived by Raid, 278, 279
Spreckley, J. A., officer in Rhodesia Horse, 106
  receives orders as to mobilisation, 106, 149
Staats Artillerie, 214
  released to engage Jameson, 218
Stellaland, freebooters, 256 (footnote)
Stevens, J. A., unauthorised reference to *Times*, 120
  receives final telegrams from Jameson, 196
  abortive attempts to reply, 197
Surrender of Jameson's force, terms of, 189
  details of, 190
Suzerainty, flouted by German Emperor, 238
  discussion of, 296

Telegraph wire, cutting of, 125, 137, 150, 152

Telegraphic correspondence between conspirators, methods of, 116 (footnote)
Thompson, F. R., and Matabele Concession, 8
  at Bulawayo, 11
  flight from Matabeleland, 14
Times, The, unfounded reference to, in connection with rising, 119
  publishes letter of invitation, 222, 223
Times special correspondent, see Shaw, Miss F.
Transvaal, Boer population of, 25, 28
Transvaal National Union, 31
Trimble, Andrew, organises police force in Johannesburg, 209

Uniforms of Jameson's force, 293
Uitlanders, position of, in Johannesburg, 26, 27
  numbers of, 28
  grievances of, 28–31

Vallé, Bugler, carries last message from Jameson, 186, 220
Victoria, raided by Matabele, 21
Villiers, Captain C. H., accompanies Major White on tour in Transvaal, 48
Vintcent, Mr. Justice, 98
Vlakfontein, scene of Jameson's last stand, 185, 187

White brothers, the, ascendancy of, 45
White Hon. C., Chief Commissioner of Police in Rhodesia, 45
  at Johannesburg, 211
White, Hon. H. F., appointed to command Mashonaland Volunteers, 45
  surprises Boers near Krugersdorp, 180, 181
  frontal attack on Boers, 183
  tried and sentenced in England, 269–271
White, Hon. R., appointed Chief Staff Officer of Volunteers, 45, 46
  visit to Rhodes, 47
  tour in Transvaal, 48
  magistrate in Southern Protectorate, 64
  selects police camp at Pitsani, 65
  his despatch box, 65 (footnote)
  starts from Mafeking with B.B.P., 160
  tried and sentenced in England, 269–271

White, Sergeant, B.B.P., carries despatches to Jameson and officers, 168, 169, 232
Williams, Gardner, and smuggling of arms, 100
prosecution of, 259
Willoughby, Sir John, friendship with Jameson, 15
character of, 16
military adviser in Matabele war, 22
in command of Rhodesia Volunteers, 45
his cognisance of Jameson's schemes, 47
arrangements for mobilising Rhodesia Horse, 95, 106, 107

Willoughby, Sir John (*contd.*)
assurances to his officers, 156, 157, 158
Report on Raid, 164, 165
reasons for not obeying High Commissioner, 169
letter of surrender at Vlakfontein, 189
tried and sentenced in England, 269–271
Wolff, Dr. H. A., organises stores and remounts, 101, 102
responsibility for cutting telegraph wire, 150, 152
disappearance of, 170 (footnote)
last letter to Jameson, 173, 174

www.ingramcontent.com/pod-product-compliance
Lightning Source LLC
Chambersburg PA
CBHW020731160426
43192CB00006B/193